Wine Lovers' Guide

to Australia

Wine Lovers' Guide

to Australia

edited by Jill Sykes

MACMILLAN

Pan Macmillan Australia

First published 1999 in Macmillan by Pan Macmillan Australia Pty Limited
St Martins Tower, 31 Market Street, Sydney

National Library of Australia
cataloguing-in-publication data:

Sykes, Jill.

Wine lovers' guide to Australia.

ISBN 0 7329 0979 1.

1. Wine and winemaking – Australia. 2. Wine districts – Australia. I. Title. II. Title:
Wine lovers' guide to Australia (Television program).

641.220994

Design by Robyn Latimer

Typeset in 11/14 pt Caslon 540 Roman
Printed in Australia by Sands Print Group

Published to accompany the SBS TV series entitled Wine Lovers' Guide to Australia *for which the presenters were wine experts Maryann Egan and Grant Van Every and television personality Pria Viswalingam. The series was produced by SBS Television and first broadcast in 1999.*

Series producer: Margaret Murphy

Segment producers: Mika Nishimura, Jacqui Sykes and Pria Viswalingam

Logo and map design: Annalisa Appo Van Commenee

Photography: Peter Clarke, Jerzy Starzynski, Aaron Gully, Tom Gelai, Mike Piper, Canberra Tourism & Events Corporation (page 156), South Australian Tourism Commission (pages 149, 173, 177), Tourism Victoria (pages 69, 128, 164, 181, 189)

Research: Muditha Dias

Contents

Introduction

From a nation of beer drinkers, Australians are turning into a nation of wine lovers. Around the country, the making of wine and the enjoyment of drinking it are becoming an intrinsic part of Australian life.

Wine Lovers' Guide to Australia captures this moment at the turn of the 20th century. Like an oral history, it shows the way that winemakers are thinking, the wide range of opinions on just about every aspect of bringing grape to glass. It is a guide to the way Australian traditions in winemaking are developing and new regions for grape growing are being found. It's about the characters in the industry — people with such a passion for wine that making the best wine they can has become a driving force in their lives.

It's also about wine and food. The pleasure of wine is greatest when it is matched with food that enhances it — and the other way around. Great relationships between food and wine are explored on these pages.

There are hints about buying wine, tasting it at the cellar door, collecting it and keeping it for mature enjoyment later. The book may not include everything you want to know about wine, but there is more than enough to set your taste buds for new experiences in a form of shared enjoyment that has delighted communities and families for several thousand years.

Winemaking in Australia

The Australian wine industry is booming. How it got that way is one of the many topics winding their way through this book. Several factors stand out. One is the history of winemaking, which began in the first days of European settlement in Australia, had its own boom in the 19th century and experienced startling changes at the start of its recent revival. Another is the development of an Australian wine which gained world attention for its distinctive quality far in advance of the many premium wines produced today — Grange, of course, made by Max Schubert for Penfolds. Yet another is the energetic promotion of Australian wine, a process which has involved more than one wine lover with professional writing and promotional skills, but is personified by the indefatigable and pioneering Len Evans.

Historic Glimpses

Grape vines arrived in Australia with Governor Arthur Phillip and the First Fleet in 1788. They were brought from Rio de Janeiro and the Cape of Good Hope, and planted at Farm Cove — just around the point from where the Sydney Opera House is today. Initially, grapes did well in the new British penal colony, but disease and the lack of proper management took their toll. There was considerable determination to get grapes growing and wine made nonetheless. Two French prisoners of war were brought to Australia with full instructions and supposed knowledge of these important matters, but they failed in their attempts. Others planted vines that flourished, then faltered.

Gregory Blaxland — best known for his crossing of the Blue Mountains with Wentworth and Lawson — experimented with varieties, cuttings, training the vines and keeping up the water in summer. He became the first person to export wine from Australia in 1822, earning a silver medal in London from what became the Royal Society of Arts. In 1828, he was awarded a gold medal for a tawny red wine. The Macarthur family, best known for their wool growing, also succeeded in growing grapes and making wine.

It was James Busby, however, who had the strongest and longest influence on winemaking. He arrived in 1824 after equipping himself to lead a colonial wine industry by studying viticulture in France. It was not so much the vines Busby planted as the cuttings he collected and distributed, and the books he wrote. First, it was a translation of French writings in his *A Treatise on the Culture of the Vine and*

the Art of Making Wine. Then, to encourage settlers to plant vineyards, he published *A Manual of Plain Directions for Planting and Cultivating Vineyards and for Making Wine in New South Wales*. Busby's later writing included *Report on the Vines Introduced into the Colony of New South Wales in the year 1832*. These were vine varieties that he collected from Spain, France and England, and shipped back to Australia, planting many of them on his property Kirkton, in the Hunter Valley in New South Wales. When Busby moved to New Zealand to take up a major colonial position, his books and his vines continued to have an influence — as they do even today, with clones of chardonnay and shiraz in Australia being traceable to his imports.

The 1830s saw a boost in viticulture as plantings were extended in New South Wales and begun in Victoria, South Australia and Western Australia, where, in 1829, the Swan River valley was chosen as suitable for grape growing by a syndicate of Richmond Houghton, Ninian Lowis and Thomas Yule. Houghton continues to be a leading West Australian winery.

Jump about a century and there is more wine history being made in the Swan Valley, a half hour's drive from the centre of Perth. John Kosovich, best known for his Westfield winery's award-winning chardonnay, is the son of an immigrant from Dalmatia who worked in the goldmines and earned enough money to buy land in the Swan Valley. In 1922, Ivan Kosovich set up the vineyard with his brother, and then went out cutting railway sleepers to support the venture until it was established. John Kosovich continues:

In about 1926, he was able to come back and play his part in the viticultural side of things here. In those days, the area grew a lot of table grapes, more for dried fruits like currants and sultanas. That was quite a good earner in those days. Then they started up winemaking.

This area was mostly fortified wines, as indeed most of Australia made fortified wines. In 1961, I believe the figure was 80 per cent of the wine made in Australia was fortified, and it took 20 years to reverse those figures from 80/20 to 20/80. It's probably gone further towards 90/10 I would suggest these days — it's all table wine. In those days, people wouldn't drink what they called 'that sour stuff'. They just wanted to drink sweet, rich fortified wines and that was the earner in those days. So they made muscats, sherries and ports — they were the three basic ones.

I came on the scene in early 1953, when I left school. It was in the 1960s that there was a big move towards the table wines and that's when we started to plant. We already had shiraz, but we never had any of the classic white varieties then. But it was all different in those days. The technology was so far behind. We were all making wine in old concrete tanks which were just wax-lined — totally unsuitable for the job. You couldn't seal them properly, you had flat lids and you couldn't get all the air out. You'd get a bit of expansion on a hot day and the lid would lift. You'd walk into the winery and there'd be the telltale drips of wine running on to the ground … It was almost impossible to operate efficiently.

When I started, you might have crushed the grapes at about 20°C and two days later they're fermenting at 30°C and on the third day at about 35, 36 or even 37°C. We had no way of cooling them off except to run into Perth, bring home a ute load of ice and throw it into the wine. Today, we just put a coil into the wine or pump the wine into a tank which already has its coil fixed inside and press a button. Within hours, we can get it down to the temperature that we'd like to run it.

John Kosovich, winemaker,
Westfield

We used to have steel crushers that had to be painted two or three times a year and we operated with an old manual basket press or perhaps a hydraulically driven one. Today you've got automatic horizontal presses and you just fill them up and sit down and have a cup of tea, press a couple of buttons and it's all over. I can tell you, it was hard yakka in the old times. It'd take you all day long just to press a couple of tonnes of grapes, but today it's really been made easy with technology.

While Kosovich celebrates Swan Valley and the new technology, Frank Tate is taking his winemaking business south to Margaret River, where the company already has a larger and very successful operation. His grandfather came to Australia from the Ukraine in 1909 when he was nine; when his older brother arrived, he opened a wine saloon in Fremantle. Through this connection, Tate's father became interested in making wine and set up business with a colleague by the name of John Evans. And so, in 1971, Evans & Tate was born, and had a huge impact on the reputation of Swan Valley red wines over the next decade.

As Frank Tate says: 'In 27 years we've made a lot of wine and this vineyard, as a supply source of the overall production of our wines, is representative of five per cent of our intake. In other words, the total amount of vineyards to supply the winery we've been operating here is 20 times what we have here, so we've had a very good growth.'

In contrast, Beverley Atkinson, who runs Jane Brook Estate Wines with her husband David, is talking up Swan Valley's individuality and wine prospects:

The future for the Swan Valley is very exciting at the moment. We've just been part of a funded strategy for the marketing and the branding of the Swan Valley for its future development. Within the next two to three months, you're going to see the launch of the new Swan Valley logo and brand. All facets of industry have joined together on these committees …

The need to work together has been heightened by the pressure put on the area by industries other than viticulture and its proximity to Perth.

I think that areas close to cities will always have pressure upon them. We have been involved in some quite hefty discussions and problems over the past 12 months. There is, however, a very strong increase in grape growing in the valley.

There is a very strong belief by the people who live here that they want to live in a rural atmosphere and I think we all have faith and hope that this problem will solve itself. There has been a strong tourism development because we're only 30 minutes from Perth and 15 minutes from all the airports, so we're in a very, very lucky position in the Swan Valley.'

Grange

Bottle of Grange Hermitage

Grange, which began life as Grange Hermitage in the days when the French were not so concerned about appellation rights and the description 'hermitage' was synonymous with shiraz in Australia, is Australia's most famous and expensive wine. Yet it was at first an unwanted addition to the Penfolds range and its winemaker, Max Schubert, had to keep the results of his project very quiet until it took a grip on the palates and imaginations of his employers. To begin with, they didn't like it at all.

Schubert made his first, experimental vintage of Grange in 1951, followed by a commercial vintage in 1952. As chief winemaker, he had been sent on a sherry-making study to Spain in 1950 and travelled on to Bordeaux in France. There he was introduced to the joys of mature claret, wines 40 to 50 years old with magnificent bouquet and flavour. He returned with inspired plans to an Australian company that, at the time, was mostly concerned with producing fortified wines.

'I didn't set out to produce a French wine because I knew I couldn't,' he said in an interview before he died in 1994. 'I wanted to produce an Australian wine with individual Australian characteristics, but a wine that would be rated on par with the French.'

Of the early Grange, he said: 'It had tremendous flavour, it had tremendous balance. The character was tremendous. It had all the earmarks of the style of wine that would live for a very long time and would improve, would really become a fine, intelligent wine. If kept long enough. I could not understand why people to whom we submitted this thought it was a dreadful wine.'

Then the 1955 vintage was entered in the 1962 Sydney wine show and it won a gold medal. 'From that time onwards, Grange Hermitage never looked back,' said its proud maker.

Max Schubert, winemaker, at work in the laboratory

But Schubert went through some extraordinary experiences to get to that point. When the 1952 vintage was released in 1955, it was condemned as 'a very good dry port which no one in their right mind will buy, let alone drink' and 'a concoction of wild fruits and sundry berries with crushed ants predominating'. It was a costly wine to make, involving winemaking innovations such as refrigeration to control the rate of fermentation, and the storage and maturation of the wine in new oak casks — all standard practice today, but new to Australia at the time.

Schubert was ordered to cease production before the 1957 vintage, but he continued to make the wine secretly until production resumed officially with the 1960 vintage. Peter Gago, an oenologist for Penfolds, explains how the clandestine vintages were hidden underneath the winery at Magill, now a suburb of Adelaide, but still boasting a vineyard that grows grapes for Grange:

> There was a masonite wall reportedly built at the end of the cellar. Back in those days, after bottling, the wines were stored in these underground drives or bins, and sticks of wood were used to calculate the numbers. You pushed in sticks and if they went back four feet there were X hundred bottles; five feet, so many more. And the Grange was behind the masonite.
>
> The company's board at the time didn't like the concept of a red wine that couldn't be drunk soon after release. They didn't understand the style. It had never been made before in Australia and it was almost as rich as a port. It was a whole, new, revolutionary style of wine and it was misunderstood.

Len Evans, wine guru, at home in the Hunter Valley

Fortunately for all those who have come to understand Grange only too well, Schubert persevered and Australia's greatest wine went out to the world as a flagbearer for the premium wine industry that was to develop in its wake.

Len Evans

You really know how completely Australia's wining and dining habits have changed over the past fifty years when you talk to Len Evans about it. A wine guru who has enjoyed wine, served it at his restaurant, written about it, promoted it and made it, he came to Australia from the United Kingdom in 1955. Not long after, he recalls going to work in the

Queensland outback mining town of Mt Isa and making the mistake of asking for a bottle of wine at the pub. 'What are you, some kind of pansy?' replied the publican.

Evans came to Sydney in 1958 and was astonished to see beer was 'the tipple' on every table, even in the great restaurants of the day where the male diners wore black tie — even white tie. 'And they still had an open bottle of beer on the table — it was fairly incongruous to me. I think that people hadn't got around to understanding what great wines were available. You know, it's come a long way in a very short space of time.'

So, how did the change come about? 'I think the promotion I was involved in certainly had an effect. I think the migrants had a great effect. The wave in the 1950s of the Greek and Italian migrants not only showed how to live life a little more cheerfully, but they also set up the first continental restaurants.' Those were the days of carpetbag steaks and onion rings even at top echelon nightspots such as Prince's and Quo Vadis, although the Silver Spade at least sold wine to go with them — encouraged by Evans, who wrote his first wine column in 1962 and began promoting wine for Australia in 1965.

Evans reckons Australia is up amongst the big seven wine-producing nations: better than Portugal's table wines, though not equal to its great ports; better than the top Spanish wines; not to be compared to the great wines of France or Italy; on a par with America.

Their quality is high, like ours here. I think our reputation has come by providing great value for money. We provide good varietal wines with value for money — possibly with the exception of pinot noir. But the rest are very good value and the world understands varietals. Thank God, France aren't using them as heavily as they should, if hardly at all. That gives us an edge, and what it means is that people can pick up a bottle of Australian cabernet or chardonnay or shiraz with great confidence.

Very simply, when you make very good varietals at a reasonable price, there's a very big market to be gained around the world. And don't forget that commodity wine, ordinary wine — three or four pounds, five or six dollars in America — is still 60 per cent of the market, so we're going for the niche above that. Now above that, you have the very high premium and then the super premium — and we're just touching those now with Grange, with 707, Henschke, Petaluma, Leeuwin Estate. We're starting to show around the world that we can have exceptional wines that are very expensive. But I'm not against that because I think that helps every wine.

I think it's safe to say our best wines, our best vineyards, are still to come from areas we don't understand or know yet. I mean, I think there are literally tens of thousands of acres of potential vineyard country in

Australia. The great thing about Australia is that it's not one big blanket of vineyard sitting under the same gorgeous sun all the time. It's really very varied.

The Hunter wines are much different to the Yarra Valley, to Margaret River, to the Barossa, to McLaren Vale, to Coonawarra — and thank God for the difference. Vive la difference because you get this great joy out of tasting different flavours. What's your favourite wine? I get asked. I mean, what a stupid question. What's your favourite piece of music? It depends how you feel. And the great thing about Australia is the range.

What we have to do now overseas is to teach people more about that range, and then we have to go into genuine single-vineyard wines to identify the best parcels of five acres, two acres, ten acres, and to really cultivate those properly to the nth degree. To make the very best wines we can, to have single vineyard names — because we have *terroir*, just as the French do, it's just never been that important to us, and now it's got to become more important.

Exporting is a key to the future of the Australian wine industry, according to Evans:

We've gone from a million cases in 1975 to two million in 1985 to more than 20 million today. It just shows what can be done. The local market is not going to grow that much in the quality market, as people switch from case and flagon to bottle and to higher and better bottle. The world is drinking a bit less, but a bit better all the time, and this is very much a help for Australia. As far as I'm concerned the potential is enormous. We still have two per cent or less of the world's wine exports. We have less than one per cent of the total wine drunk in America. I think we have seven or eight per cent of the English market and 14 per cent in value. I think we have 15 per cent in Ireland. So, if Ireland can do it, why can't the world do it. And that means you could become a vineyard to the world.

But the last thing I want to do is just ape French wines. I want to bring out distinctive wines or distinctive flavour from Australia. I looked at a very good South African chardonnay the other day made by a very able winemaker trained at Roseworthy, a New Zealander living in South Africa. I said, this is undoubtedly one of the best chardonnays I've seen to come out of South Africa, but what the hell about it is South African? Just tastes like a New World wine, you'd think it was made in Australia or New Zealand. It had nothing to do with South Africa at all. And there's the danger if you don't establish your national, regional, varietal and then your vineyard identity, you're just a mishmash.

Sparkling

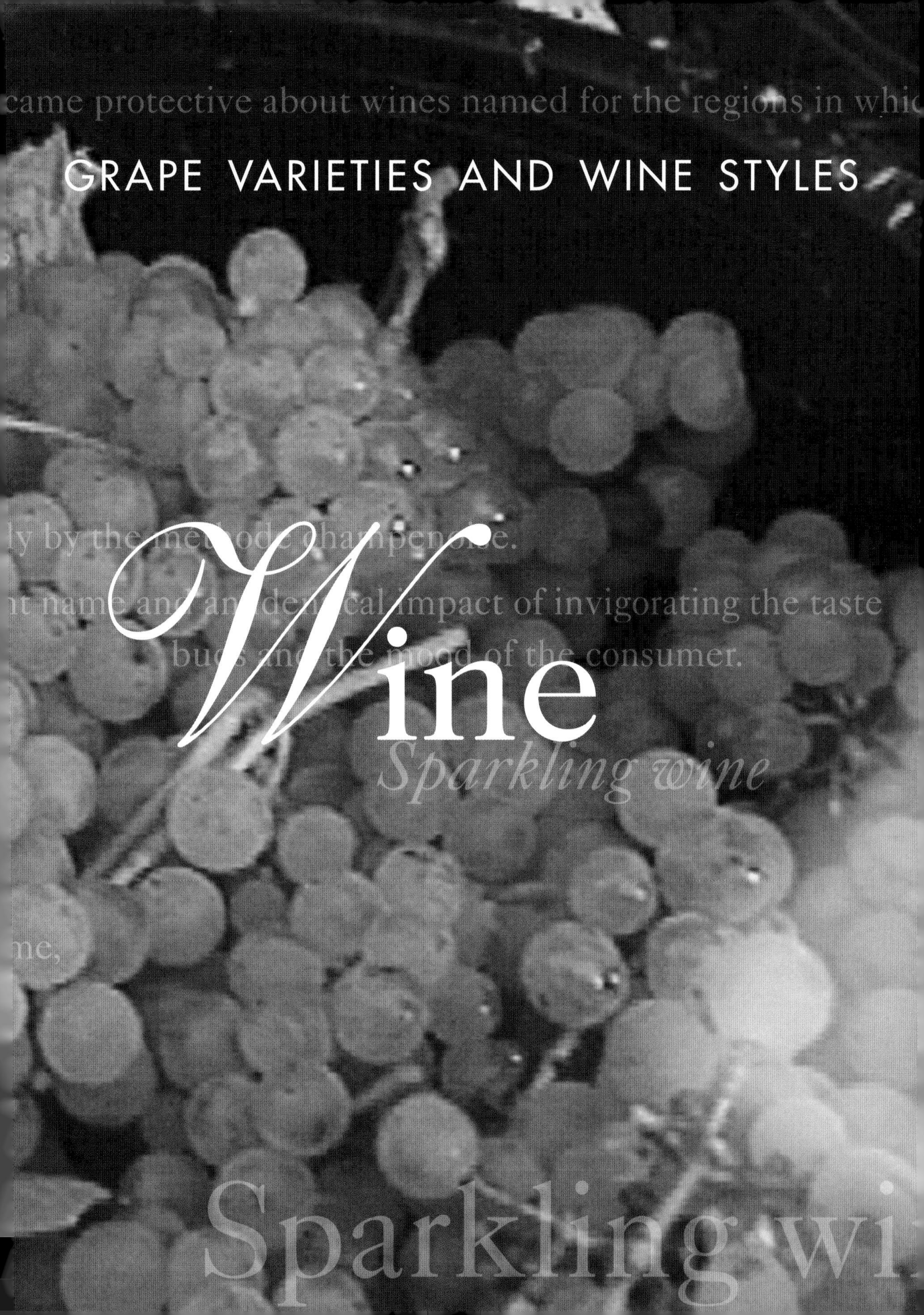

GRAPE VARIETIES AND WINE STYLES

ly by the methode champenoise.

t name and an identical impact of invigorating the taste
buds and the mood of the consumer.

me,

Wine

Sparkling wine

Sparkling wi

*W*e used to call it champagne. But the French, understandably, became protective about wines named for the regions in which they were developed — and Champagne was one of them. So now we in Australia are making sparkling wine, usually by the méthode champenoise. It's the same wine with a different name and an identical impact of invigorating the taste buds and the mood of the consumer.

Australia has been in the sparkling wine business for a long time, as Ian McKenzie, chief winemaker for Seppelt Great Western, 220 kilometres northwest of Melbourne, explains:

Maryann Egan with Ian McKenzie, chief winemaker, Seppelt Great Western

Seppelt have been making sparkling wine since 1918, but the history of sparkling wine in Australia in this region started well before then. The vineyards and winery were established in 1865 by Joseph Best. But in the late 1880s, a guy called Hans Irvine was really the instigator of sparkling wine production at this site when he bought the vineyard, took himself off to the UK to see if there was a market, decided there was, brought a champagne maker from France back with him and set up a sparkling wine operation. The Seppelt family bought this operation from Irvine in 1918.

In those days, there were very few people making sparkling wine in Australia. Coincidentally, another Frenchman was producing it in South Australia — and they both, independently, began working on sparkling reds at the same time.

The traditional méthode champenoise is still used for the premium sparkling wines today:

We start off with a base wine that is made much the same way as any other dry white. We add sugar and yeast, and that is put in a bottle with a crown seal. The wine undergoes a secondary fermentation and that produces the carbon dioxide of the gas that makes the cork go pop. After a period of maturing in the yeast — by law, a minimum of nine months, but it can be whatever the winemaker wishes after that — the time comes for disgorging the product, where we have to somehow remove the yeast sediment from the bottle and finish up with a nice clear wine.

You can do that by hand, where you put the bottles into wooden shaking tables, or by machine, and you can achieve the same result where the yeast is moved down on to the crown seal. Then a plug of ice is frozen in the bottle by a machine, trapping the yeast, and by pulling the crown seal off, that plug of ice is blown out and you finish up with a clear wine. A little bit of sugar is put back in to make it taste nice. And then it is corked.

Unexpectedly, the popularity of sparkling wine in Australia is producing a different range from those in countries overseas:

Bottling sparkling wine

> The Australian market has embraced sparkling wines as almost an everyday drink, which is different to the rest of the world. Most places, they regard sparkling wine or champagne as a celebratory drink and it really is only brought out on special occasions, whereas we in Australia tend to treat the wine style very much more as an everyday drink. As a result, we are now seeing some really innovative products coming on to the market which are nothing to do with traditional champagne, if it can be called that, but are aimed at people having a good time, often outdoors. We're getting some really interesting sparkling products which are just concept driven with frosted bottles, blue and pink bottles, and so on. They're fun, everyday wines, which I think is great. We're hoping that maybe we can start developing some of that usage, particularly in the United States because there's obviously a huge market over there.
>
> We tend to be very market driven in this company, which is the way it should be. And the market researchers keep telling us that there is a market out there for wines that have got quite a bit of fruit still, a bit of sugar. Even though people talk about brut and dry wines, they still drink very sweet wines, so we're just following that trend. And that's where a lot of these concept products are really. They are relatively sweet in sparkling white terms. They are fresh, fruity and they're easy to drink. That's what it's all about.

At the less expensive end of the Seppelt range, the Great Western Imperial Reserve and Brut Reserve are made using a bulk tank fermentation method, 'where it is still a natural fermentation for the secondary fermentation. But instead of being done in a bottle, it's done in a tank and then the wine is bottled at the end of that fermentation.' This is obviously a more cost-effective way of making sparkling wine. Ian McKenzie continues:

Taltarni vineyards, Tasmania

> The next price point is the transfer method wine, which is bottled, with yeast and sugar added, and it is fermented in the bottle — as distinct from the tank method. At the end of the time of fermentation, which is usually six months or so, the wine is transferred in its entirety with the yeast, with the sediment, into a pressure tank and filtered. The filtered wine is then put into a new bottle — and that's the bottle you buy the wine in.
>
> From the winemaking point of view, the transfer method gives winemakers much more flexibility. Because, at the end of the day, you

OPPOSITE:

*Dominique Portet and
Maryann Egan at Clover
Hill, Tasmania*

can have a whole lot of components which have been fermented individually in the bottle, from a whole host of different varieties. You can blend them right at the very end of the process to make whatever wine you like. Whereas the wine you're going to sell as méthode champenoise, where the wine is fermented in that bottle, you can't play with the blend. What you start with is what you finish with.

Sparkling red is one of McKenzie's passions:

I was a great collector of the old Seppelt sparkling burgundies made by that famous winemaker Colin Preece from back in the 40s and the 50s.

Wine & Wherefore

OPENING SPARKLING WINE

Sparkling wine is the ultimate drink for a celebration, but the occasion can be marred when popping corks turn into projectiles and damage the roof or furniture or, worse still, a guest.

Here are a few tips to make life with sparkling wine a bit easier and safer.

🍷 Sparkling wine should be served cold — about six to eight degrees Celsius. One way of ensuring this temperature is to put a mix of ice and water into an ice bucket and putting your choice of sparkling wine into the mix about 30 minutes before opening it.

🍷 If you are short of time, put a generous sprinkle of salt into the ice water mixture. Salt will chill the water temperature and the wine will be ready in about ten minutes.

🍷 As you prepare to open the bottle, put a clean table napkin over your left forearm — assuming you're right-handed. Remove the foil cover and underneath is a wire casing with a little circular piece. Pull that out,

give it six half turns anti-clockwise and it is ready to go.

🍷 Now is the time to be careful. If the pressure is really high, the cork could explode, so here's where you use the napkin. Place it over the top of the cork and gently remove the wire casing. Hold the base of the bottle with your left hand and, with your right thumb, firmly push the cork up.

🍷 If you don't have the strength to push up with your thumb, use a pair of pliers. There are some on the market designed specifically to open sparkling wine, but the pliers from your tool kit, or even a nutcracker, will do. Sometimes when you get to this stage, the cork breaks. If this happens, simply remove the remaining piece of cork with your favourite corkscrew.

🍷 All being well, the cork will remain intact as you loosen it and ease it out. You can still have a big pop. Pour the wine into your glass and have a taste. Even champagne can suffer cork taint.

Dominique Portet,
winemaker, Taltarni

I had a nice collection of those in my own right long before I thought of joining Seppelt — an opportunity that arose in 1983 — and that has allowed me to follow on, making a style of wine which I think is one of the world's unique wine styles and one of the great wines of the world.

Seppelt has traditionally used shiraz, right from the wine's inception, and it really started back in the 1880s. A lot of people don't realise that sparkling shiraz — or sparkling burgundy as it was called in those days — has such a long history here in Australia and is now regarded as a unique wine style of the world. It's something that the Seppelt family, in particular, carried on that tradition for many years, right through the time when there was no market for the wine. They still continued to make them. And I'm pleased they did, because I think it's led to the resurgence of the style. Now there are many producers making this lovely fun wine, and it's really great to see.

For sparkling shiraz, we look for softness and richness and nice full flavours, without too much tannin. The wines must be soft, otherwise they get too aggressive and not very pleasant. And, of course, to help that along, we have quite a deal of sugar in them. They're much sweeter than any normal sparkling wine, but they must be sweet to balance that tannin astringency that you naturally have in a red wine. It wasn't that many years ago there were only three or four producers of sparkling red. At the last count I did, there were more than 50. So it's obviously a style that's selling, and we're also starting to get a bit of interest from overseas.

John and Ann Ellis are on the small-scale end of making sparkling wine with their Hanging Rock Macedon, a name that links two famous places around 60 kilometres northwest of Melbourne in the area they chose for their vineyard:

The Macedon Ranges are climatically just exactly what we wanted for sparkling wine. It's cold here. In fact, this property is at 650 metres elevation (which, if you haven't converted, is 2,000 feet). And we get snow here. It really is a cold place to live and work. But that makes it ideal for growing grapes for sparkling wine. I guess the test of that is that the grapes *just* ripen. And that's what happens in the great sparkling wine area of France, Champagne, and that's what we were really looking for. Something that was as close as we could get to the climate of Champagne.

Starting as a maker of table wines, John's life changed in more ways than one when he got to know Ann Tyrrell, who became his wife:

I started making wine in the Barossa and then went to the Hunter Valley. I guess it was my father-in-law, Murray Tyrrell, who challenged me one day and said 'Well, you're not a bad winemaker but what do you really want to be?' And I had to think about that. I had to ask him what he really meant, you know. And of course he said, 'Well, my bag's pinot noir and chardonnay, what's yours?' And I really hadn't thought about it. I just thought at that stage — this is 20 years ago — that winemaking was winemaking. It wasn't a particular wine that was the thing to concentrate on. Well, it took about another 10 years to work that out…

A number of things happened along the way, significantly Ellis being shown by a French champagne maker how to process cool climate chardonnay for someone else's sparkling wine, and it intrigued him:

It was the challenge that was obvious. That here you started with a grape that you had to take all the way through to the bottled wine over a period of three or four years. And so many steps along the way. I guess it was that challenge which really got my interest, so then we went looking for the right property … and here we are.

He and his wife are in the middle of blending as they talk, sitting down with a line-up of wines, chardonnay and pinot, to blend in a way that, after fermentation with yeast and sugar, will taste like the three-year-old vintage, Macedon 6, that they were now selling:

Of course you've got to transport your mind a bit because that wine was on the tasting bench like this one three years ago. And a lot happens in those three years. But we're tasting Macedon 6 so that we can get a pretty good idea of the style that we're aiming to make. And we've had a few years' practice now at selecting the wines that will deliver the various attributes of this wine.

Maryann Egan tasting with Hanging Rock winemakers John and Ann Ellis

When we bottled Macedon 8, we kept a very large volume of wine in the winery which is destined to become probably 40 to 50 per cent of the blend that we're going to put together today. When we put this blend together, we're going to take a fair bit out of the blend again to put back into the winery for another year so that we can roll it on every year consistently. We can look at the wine that we started with last year, and it's changed a little bit because it's a year older. But, in essence, we've got those two reference points to look at: the one we're currently selling and the last one we bottled. Those reference points, and knowing what's going to happen, mean that we can predict pretty well what it's going to taste like. And just how good that prediction is, that's the big test.

FOLLOWING PAGE:
Growing grapes for sparkling wine, northern Tasmania

You've got to understand a bit of history of this wine and that is that, when we got our first vintage in, which was in 1987, we'd experienced a very normal year. A mild, good year. And the result in the barrel was: Wow! This is the great stuff. And then in 1988 we got a stinker. It was hot, it was dry and the grapes ripened a month earlier so they didn't have anything like the same flavour. And then, in 1989, we had 14 inches of rain during vintage. So everything was diluted, if you like. That gave us an idea of what the spectrum of experience was going to be. And if we were going to make a single wine from this one vineyard, we said well, it can't be a vintage wine. It's got to be a non-vintage wine.

And as those original wines from 1987 were maturing and we got to 1990, that's when we thought we were ready to put our first blend together. They'd been maturing in oak and gathering flavour. And we realised that what we had was the potential to make the wine that resembled, somewhat, the wines that we really enjoyed drinking the most. Which were Bollinger and Krug. So we decided that was going to be the style we would chase: a big, flavour driven, complex style of wine. Not the finer fruit driven styles that, for example, Chandon makes.

So that was the choice we made. We could have put more of the younger wine in there and fined it up, but in fact we thought, if we do this well, we'll be known because it's different. Rather than joining in the big, long queue with Seppelt, Croser, Chandon … little old us. We've got to be different. So the point of difference then was, what style of wine are we going to make? And it happened to be the one we like the most. Controversial, yes. It's had a lot of people talking about it. Fortunately enough of them love it and say so, loud and strong.

Ellis is again immersed in blending:

Now, I think the first base wine that we should look at is this one … Macedon 8. This is Macedon 5 and this is Macedon 4. We put it back on yeast lees in the barrel, so it's now had four years on yeast lees. So when we get to this, we'll find it's incredibly complex. There's only a little bit of it: three barrels, 675 litres … This one's on yeast lees in a tank and there's 9,000 litres of that. So we might put in a bit of these to balance up some of those that are very young, the 1998 vintages. You can see from the clarity of them that they're not quite finished yet, so they're not going to have the same depth of richness and complexity. Now, as well, we've got a couple of wines that have been deliberately kept back to give us some really rich, toasty, yeasty characters — so we can sneak a little bit of those in to balance the vast majority of wine which is younger and fresher to get the same complexity you're seeing in that glass there.

Sparkling

Food Match

SPARKLING WINE

Sparkling wine is known as the wine for a celebration, as an accompaniment to freshly shucked oysters. But there is actually a diverse range of dishes that can go deliciously well with sparkling wine.

For instance, the Italian style antipasto platter has a feast of flavours that set off sparkling wine. The soft texture of roasted capsicum is a lovely contrast to the bubbles in the wine. The prosciutto, the salami, the olives and the parmesan have a saltiness that draws out the wine's flavours. The fresh herbs in a garfish dish with fresh coriander or carpaccio with rocket and parsley are a lively complement to the fruity flavours in the wine.

Another perfect match is a glass of sparkling wine with a lazy Sunday morning yum cha, teaming it with the delicacy of steamed dumplings.

We've never, ever put any Macedon yeast lees down the drain.
They all go into the bottom of this tank. So there's actually less and less
wine in that tank every year, but that means we've got a consistently
renewing resource of yeast in the bottom of the tank. And what's
happening there is that the yeast cells are … I guess you could call it
decomposing. Autolysing is the real word. But as they decompose, the
contents of the yeast cells are absorbed into the wine, and that's where
the real richness and body of the wine comes from. Also the feel of the
wine. And when you overlay that with bubbles later on, that's where the
real softness starts to show through.

Later, much later:

Well, I think we're there. We'll put that together in the winery — and
some of those quantities are a little bit of a guess anyway … You
couldn't take that cloud out once it's in the bottle, so it will have to be
filtered and then it will be ready for bottling. If it passes the test again.
So when we've got it together, we'll get the old Macedon out and do
the comparative tasting again. And perhaps look to see whether some
of the other wines — like those older ones, like the pressings, like the
fruit driven younger wines — could be increased in quantity. Our
experience is that we get it pretty right.

I'd just like to say that this is the bit — this is IT. You put all of your
work into making these wines, you keep them separate all the way
because you know in nine months' time — today — we're going to sit
down and taste them in a line-up like that. And wow! All these choices
to make. This is the fun bit.

Dominique Portet has brought French bloodlines to the sparkling wines
he has made for Taltarni in the Pyrenees region of Victoria, around 220
kilometres northwest of Melbourne, and in northern Tasmania, where
Clover Hill was established in 1986 for the sole purpose of producing a
premium sparkling wine.

We were determined to use a French technique and to use French vines,
which are very well suited to sparkling wines and to the méthode
champenoise. They are quite energetic and not very high in alcohol.
They make very pleasant wines, very round in the mouth and very high
in quality. We haven't managed to emulate French champagne, but
we're very close to it. We still need another 10 or 15 years for the vines
to be old enough. Only then will we get that infrastructure, that feel in
the mouth, specific to champagne.

From 1975 up until now, quality has improved dramatically. Vine selection and techniques have changed in a major way. The next 15 years will be very important because, during that period, the vines will age. There is only one champagne technique, but the blends will change and so will the locations. It could be Clover Hill, Pipers Brook, Yarra Valley …

It's a pity that so many producers make sparkling wine just for the sake of it. For example, some parts of Victoria are hot, too hot. Yet people make sparkling wine. I don't mind. It's up to them. But it's a pity to lose the quality of sparkling wine.

Dominique Portet and Maryann Egan at Taltarni, Tasmania

Portet is enthusiastic about growing grapes in northern Tasmania, although he says it is a tricky region:

The climate is oceanic, we're very close to the sea — about 15 kilometres — and the soil is volcanic. We plant 5,000 vines per hectare, it's very high density — that's three times higher than at Taltarni in the [Victorian] Pyrenees. We control the growth rate and grow very high quality grapes. They're only ready to be picked quite late. A long maturity period and high acidity are the qualities for champagne and good sparkling wines.

In a young country like Australia, the problem is in educating the consumers, telling them what to expect in a wine. I arrived here in 1976, my first harvest was in '77. I was making dry wine, a dry riesling, and most wines on the market were sweet. So it was hard to develop the market. Now everyone drinks dry wine. It's funny, but that's the way it happened. It was quite a gradual, logical evolution.

He is his family's ninth generation of winemakers and vignerons from the Cognac region. About 40 years ago, his father took charge of the Chateau Lafite-Rothschild estate, almost legendary in its renown for red wine.

That's the environment in which I was brought up. I spent my youth learning firsthand about wine, so it's in my blood. I've got vintage blood in my veins. For a wine producer like myself, with longstanding experience, working in a young country has been amusing and enriching. Now I'm ready to move on and do other things.

Characters of the Industry

Prue Henschke, viticulturist, and Stephen Henschke, winemaker

Stephen and Prue Henschke

Henschke's Hill of Grace is next to Penfolds Grange in the scale of price and greatness of Australian reds. But Hill of Grace has something that Grange does not — a vineyard of its own. This is a vineyard planted about 130 years ago: the wine is made exclusively from its shiraz grapes. Whereas Grange is sourced from several vineyards and blended.

The fifth generation of Henschke wine producers, winemaker Stephen Henschke and his viticulturist wife, Prue, are justly proud of their historic vineyard and winery in Eden Valley, which is in the Barossa Ranges just a little to the east of Barossa Valley in South Australia. Prue says:

We believe they've lasted so long because of the soil profile here. There's a creek over there, we're in a sort of deep silt here, and we've dug holes to investigate where the roots are actually going. We've got down to 1.6 metres, we haven't met any sort of problem or layer that stopped the growth of the roots, and there's still roots growing down through that profile. So we believe that's the reason why — because they've got access to moisture right through any drought or bad weather, and it's kept them living on over the centuries.

Prue Henschke is spearheading a program to propagate new vines from the best of the old, making sure there is a new generation from this priceless genetic material. She is credited with playing a vital role in establishing Henschke's Lenswood vineyard in the Adelaide Hills, as well as introducing different pruning and trellising styles at Eden Valley.

Shiraz loves long plants. We give them long canes because they are very vigorous vines in that situation. You can imagine, when the buds burst and we get shoots developing with their bunches, it's going to be pretty shady, and that's not helpful when it comes to developing flavours in the fruit, which is what wine is all about. So what we've tried to do is take the foliage upwards, and we've done this with a Scott Henry trellis.

We've pruned back the vigour on these vines and then divided the canopy so that we've got sunlight on the top canopy with the fruit well exposed, and then down the bottom as well. We've got good light penetration on the leaves which are our little flavour factories. They photosynthesise and produce the flavours and the more sunlight they get, the better the flavour is. There's some actual flavour development through the receivable sunlight on to the berry itself, and it helps develop the colour of the berry.

Around the vines there is straw:

These are dry grown so what we're doing is conserving the moisture in the ground. We get an extra month of moisture, so that gets us through the growing season of the vine and, at about the point when the soil dries out at the top level, that's when we want the vine to start going into flavour production and not grow. So, we're helping the vine adjust to the drier conditions of an Australian summer. Plus, we've got weed control — as any gardener would know, controlling summer weeds is horrific. We've actually removed that process from our management, which is wonderful.

And between the lines of vines a healthy growth of grass:

We have inherited vineyards that have been cultivated regularly through the growing season, and we've seen them disappear over to the neighbour's paddock in the winds — wind and water erosion — so what we've done is develop a permanent grass cover that also helps us regenerate the soil, so it's rich in organic matter. They're able to contribute a small amount of mulch and other important

minerals into the soil and then for the vine to use them so that we don't have to use fertilisers either. We are growing early maturing rye, which won't use any moisture, or very little moisture, during the vine's growing season. We may get a native grass that will go dormant earlier, but that's still experimental.

Stephen continues:

I think probably we're at the stage where, in the fifth generation, there needs to be some sort of awareness of where our vineyards are going and where our wines are going. Because our vineyards are anywhere up to 130 years old, Prue's filled a role in terms of research and development in trying to hold those vines together. We almost consider ourselves more as custodians or curators of a museum in terms of the vineyard and the winery, and making sure it stays — using our scientific background to do that.

Certainly, if you want to try to use the advances in technology with flavour, you've got to start looking at different trellises, but then you've got to look at the value of something like Hill of Grace, where everything seems in balance and we do get that flavour in its present state. So there you're preserving, whereas in other areas you're advancing, which involves different technology.

We're both aware that the quality comes from the vineyard and that's the most important thing in terms of using the best of the light and sunshine and management techniques to get the best of the flavour and the colour. Prue's botanical background and scientific mind help to work those things through and it just needs a bit of discussion to come out with a workable solution — and, when it leads off in a positive direction, it's terrific! You always have to think of the practical things like the economy and the bottom line, whether it's justified in terms of how low can you go in yield before you start sacrificing the ability of the consumer to pay for the product. There are all sorts of issues you need to think about.

Different issues, no doubt, from when Johann Christian Henschke arrived in South Australia after a 98-day voyage from Silesia, during which his wife died. Settling initially at Krondorf, where he remarried, he bought land in what was to become Keyneton. He cut fence posts, dug soil and sowed wheat by hand. He and his sons pulled the bagged wheat they harvested about 100 kilometres to Adelaide on a hand trolley they built. Like other pioneers in the district, Johann Christian planted a few vines to make wine for the family. He probably made wines from the mid-1860s; records show he started selling them in 1868. His son, Paul Gotthard, continued to produce and sell wine, as did Paul Alfred of the third generation.

When his youngest son, Cyril Alfred Henschke, took over in the 1950s, he phased out the fortified wines and concentrated on high quality red and white table wines — not easy to sell to start with, but the foundation of the great winemaking firm that it is today. Stephen Henschke took over as winemaker in 1979, bringing practical and academic experience, which included two years' study in Germany.

I think what the German wine education taught me was care and attention. They are very disciplined and very scientific. I think that as I've grown — now that I've

been making wines for nearly 20 years — I've tried to work the wines back towards the way they would have been in the 1950s. That is, making wines with minimal handling so that the wines sort of evolve a bit more by themselves.

It was interesting for me to look back on retrospective tastings to see what the wines were like. You can see a snapshot of time — of what the technology was like in those days — if you look at the wines in the 50s, 60s, 70s and 80s. They're all different, the eras are all different and the flavours are quite different. Things that we'd done in the 70s, you wouldn't do to wine now. It was an awareness time of technology and they started using soft oxide in a controlled way, they had the analysis to see things and they started to use more finings. I've gone away from that sort of thing. We use very low levels of soft oxide and we do no fining.

I haven't fined a wine for nearly 20 years. If a wine's in balance in the beginning, it doesn't need it. Using Prue's skill, we try to get the wines in balance actually in the vineyard before they are even made. From then on, we do no rackings, we basically just ferment the wines on skins, press them out and then mature them in barrel for two years.

The conversation turns inevitably back to Hill of Grace and a comparison with Grange:

From our point of view, we don't really relate them because we try to make the best wine possible out of that little unique vineyard that we've got. So for us it's a good example of a museum vineyard that we don't fiddle with. We just let it do its own thing and it's in balance — it's been in balance for so long — and really just take the best care of the wine, just leave it alone effectively and let it develop by itself. It's a very different process because we accept the seasonal changes, where I guess with Grange, you can go to whatever vineyard is producing the best material in that season. It's a different way of going about it.

There is quite a difference between the two wines … the uniqueness of Hill of Grace, the fact that it's made from such old vines and from one individual vineyard and that's all there is. I mean, it's a designated vineyard and I guess it's a bit like a part of Europe, reflecting the flavours of Europe, middle of last century, and sitting in a little vineyard tucked away up in the Eden Valley hills. It's quite unique.

What about the way that Hill of Grace is going for so much money at wine auctions?

We don't like it that much because, for us, Hill of Grace is a different thing. Some people say it's just another wine, which it is, but it's the sort of wine you put a huge amount of effort into. It's like bringing up children. You know it from vintage to vintage, you know the colours and flavours and changes that happen. When you see it develop and grow, you'd rather have somebody buy the bottle of wine and put it in their cellar and, in a few years' time, open it up for a special occasion. Just have a glass of wine and enjoy it rather than trading it as a commodity. You can't stop that, but it's not what we make the wine for. We make the wine for people to sit down and say: 'Well, wasn't that great!' … and we love it ourselves.

Hill of Grace vineyard

New Regions

Tasmania

It is not so long ago that Australians thought of grapes as a hot climate product. Cool climate viticulture was in its early days in Australia when Andrew Pirie began planting vines in Tasmania a little more than twenty-five years ago for his Pipers Brook winery, around 70 kilometres north of Launceston. Vines had been grown in Tasmania's early days of European settlement, and then again in the 1950s, but most people didn't see grapes as a viable commercial crop. Pirie believed he could change this.

Looking for the original investors was, I guess, a challenge. But I told potential investors the story of cool climate viticulture in France — how it all happened in France and that it could happen the same way in Australia. Cool climates make great table wines. People knew I was serious, that I have the right background and I'd spent time in France, and they believed me. I didn't have a lot of trouble in getting support from the close circle of friends who put in some of the seed money for the business.

It has been a tough call for Tasmanians to take this thing seriously. The idea of viticulture in Tasmania has come way from left field as far as Tasmania is concerned. I think it wasn't until we won our white wine of the year award in the UK in 1995 that suddenly there was full support for Tasmanian wine. It's been a difficult thing for people to comprehend: that something which wasn't here could now be a world success. But now we're through that hurdle and Tasmanians are major investors in their local industry.

Pipers Brook started with the search for a climate/soil combination in some part of Australia, and Tasmania was eventually the place that my climate studies said, 'Well, this is the closest you're going to get.'

That was to do with the humidity, the rainfall, the rainfall distribution — a whole lot of things. The soils were important and we started the search just down the river at Freshwater Point, then moved out to the Pipers Brook district. The original site became successful from the 1980s — it was actually profitable, which was a great achievement, and that led to the growth of the business. The demand for the wine style was strong and we decided to keep on supplying the demand, so it evolved organically and we've now gone from one vineyard to ten vineyards in the district.

But the unusual thing about it is that we're staying Tasmanian. That's our business plan. We want to focus on Tasmania as our marketing niche. Normally, when a company gets to our size, it would start to spread its risks by going interstate to other regions. We've decided no, we're going to stay within this territory. We will be 100 per cent Tasmanian, and the reason is that we think people enjoy tasting the difference between Tasmanian wine and other wines. We don't want to make that confusing by having a bit of Victorian, a bit of West Australian. We want to keep it pure. So when people taste our wine, they know that it's Tasmanian.

I think the biggest challenge, within one lifetime, is to get the climate/soil/variety/management combination to produce great wine in a short period. And that's a balancing act because if you get it wrong it takes another 20 years to get a mature vineyard to get it right. I think we've been lucky in that we've got it right in a couple of instances. At Pipers Brook, that site, the way we pruned it, the way we made the wines, all came together and gave us a unique wine style. We're now trying to repeat that in all the other wine styles — some ticks there and a lot to do in the future.

Andrew Pirie talking to pruners at Pipers Brook

The core varieties Pirie has planted at Pipers Brook are riesling — 'one of the best sites for it in the district' — chardonnay, gewürztraminer and pinot noir. Cabernet sauvignon was the only one that did not survive on vineyard land that Pirie, who spent a year working in French viticulture and winemaking after gaining a master's degree in agriculture science, equates with a patchwork of European wine regions: 'I guess we've got a bit of Alsace, a bit of Burgundy and, in the far corner, a bit of Champagne.'

I think over the years we've learned what sort of knife edge we're on and, if you're on north-facing slopes in a nice soil type, you can make fantastic table wines. But as soon as you go into lesser soils or lesser aspects, you're starting to look at a marginal ripening, which means either sparkling wine or special varieties such as pinot gris, where you're going to get very early ripening. The advantage of this climate is very slow ripening, and in the best sites you get slow ripening and full flavour and full structure.

The negatives are in cool years you're picking late to get your full structure, but over the 20-odd years of winemaking, we've never made a riesling under 11 per cent alcohol. We've never made a chardonnay under 12 per cent alcohol. So it's actually not as marginal as some people might think. The truly marginal areas are yet to be planted. That's going to be out at Devonport or somewhere else, so we're still pushing the boundaries forward. Clearly, if you go down on to the flats into the heavy soils, you're going to be struggling, particularly if you plant cabernet or a late-maturing variety. With the experience of 20-odd years, I think it's all possible, but you've got to be fairly selective.

We started as a traditional family winery crushing 30 tonnes, then 50 tonnes, all done by ourselves on a one-tonne press, totally hands-on. Then we started the growth pattern that many wineries go through to an automatic press, with 100 tonnes in the late 1980s, so that's a measure of the growth. I guess we've gone from the basics through to a modern Australian winery. It's fantastic to have done it all — you get a total hands-on feel for the job. I appreciate having that experience both in the vineyard and in the winery.

We had the opportunity at the end of 1997 to take over the Heemskerk group of vineyards. We had always been constrained by the inability to grow our vineyards quickly. We detect a demand, but we have to go and plant our vineyards, wait for them to produce and then have more wine. The Heemskerk group were in the same area, they'd changed their vineyards to the same style as ours recently, so there was a greater opportunity to have more vineyards producing from mature vines fairly quickly. We jumped at that chance and now that absorption is complete — we feel as though we've been running those vineyards for some years now. It's been a very smooth and logical move, and I think we'll see the advantages from that roll forward in the next few years.

We have two labels, Pipers Brook and Ninth Island. We make them for very different purposes. Pipers is generally from older vineyards and it's made to be able to age. While it often can be good young, it has the capacity to age. Ninth Island is to drink now. It'll keep two or three years, but the idea is to drink it young. We separate the two when we're winemaking. We make the Ninth Island in a totally different way. We call that our bistro wine.

With the company he founded now hugely expanded with the support of its shareholders to be capitalised at $25 million, and providing about

35 per cent of winemaking in Tasmania, Pirie still keeps a focus on the creative side of his work:

> Pinot is such an important wine because it goes with so many foods that a very dry cabernet style won't go with. You need a pinot in the world because with game, with soft ripened cheeses, with slightly sweet sauces, pinot adds that element of sweetness which makes it work. If God hadn't invented pinot, we would have done so. I was drinking one of the greatest wines in my life in my first week in the wine business. That was a 1945 pinot from Burgundy, and it was a great experience. That's where I'd like to finish — making that wine. So I certainly know what I'm wanting to do.

In southern Tasmania, at Cambridge, 15 minutes drive from the heart of Hobart, Andrew Hood runs the island state's second-largest winemaking operation. It is a winery without a vineyard and the production is considerably smaller (at 250 tonnes, about one-quarter the Pipers Brook annual crush), but it makes an important contribution to the industry. It consists not only of Hood's own label, Wellington Wines, but also of contract winemaking that he provides for around 35 vineyards in various parts of Tasmania:

> There is variation between the vineyards because of the different regions they are in. They also vary a lot in size and the level of management. Obviously, the bigger vineyards are going to be more professionally run on a fulltime basis, whereas a lot of the smaller vineyards are run on almost a hobby or weekend basis by their owners. The style of wine I make tends to be fruit driven — I don't like to introduce a lot of winemaking contrivances. But it is interesting that, despite the fact that most of the wines get fairly similar winemaking treatment, there is quite a variation which I see as reflecting the original fruit.

The vagaries of the weather can be the opposite to what is happening on the Australian mainland:

> I've noticed — and other people have noticed — that, in the years where some of the mainland areas have got a lot of tropical influence, the normal stable high pressure systems have moved further south and influenced Tasmania a lot more. So in those years we can have really good weather … when some of the mainland areas are having wet weather. Vice versa can also happen. The system's moved north and we're stuck in what most people in Australia would regard as winter. The trouble is, it's summer months.

This makes it more important that the vineyards in the marginal areas have got earlier ripening varieties. And that's really happened to a large extent already. That's why pinot is such a widely planted variety in Tasmania. Chardonnay also, although it's a little bit later than pinot, but it's the earliest ripening of the major white varieties. So it works pretty well here.

Riesling is an interesting variety in Tasmania. It works really well in the warmer areas and that's where we try to source most of our fruit. But it is interesting that even in cooler areas or cooler years, it's a remarkably forgiving grape variety. You can have riesling which is only marginally ripe, yet, particularly with a couple of years age in the bottle, the wines can be fantastic. But this doesn't work with a comparatively late-ripening variety such as cabernet. Unripe cabernet never gets any better. It always stays mean and green.

But the cool climate of Tasmania is not cold enough for one of Hood's specialities. He not only makes a straightforward, floral dry riesling, but also a sweeter iced riesling:

Andrew Hood, winemaker,
Wellington Wines

In Europe and North America, they make traditional iced wines by leaving the grapes on the vine until the dead of winter and they actually pick the grapes and press them while they're still frozen. And a lot of the water in the grapes remains as ice in the press and the juice that comes out is concentrated by that removal of water.

It's got to be seriously cold to achieve natural iced wine. In North America, they don't even think about it until it's minus 15°C at night — far colder than we ever get here. I'd seen a few examples of European and North American iced wine which I found really attractive and I decided to try to make something similar using freeze concentration procedures which I apply to the juice. We've been doing it since 1995 and I am getting a handle on how to make that wine.

I started doing this as a bit of a hobby because I like that style myself. But it's taken off. The attractive feature of the wine is that it has concentrated riesling flavour without the added complexity of botrytis. You have intense floral characters and the concentration procedure also concentrates the acidity, so while it's a sweet wine, you also have a very zippy fruity acid balance as well.

Couldn't that be achieved by getting the grapes riper in the first place, then adding acid?

You can't get it that ripe. I don't start fermenting this juice until it's almost twice as concentrated as the original grape juice, and you can't get fruit that ripe without a lot of botrytis. And also, I might say, without losing a lot of the fruit because you'd have to leave it hanging on the vine well into winter and you've got botrytis, birds and the fruit starting to fall off the vine in the wind. Where they do these wines naturally, they suffer huge losses of fruit.

We use the same juice that we make our dry riesling from and freeze it artificially in a tank — an old milk vat. It holds about 1,500 litres of juice and we remove about 150 or 200 litres of ice at a time, so it's a fairly intensive, laborious process.

Eric Phillips, vigneron, Elsewhere Vineyard

It is frozen seven or eight times and the ice is just water: the actual grape juice with the sugar in solution doesn't freeze at that temperature, it just intensifies its fruity flavour until it is ready to start fermenting. 'The next step is for the juice to be pumped out of this tank and the ice will float down as the juice disappears. Over the next day or so, the remaining juice will seep out.'

Once made, what food do you choose to drink with this iced riesling?

You have to be careful. I know everybody thinks that sweet wines are for dessert. But it's got to be a fairly delicate dessert because this is really a delicate wine. Something fruit based — citrus soufflé or something like that. Or a crème caramel. Or it goes very well with a delicate blue cheese. And if you haven't any cheese or crème caramel, it doesn't go so badly on its own.

Eric Phillips has been growing flowers commercially to the south of Hobart for two decades, but vines have gradually been pushing the flowers aside at his Elsewhere Vineyard:

First harvest was 1988 as a commercial harvest. Prior to that we had a tiny vineyard by the house, where we experimented with pinot noir, had lots of fun … and sometimes we yearn for those felicitous days when life was far simpler than it is today. The first winemakers were ourselves — my wife and I, and friends — and our daughter crushed the fruit with her feet covered in plastic bags in a rubbish tin.

Richmond Bridge, Tasmania

By 1988, they shared both the winemaking and the fruit with Moorilla Estate. Then Andrew Hood returned to his home State in 1990 with 17 years of academic, technical and practical wine science experience, and set up a contract business dedicated to small vineyards:

This arrangement works very well for us and I think that at the infant stage of the industry in Tasmania it's absolutely critical to its future development because it's actually defining grape growing areas — sometimes very small areas — with potential for the future. And the industry will benefit very much by having had this opportunity to experiment with lots of wines in lots of different places in the State.

We make principally pinot noir. Half of the vineyard is planted to pinot, and that's both as a still table wine and as the base for our sparkling wine. In the future we will be producing sparkling from both pinot noir and chardonnay. We are growing dedicated cool to cold climate varieties. The clones that we have of pinot noir have been grown here for quite some time now and have proven their point. Our pinots have taken gold medals at the national show and our sparkling wine was the trophy winner for the best Tasmanian sparkling wine last year.

Having said that, the coast of Tasmania always presents warmer climates. We are very close to the open sea and we're on an estuary that is very close to a kilometre wide. We've lived here and grown flowers here long enough to know the climatic limitations of this property — and of the neighbouring properties for that matter. One hundred metres further up our hill it's quite impossible to grow grapes. It's simply far too cold and frosty. We're protected here in the lower levels by a mist which guards us to a large extent against frosts in the springtime and, further out towards the sea, the sea breezes are so strong and salty I think grapes would not do very well. I think that's essential information one must have before planting. To anyone coming into the business, I'd say live on your property for at least two years before planting a vine.

We attempt to present to Andrew perfect fruit. That's our job — to make his job as easy as possible by giving him blemish-free fruit. Our cooperation from the moment we start to deliver to the winery is very close. He's always available on the telephone. We get results back. If we need to wait a little bit or pick one part of the vineyard before another, we have that immediate feedback. After the wine is made, it's then a question of keeping up our contact and tasting the wine with him. We're invited to go to the winery and check out the progress of the wine and the critical decisions then as to when to bottle etc are ours — but always in consultation with Andrew. The choice of wood is ours, but in consultation.

Andrew's hallmark is clean, bright wines. But, at the same time, each district or vineyard is expressing its own individuality, which then points to the direction that small districts and subdistricts will be making wines of great interest. We don't drink our own wine all the time, we're very happy to drink wines that Andrew has made from other districts —

and they vary quite markedly and delightfully in their flavours and their colour even. And from year to year, adding the weather dimension, which then opens up a whole possibility of taste enjoyments.

And the future of the Tasmanian wine industry?

My view is that it's very rosy. It's going to require a commitment from the investors. A very long term commitment. There will be no quick returns. There will be a great satisfaction, probably after 20 to 25 years. It's going to require patience and some people are going to have to accept that there will be failures along the way.

Say white wine to an Australian and the instant reaction
variety has gained throughout the population in a very sh

Chardonn

Char

And not only in Australia, where it has leapt fro
to being the country's i

hardonnay

Chardonn

Why such popularity?

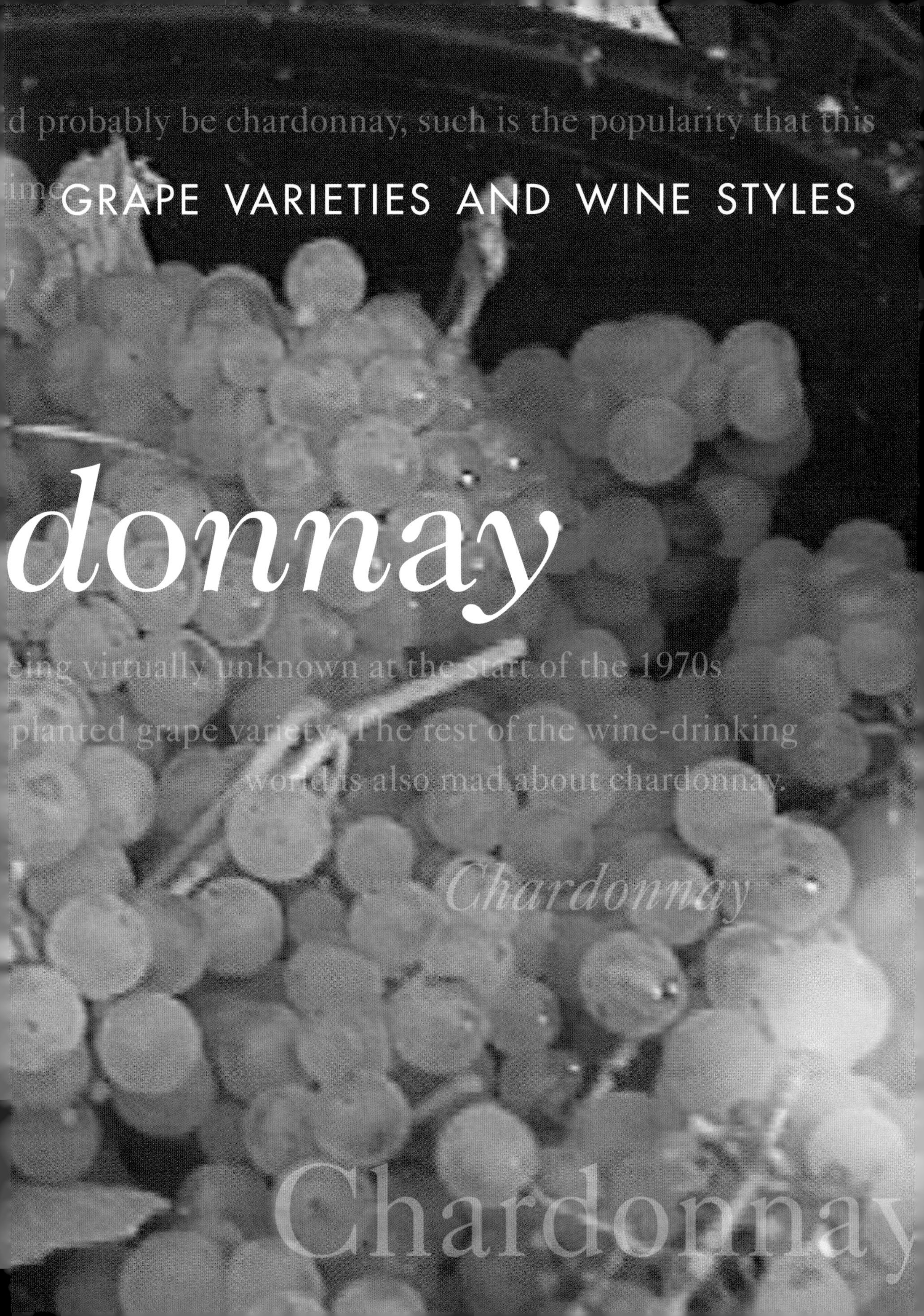

d probably be chardonnay, such is the popularity that this

rime...

donnay

eing virtually unknown at the start of the 1970s

planted grape variety. The rest of the wine-drinking

world is also mad about chardonnay.

Chardonnay

Chardonnay

*S*ay 'White wine?' to an Australian and the instant reaction would probably be 'chardonnay', such is the popularity that this variety has gained throughout the population in a very short time. And not only in Australia, where it has leapt from being virtually unknown at the start of the 1970s to being the country's most planted grape variety. The rest of the wine-drinking world is also mad about chardonnay.

Why such popularity? Keith Mugford, owner with his wife, Clare, of Moss Wood in Western Australia's Margaret River region, has an answer:

> My attitude to chardonnay is that it deserves its highly sought-after status because it is a very complex grape variety. It has a flavour profile which is really interesting: multi-layered combinations of flavours which most of the other varieties can't deliver. And then you have the added complexities that are associated with the oak handling.
>
> Chardonnay can also be made quite delicious because ripeness, softness, suppleness … it's quite a part of the style. So, for me personally, it's a pretty interesting grape variety. Whilst I acknowledge the quality of wines like riesling, semillon — and indeed will enthusiastically consume any of those wine varieties — and acknowledge the selling potential of, say, classic Hunter Valley semillon or whatever, the thing about chardonnay is that it makes a really interesting, complex wine. And that's why people like to drink it.

Mugford also makes it at Moss Wood, one of the small wineries in the Margaret River area, which is 280 kilometres south of Perth on a scenic stretch of coastline with very good surfing. His chardonnay was declared one of Australia's top 20 by *The Wine Magazine* in October 1997. Yet his vineyard is not quite nine hectares, with 14,000 vines — so few in comparison to the big wineries that the local joke is that he doesn't need selected monitor vines to work out the big picture of what is happening in his vineyard, he can monitor them all.

> We have the opportunity to be in them and around them all the time. We value people's time in the vineyard as being a very significant contributor to final wine quality. It's true, too, in the winery that, when we're dealing with small batches, we have the opportunity to be as careful as possible in all the stages of the process. And I guess that allows us to have a consistency and a uniqueness that a bigger organisation may not necessarily have.
>
> On the other hand, a large organisation has enormous technical resources that we don't. So, I guess if I see a strength for small wine production, particularly on really good and interesting sites, it is that we

have the opportunity to maximise the quality that comes from our vineyard because of the level of our hands-on input. And if we play our cards correctly, we can do it consistently — if you look back over a range of our wines, you can see that the style is consistent. It's come from the one place.

Over two decades, Mugford's approach to making chardonnay has changed from being 'traditionally Australian' to 'working out how a more traditional Burgundian technique may suit our chardonnay style'.

Keith Mugford, owner/ winemaker, Moss Wood

We've introduced malolactic fermentation and extensive lees contact. We still, of course, use all new oak and those sorts of things, but the level we have used this — for want of a better word — Burgundian technique has chopped and changed to a degree. Underneath it all, what we have wanted to do is to make Margaret River chardonnay which basically gives a statement for the region.

Burgundy is, of course, the French province renowned for chardonnay (as distinct from its great red wines), and it is one of the many compliments given to Leeuwin Estate's premium chardonnay from Margaret River that comparisons are made between Australia and France at this level. James Halliday has referred to the best vintages of the Leeuwin Estate Art Series Chardonnay as having 'many of the attributes of a top-flight French White Burgundy', the wine made solely of chardonnay grapes, but named after its home province. Halliday is also quoted as saying these wines are 'on a par with the greatest of the New World and perilously close to the best of France'.

Leeuwin Estate's executive winemaker Bob Cartwright is contrastingly down-to-earth about chardonnay, why it is so popular and why he makes it so well. First, on the reason for its popularity: 'I think because people like it. I think in Australia, generally, chardonnay is a bit more full-bodied than a lot of the other white wines and a lot of red wine drinkers just like that extra, fuller body that you can get with chardonnay.'

And why should some of the Australia's best chardonnays come from Margaret River?

That's a bit difficult to answer because the Margaret River area is spread over quite a big distance, and the climate from one end to another varies quite a bit. I think it's because some people down here have made some very, very fine chardonnays, and I guess that's brought Margaret River to the forefront as far as chardonnay is concerned.

I think part of the story is that we're using a clone which is a low yielder and produces very good, strong flavours. And we've got a very good viticulturist who knows and understands chardonnay and that's very important. I think a lot of people, particularly in the bigger vineyards, don't know and understand the variety perhaps as well as they should. In other areas of Australia, they're using a lot of clonal material which is high yielding and it just doesn't have the flavours. But I guess at the end of the day we need that anyway because you'll always have people who want to buy a Rolls Royce and people who want to buy a Holden Commodore, and you need both levels.

Chardonnay grapes

When I came down here, there was only a handful of wineries and we were all pioneers in those days. The most successful wine at that stage was a Rhine riesling from Vasse Felix. You know, no one knew at all the potential of chardonnay. But once we started making it, we said, 'Hey, we have something fantastic here.' And we were very lucky because our viticulturist arrived about the same time and he'd had experience in Cowra with chardonnay, and perhaps knew a lot more about it than most people because chardonnay was a new variety to Western Australia at that time.

Initially, the styles were very much more concentrated on the big, fuller chardonnay characters that we got ... You must also remember that in those days things like barrel fermentation of white wines — even though they'd been doing it in France for centuries and in other parts of the world for some time — in Australia were something almost new. And so in the early days we were very cautious and we were only doing 30 per cent or 50 per cent maximum of barrel fermentation. Now it's 100 per cent.

This adds a lot of complexity to the wine because you have the oak flavour, and I think from the fermentation in the barrel you get a lot of fine oak flavour rather than just a straight oak character. Also, by keeping it in oak for that period of time, if you've got a really good fine-grained oak it's not that obvious because a lot of the volatile oak flavours are blown out with the fermentation. It's a different oak character from just storing it in barrels.

Leeuwin Estate wines 'don't really start looking 100 per cent until they're three or four years old, and so we're releasing them as an aged wine'. He talks about a three-year-old chardonnay that 'still looks very much a youngster. And that's part of the whole thing about this part of the world and this vineyard. We've got the fruit that we can age for a long time.'

This, of course, adds to the winery's costs which are quite considerable when it comes to chardonnay:

It is labour intensive all the way through. I mean, fermenting in barrels is a lot more work than fermenting in a tank. If you've got a tank, you have one unit and, if you put it in barrels, you might have 50 units. So a lot more work is involved: the topping up all the time, the lees stirring, the malolactic fermentation in barrels, if you need to do some. It's very time consuming. And, of course, for our Art Series Chardonnay, we use 100 per cent new barrels. With the value of the Australian dollar, it's more than $1,000 each. And that effectively puts — if you just run it straight out from $1,000 — $3 a bottle for the wood for that particular vintage without all the other associated costs.

Bob Cartwright, executive winemaker, Leeuwin Estate

Yet even while commanding peak prices for an Australian white wine, chardonnay is in huge demand:

We're planting more and more because the demand for our chardonnay is so great that we just cannot meet it and we see a lot of potential in expanding our own production to cope. In the rest of Australia, I don't know. We're hearing all these comments — 'ABC, Anything But Chardonnay' — and maybe there's a bit of a general trend away from it. At the moment, you're seeing products where you've got chardonnay blended with semillon. Perhaps this is an indication that, maybe, in the bottom end of the market anyway, the chardonnay situation is a bit saturated.

But not at the top. In 1998, when Leeuwin Estate's premium chardonnay was the highest priced release commercially available in Australia at $67 a bottle, Penfolds brought out a chardonnay called Yattarna and set its price at $70. What drove this first-time release up to that level? Penfolds chief winemaker John Duval has a simple answer: 'Us as winemakers telling sales and marketing that it's a great wine — and over to you, guys.' Prices for both wines rose immediately through retail demand, with Yattarna going to $180 at auction soon afterwards.

Although Yattarna has only just arrived on the scene, it had six years incubation through experimentation and a series of trial bin wines. As John Duval says:

We were very happy with the '95 straight away, but we wanted to make sure that we had the consistency to continue afterwards. We wanted to make sure that the '96 was great and the '97. The first release, the '95 vintage, is a blend of Adelaide Hills and McLaren Vale. Our resources in each of the sites are a little bit different — different elevations, aspects and, in some cases, different age of vines — and those blending options are great to have. Grange is exactly the same: a blend of many vineyards. But it's blended to a style and certainly that's our intention with Yattarna: that we've formulated a style which we're very happy with and we'd like to continue.

Is it important for this wine to age well?

Yes. The criteria with Yattarna was to make a wine that was, perhaps, a little bit more austere as a young wine. It was to be an elegant style with, I guess, a finer flavour profile. And one of the really important things about great white wines is the intensity of flavour and the length … that sort of persistence that stays in your mouth a long time after you've swallowed. That's why we've got to look for cool climate areas and are focused in on that.

And why chardonnay?

We've taken a lot of advice. We've spoken to people in the industry. And what it boils down to, we're very much an international or global wine company now and we'll be selling our wines overseas, not just to Australia. Certainly we're very keen to look after Australia, but we want it to be an international wine. Riesling, semillon and chardonnay were the main varieties we considered. Now, as much as I like drinking riesling, and we make some great rieslings in Australia, it's a really tough sell to take that internationally and say: 'Look, this is our flagship white wine.' To a certain extent, that's the same with semillon. People say, 'Grange is made from shiraz, why couldn't Yattarna be semillon?' But shiraz is much higher up the pecking order in terms of red wine than, perhaps, semillon is in terms of the whites.

So, again for that reason, we thought it'd be a pretty tough sell to take that around the world. And it would take a long time to build up that reputation. But we really haven't eliminated the fact that, OK, the '95 Yattarna is 100 per cent chardonnay. But at some time down the track, it may well develop that we use a small proportion of another variety — just to add complexity and still remain within the style parameters of Yattarna. Just as with Grange: in some vintages there's a little bit of cabernet in the blend. It's consistent with the Penfolds philosophy to make blended wines.

Interestingly, these conversational links are far from the first to be made between Yattarna and Penfolds top-priced, internationally prized Grange. No one in the company tried to stop its nickname of 'white

Grange', even when 'research from the marketing people came across Yattarna, an aboriginal word meaning "little by little" and "gradually", and it was felt that did embody the whole project because it's been gradually developing over six years, one step at a time with all the trials we've done. So, Yattarna it was.'

Characters of the Industry

Joe Grilli, winemaker, Primo Estate
OPPOSITE: *With his wife Dina*

Joe Grilli

From the moment Joe Grilli's father, Primo, arrived in Australia, it was his ambition to plant grapes. He had grown grapes and olives in central Italy on the Adriatic coast and, when he settled in Virginia on the hot, dry plains at the northern outskirts of Adelaide to run a market garden, it didn't matter that there were no other vines around. His dream remained. Joe Grilli tells the story:

It took him from 1953 to 1973 to plant a vineyard. A bit of a crazy thing to do really — he hocked up his previous 20 years' work to plant a vineyard in 1973. He was one of the first people to plant in the Adelaide plains area. He just planted vines here because he knew the soil was good and the climate was more Mediterranean than the Mediterranean, it was a beautiful climate and he planted grapes just going by his own feelings.

By the late 1970s, his two sons — one of them myself — had grown up to the stage where we were looking at our careers and my father basically said, if you want to go into the wine industry, we can build a winery here next to the

vineyard that I've planted. It's up to you. My brother and I decided in 1978 that we would build a winery for the '79 vintage. And so my father, out of love for his two sons, once again put all his previous 25-plus years' work at stake. Which is really an amazing story. I don't know if I'd do that for my two sons, but that's what he did. He had complete faith in his two sons to get into the wine industry.

Joe and Peter Grilli were only 20 and 18 respectively when they made the decision to build the winery, and Peter left the business in 1985 to do his own thing. That first Primo Estate vintage in 1979 coincided with Joe's graduation from Roseworthy Agricultural College as Dux of the Year. He is Primo Estate's winemaker and he shares the marketing responsibilities with his wife, Dina. Their approach to winemaking has always been to try something different.

From our very first vintage in 1979, we produced a double-pruned cabernet sauvignon — just a few acres of our three-acre patch of cabernet that we

double-pruned. Now, without going into it too much, it's a reasonably abstract thing to be doing to some vines: pruning them twice and making the fruit ripen well into May to try to develop a unique style. What we got was a very small yield, very small berries, very fine berry fruit characters in that fruit — and we made a very different style cabernet sauvignon to the more full-bodied style that this area can regularly produce. We were after a finely textured wine, which we achieved, but it was one of those things that was just impractical. It was different and we had a lot of fun making it. It was my brother, my dad and I pruning those vines a second time and this required a particular skill, and when that was not possible any more we really couldn't hire people to do it. So that was one of those things too crazy to do.

After 1991, they stopped. By then, Primo Estate had made its name in other areas. First, it was a sweet white wine made with botrytis riesling, produced from 1981 when few Australian winemakers were making it and it put Primo Estate on the map. 'We developed that and it was really quite a thrill. It's still an important part of what we do.' At the same time, they introduced new varieties of grape into what was very much 'a riesling, cabernet sauvignon world', as Grilli describes it.

We planted colombard in those days purely on the theory that it's a grape that's very late maturing and is suited to warmer areas and has a really good propensity to retain acidity. All things that were supposed to be good for sunny climates like here at Virginia. We really didn't know what wine we were going to make. We just planted on that theory and

our first vintage of colombard was 1982, and it grew steadily to the stage where it's now our main wine. It's given us a lot of satisfaction that it has developed into a very sought after wine and it's not a riesling, it's not a chardonnay, it's not a semillon, it's something very much that Primo Estate has developed.

They were good times back then because, you know, when you crush a grape and you don't know what sort of wine you're going to make, it's a process of discovery and sure, there are disappointments, but when it works it's a real buzz.

I think if you're a small winery, no matter where you are, it's our role to make some experimental wines. When you look back at the history of the Australian wine industry, a lot of the mainstream styles began with a small producer somewhere trying something different. Chardonnay began with small producers, and even the trend now towards unwooded chardonnays began with the small producers. As the bigger companies tend to see the successes, if they see an opportunity, then they develop it in a more commercial sense. That is a continual process, but for the small winemaker, really, that's our reason for existing: to try these different things. And for people who buy our wines, I think they're looking for that from small wineries.

Grilli places Primo Estate as a bridge between the old world and the new in terms of winemaking:

We have all the technology at our fingertips, but we are very mindful of using as much of the traditional part of winemaking that works. For example, the botrytis wine came into being by using some pretty cheeky technology to culture the botrytis spores and inoculate it onto the fruit. But that doesn't mean Primo Estate is a high-tech winery. You won't see a rotofermenter at Primo Estate. All our reds are still fermented in open fermenters, which I reckon produce a beautiful, satisfying red wine. You can't even say why open fermenters produce a better wine but there's just a bit of something in the wine, a bit of a mystery that comes from having them used. So that's an example of how we use both technologies.

Primo Estate is all about making very individual, very personal wines. Making wines that, really, you can't get anywhere else. If you look at everything that we do, it's all geared around that philosophy. My dad, I think, has probably looked at what we've done with bemusement, but I think he now understands more than anyone where we come from as far as trying all these different things. When I think about my family back in Italy ... my grandmother's still alive and I think that she would look at what we're doing and she'd be very proud of the way that we've used a lot of Italian influence to inspire us. But she's also very well aware that her grandchildren here in Australia are very much Australian. We're a mixture of Italian and Australian influences and we feel very lucky to be in that position.

Grilli's Italian inspiration includes wine styles such as his Joseph Sparkling Red and grape varieties such as barbera and nebbiolo. And, of course, the olive. Since 1989, he has been making extra virgin olive oil from the thousands of olive trees planted by Italian and Greek migrants who settled after World War II in the Virginia area. On a visit to Tuscany in 1987, he and his wife, Dina, saw wine and olive oil produced on the same estate. Back home, he negotiated with the olive growers all around him and the Joseph Extra Virgin Olive Oil came into existence.

The olives are picked by hand on to these mats. We have to go to a fair bit of trouble to take the leaves away — a little bit of bitterness from the olive is OK, but not from the leaves. And all these olives are taken to the press in beautiful, pristine condition and then we look after the oil just like we look after the wine — and that's really all there is to making a really good extra virgin oil. The ripeness of the olives is also important. When they're half green, half black ... this is a good example of a good time to pick them. You've got a lovely green colour and a sort of peppery character from the greenness, but those slightly riper olives give a nice fullness and richness to the oil. So when I see olives like this, that's just perfect for making a really good extra virgin olive oil.

Wine, olive oil, what next? 'We're working on a vinegar.' Of course. 'We're working on a very old, wood-aged vinegar that I think will be a perfect complement to the olive oil and the wine.'

Characters of the Industry

Murray Tyrrell, wine producer, with Pria Viswalingam

Murray Tyrrell

Murray Tyrrell is a gruff sort of a character, a countryman who speaks his mind. Not for nothing is he known as 'the voice of the Hunter', being a third-generation Hunter Valley wine producer who is not far off 80, but still active in the family wine business and involved in the region where he has lived all his life.

> We're standing on the original bit of land that was selected by my grandfather in 1858. There is the original house that he built and the first vineyard he planted that we've had to pull out over the years because of soil erosion on the steep hills. Here are vines which were planted in 1879 — they're a shiraz and they make the best wine in the Hunter I think. My uncle took over at the age of 16 and his father used to drink a lot. He used to say to us that when he came home from school every afternoon, they were all drunk with a couple of jars of wine under that tree.
>
> This vineyard was easy to work when we worked it with the horses because the rows were four feet wide down the bottom and 20 feet wide at the top. You had to have silly beggars like the Tyrrells to carry the plough through the four-foot rows. In recent years, we've pulled out every second row, so we could put the tractors through because I'm getting too old to use a horse and no one else will use one.

Murray Tyrrell is credited with producing the first commercial chardonnay in Australia, the 1971 Vat 47 Pinot Chardonnay. The Vat 47 wines are still among the company's greatest, winning more awards at wine shows than any other Australian chardonnay. The Vat 1 Semillon has led the way in its field, winning more than 300 awards since it was first produced in 1963. Vat 9 Shiraz and Vat 6 Pinot Noir, also award-winners, complete the line-up of flagship Tyrrell wines.

They are, literally, the tip of a wine mountain. Tyrrell's is now one of Australia's largest privately owned wine companies, selling about 600,000 cases annually. Its range of wines begins at the Long Flat, easy drinking red and white, moving up through Old Winery, individual vineyard and the new Rufus Stone label, which takes in Hunter grapes beyond the Tyrrell property. While the company's main operations are still on the home ground established 140 years ago, it also owns vineyards at Heathcote in Victoria and in the Coonawarra and McLaren Vale regions of South Australia.

Murray Tyrrell is now chairman, with his son Bruce taking over the running of the company as managing director. Tyrrell looks back on his years of wine production, which saw the company double its size every five years from the mid-1970s, and his thoughts are in the vineyards:

I think things are getting harder. We've got too many academic idiots running around telling us what to do. You know, they came the other day and wanted to know where the prevailing winds came from. And I said, you just need to look at that tree, you don't need all your meters. It makes you intolerant, it's a waste of time because everything is there for you in nature if you've got two eyes and can see.

We have sprays, we have insecticides, and the chemical companies are brainwashing our vineyard managers, taking them to parties, filling them up with wine, telling them to use these things. Two years later: 'Oh, that's banned, we've got to use something else.' And this is a continuous thing and we don't know where we are. When it all boils down, we go back to the sprays I used in the 50s and they're still the best by far. You've got to understand what goes on naturally and, if you don't, then you're in trouble. If you haven't got the commonsense and you're not observant, you'll never get on and that's the big trouble with the industry at the moment — too many people run it

by computers. Too much science, far too much science. You can't beat nature — nature's there to stay and no way can you beat it.

Yet even nature seems to be changing — admittedly with some human assistance:

We've cleared far too much of the land. If you look behind me, look through my house across the road there, it's all been cleared. The bush fires of 1938 and 1968 were instrumental in killing such a lot of that timber. But we need that timber, we need those trees there. They affect the weather patterns, control the storms, bring more rain. The more you open it up, the less rain you've got, the more problems you have with wind and everything else. So it has changed considerably. These creeks in front of me were running all my life. But now they haven't run for eight years and everyone's got dams and contour banks and doing all sorts of things which, with the extraction of timber, have affected them.

We haven't had the big storms that we had when I was a boy and as we go on it seems to be getting dryer and dryer in this area. And that's probably a good thing in making quality wine. We don't want irrigation — anyone who thinks he can make better wine by irrigation than dry land farming ought to go to his doctor, there's something wrong with him. We need the dry weather and not too much moisture so the roots will go down. They'll follow the limestone trail in this country and get all the moisture they want. And by doing that, we get more concentrated grape juice, more flavour, more colour, more acid, more of everything. I think we're making now as good a wine as we've ever made in this area, despite the changes I said earlier about science. On this place we're still making them by hand and in the old style. We're making better wines than we were.

After 40 years, it's time I got out of the road. I'm like the bird on the biscuit tin now: on the outside looking in. I handed over to Bruce and I don't know if I handed over too many bad habits. I hope I handed over a lot of good ones. I think we've given him some great wines to go on with, and how we make them and how we've handled them over the years. So it's up to him now, as the next generation, to carry on.

Bruce Tyrrell picks up the conversation:

One of the great things of this sort of business is the flow in the family. You've got the flow in tradition, but also that brings the flow of great knowledge. When you get in a hole, being able to walk in and say: 'Listen, I've got a bit of a problem with this — which way do you think we should jump?' Having the ability to lean on that knowledge is a tremendous benefit. So often you see in any business of any type a lot of people with experience are pushed out and no longer available, and it's a tremendous loss to everyone. We're very lucky. Having Dad around looking over my shoulder is pretty handy. Hopefully I'll still be around to pass the same things on to my children.

One of the most important things in my life, from a very early age, was that this was what I was going to do. This industry is a very jealous mistress — takes a lot of time. But you work to hand on to the next generation. I think that's the thing that's been behind everything we've done here for as long as I can remember.

Discussions between the two Tyrrells and their chief winemaker Andrew Spinaze — 'who's also got a stubborn streak in him' — sound as though they can be lively. At the end of the day, though, over the choice of a blend, the decision goes to the Tyrrells because that's where the buck stops. Murray has the final word: 'You gotta be pretty sure of yourself if you want to keep that family tradition. You've got to be sure that what you're putting in the bottle with your name on the label is the highest standard that you want it to be.'

Wine Auctions

Auctioning wine may seem like sacrilege to those who buy their wine to drink, not as an investment. It has become very popular, however, with buyers and sellers — and as some people point out, it can be a way of financing the next major purchase of wine for your cellar.

Stewart Langton, managing director, Langton's Fine Wine Auctions

Stewart Langton, auctioneer for Langton's Fine Wine Auctions in association with Christie's, makes it all sound very easy. 'It is simply a wine auction, the simplest method of selling anything. It's catalogued, it's put in a lot, it's put up and you knock it down. It is sold within a few seconds. It is a very simple method of selling and very efficient.'

But isn't it intimidating? 'It shouldn't be intimidating, but I understand that it could be, and I would always recommend people to come along the first time to see how it is done — don't bid. And when you do bid, don't get carried away. Always come with how much you want to spend, how much you want to buy a particular bottle for, and if it goes too high leave it alone. Try next time.'

Langton's specialises in the top end of the market, not suprisingly. But not exclusively. 'We sell $10 bottles and we sell $10,000 bottles.' Nor is it only the obvious, well-off buyer who goes to auctions to buy wine as Langton points out.

It's a passion for a lot of people. Obviously professional people, because of disposable income. But we see lots of people — tradesmen etc — who are passionate about wine and spend a percentage of their income on wine rather than other things.

The investment is fairly recent. It's not something people considered — a bottle of wine was to be purchased, stored away and drunk when mature. What has happened, of course, is that the boom in premium wine has pushed up the prices and people suddenly find that the bottle of wine they put away several years ago is now quite valuable. And so it becomes a decision whether to consume or to sell. Some people sell half and drink half to pay for the ones they plan to drink — it's become very profitable in that way.

I think the majority of buyers are still people looking for good wine at a good price or to find something that they can't find anywhere else. There is an increased percentage of investors — of course, there is. But even then they tend to be consumers who have realised that they are on to a fairly good thing and perhaps they can finance their future drinking by buying wine.

Most of the wine we sell is under $50 and generally finds its own level. Because we sell the same thing over and over again, we can pretty much predict prices — it's very easy for us to tell a vendor about what they expect to receive. If it's satisfactory, we put it in — if not, we ask them not to put it for sale. So that's their protection really — the market.

What guarantee does the buyer have of cellaring quality? 'In principle, there are no guarantees, but as an organisation we are forced to vet everything that comes through. So we only put things in that we are happy with, depending on their price level — but, of course, anyone takes a risk with an older bottle.'

And what about the possibility of fraud, like the fake Grange which surfaced not long ago?

We haven't found another bottle. It hasn't really affected the market — I don't think. It initially made people more aware that they had to be careful. But if you come to someone like us, we obviously know what we are doing. We can spot a fake if we see one. So I don't think it's been an issue in the market since. It didn't happen before because the price wasn't high enough and the right wine wasn't rare enough. Grange — 1990 Grange — is the first wine that's achieved that: very high price, short supply, international market, then it becomes inevitable.

Fellow auctioneer Andrew Caillard has more on Grange prices and the influence of buyers who live overseas and, like prospective buyers elsewhere in Australia, put in their bids by fax.

Auction catalogue and bottle

We shove them on to the sell sheets — there is always last minute stuff before an auction because everyone leaves it to the last possible minute. People are putting in realistic bids so, unless the bids on the floor can actually beat the bids here, they will get them. So we have a pretty good idea of how the sale will be before we stand up — although we don't know the intensity of how good it is going to be or how bad.

For instance, with this sale, we are seeing that the market for Grange is beginning to flatten off. We have known that this was going to happen. The market's been very thin for almost a year — it's been supported by a couple of buyers in the United States and Switzerland — and we see a general flattening of the Grange market for some time.

In a report recently we have described the market like the

atmosphere: you don't really see the various currents that move within
it. You have got some wines going upwards and some going
downwards and others doing nothing. So it is quite a
complex market. At the moment, the market is looking pretty
strong except for Grange. The reason for that is the Grange is
seen to be overvalued. We saw prices skyrocket last year, and
they skyrocketed on the basis of two or three people — that's
what you call a speculative market. So people have to get
used to the fact that the speculative market is not there. Once
they get used to it, the prices will become firmer and it will be
easier to sell. I think it will take six months to get to that stage.

*Auctioneer Andrew
Caillard calls for bids*

Grange is an indicator. Although there are other wines that are
starting to become indicators as well, like Henschke Hill of Grace. You
have to remember that not everybody can afford to buy $200 bottles of
wine. I mean, there are lots of people here that just like to buy bottles of
wine to drink. So, it's like a retail market where you have price points,
where you have different demands of intensity and bidding at different
price points.

Most people who come to these types of sales can afford to drink
wines in the $20 to $40 mark. Therefore there is a good intensity of
bidding there. But as the prices start going up, you start seeing a
thinning out of the market. It starts becoming more eclectic, more
subject to the vagaries of speculation. Once you get over the $100
mark, the wines become different to wines under the $100 mark. It is
almost like an ultra-premium part of the market. There is no doubt that
people do drink them, although there are a lot of people who say 'I am
going to keep them and increase the value'. But their value is
associated ultimately with their drinkability.

Food $\mathcal{M}$atch

CHARDONNAY

There are many different styles of chardonnay. Not only wooded and unwooded, but light through to fruity. When it comes to food matching, there is a great variety to choose from. As a general rule of thumb, it's delicate with delicate and it's powerful with powerful.

People often assume that white wine goes with fish and chicken, but the way they are cooked — in particular, the choice of ingredients used with them — will influence their flavour and the style of wine to go with them.

A younger, more delicate chardonnay would go well with pan-fried dhufish on avocado salsa with lemon dressing because of the fresh flavours of the citrus juice and herbs.

Chicken in sage oil with gnocchi and pumpkin is richer and needs an older chardonnay with more depth and body. A mature chardonnay is also a good match for the steamed yabbies on a Vietnamese noodle and Asian green salad, as it is quite a sweet dressing and the older wine has more character and body to cope with the flavours. Recipes were provided by Flutes Cafe in Margaret River.

Chicken in Sage Oil with Gnocchi and Pumpkin

4 plump skinless chicken breasts
8 fresh sage leaves, finely chopped
$^1/_5$ fresh red chilli, finely chopped
2 cloves garlic, diced
splash of olive oil
salt, pepper

Marinate the chicken in all other ingredients and pan fry until golden brown. Finish in the oven at moderate heat and serve hot with the gnocchi and pumpkin. Drizzle with the meat glaze from the baking tray and leftover sage oil.

Gnocchi

4 or 5 large potatoes, peeled, diced and pushed through wire strainer
500 g plain flour (as needed)
freshly chopped herbs (parsley, basil, thyme) to taste
2 or 3 eggs, beaten
salt, pepper

Mix all ingredients to a semi-firm dough, roll with plenty of flour to a long roll and cut into gnocchi shapes with a floured sharp knife. Boil in salted water until they start to float, then cool in cold water or serve immediately in white wine and cream sauce.

White Wine and Cream Sauce

65 ml white wine
1 clove garlic, sliced
250 ml cream
salt, pepper

Reduce wine by half with garlic slivers. Add cream and reduce to a semi-thick sauce. Toss in gnocchi and season to taste.

Roasted Butternut Pumpkin

Slice a butternut pumpkin into 1.5 to 2 cm thick slices with skin on. Sprinkle with brown sugar, salt and pepper, and place on a baking tray lined with greaseproof paper. Drizzle with olive oil and bake in moderate heat until soft and golden brown. Place sliced chicken on top and serve hot.

Steamed Yabbies on a Vietnamese Noodle and Asian Green Salad

3 to 4 yabbies, poached and deveined, then cut in half
40 g softened rice noodles
1/2 cup tat soi leaves (or substitute very young Chinese or English spinach)
1/2 bok choy, sliced
1 stem of coriander leaves
1/2 fresh chilli, sliced
1/2 cup Asian dressing
1/2 cup macadamia nuts, toasted and chopped

Toss all the ingredients together and serve on a cold plate.

Asian Dressing

100 g brown palm sugar
250 ml sweet soy sauce
4 to 6 tablespoons rice vinegar
1/4 cup sesame oil
1/4 cup olive oil
1/4 cup vegetable oil
coriander to taste
1/2 chilli to taste
thumb-size knob of ginger, freshly ground to taste

Mix all ingredients thoroughly. Store in a screwtop jar.

New Regions

Granite Belt

Wineries in Queensland? People are always surprised by this, envisaging a tropical paradise of palm-fringed beaches and exotic fruit. Peanuts perhaps, but wine? Yet wine grape plantings in that State doubled in 1997, with almost as much again planted in 1998, and the wine industry is growing in quality and quantity from a small base.

The Granite Belt, Queensland's main wine-producing area, is a strip of decomposed granite soil which is very fertile. It is about 25 kilometres wide and stretches 50 kilometres from Cottonvale, south of Warwick, down to Wallangarra on the New South Wales border. It's only 220 kilometres southwest of Brisbane and an increasingly popular tourist destination for its concentration of cellar doors near the town of Stanthorpe.

Stanthorpe is named for its earlier focus on tin mining, a Latin and English blend of words meaning 'tin village'. Amongst the 19th century settlers were Germans who made wine, and Italians who grew fruit and table grapes — making wine for their own tables from the imperfect berries that they didn't send off to market. The elevation of the Granite Belt, where it can be cold enough to snow, makes grape growing possible, although the season starts and finishes later than usual.

Ballandean Estate is the largest and oldest family-owned winery. Angelo Puglisi's father began making wine in the 1930s, crushing the grapes by foot — a very long way from the techniques that have won awards for the winery since the 1960s. Angelo Puglisi is known as the 'father' of the Queensland wine industry for his efforts to establish the region, and speciality styles and varieties such as sylvaner.

We believe there are probably 25 growers in Australia that have this variety. It was brought in from eastern parts of Germany and it's pretty rare. It is a riesling cross variety and grows very vigorously. We decided many years ago to make it into a sweet wine and we've had huge success with it — many gold medals, many awards — so it's sort of becoming renowned right round the world.

Sunset in the Granite Belt, Queensland

It is what Ballandean Estate does with the sylvaner grapes that sets the wine apart from most others. 'We've adopted a Spanish method where you actually cut the canes and let the fruit dry in the sun and turn into raisins. We attribute that to our success with this variety because it's different from everybody else's.' He demonstrates the pruning technique used a couple of weeks before harvest when canes are selected to be cut and wired in place with bunches of grapes still attached.

The leaves will dry out, the fruit is exposed to the sunlight and it turns into raisins. Then, all of a sudden, the vine has given this extra nutrition to the other bunches and they mature into very sweet, ripe grapes. The fruit that's turned into raisins because it was severed retains all the acids that are in grapes when they're not overripe, and that gives you a fresh taste in your wine. The rest of it is very sweet, and that produces the flavour. You blend the fresh grapes with the raisin fruit and you end up with a nice refreshing drink.

While Puglisi is now trellising his vines vertically in preparation for the machine harvesting that is 'just around the corner', he has been using an Italian system in which the vineyard was trellised about two metres off the ground and the vines spread out in four directions, turning the vineyard into a huge pergola with vegetables growing underneath:

Angelo Puglisi, owner/ vigneron, Ballandean Estate

They'd grow beds of strawberries and leeks and spring onions and things like that. They really made use of the soil with very intensive farming, and that's quite important when you haven't got a lot of land. But it also produced huge quantities of grapes. Instead of ten tonnes to the hectare they were getting 25, 30 tonnes to the hectare.

Shiraz is the best-known grape variety from the Granite Belt: 'We're making beautiful shirazes in this area — lots of flavour, lots of colour — to the amazement of a lot of other people from down south, who think that it may be too hot here.'

Other major plantings include chardonnay, merlot, cabernet and semillon — and wine lovers are sensing something different about them all.

I think what we get here is a lot more flintiness in the wine. We also get this peppery character coming out of the red wines. Not just shiraz which has always got a pepper character about it, but even our merlot and cabernet seem to have a nice, spicy, peppery character about them. We feel that red wines from this area are going to be absolutely unique.

Tony Comino's family came to Australia from Greece to cut sugar cane in Queensland. Like so many migrants from Europe in the early years of the 20th century, his grandparents ended up in a country town running a café for about 30 years from 1920. But they came from a family winemaking tradition on the island of Kythera, which sparked Comino's interest in wine as a teenager when the family went back to Greece. Twenty years later, he returned on a scholarship to study winemaking, noting the 'beautiful muscat grapes' on Samos, the decorative friezes that show wine was being made in 1500 BC, and Santorini's unique trellising system of a low, basket-shaped vine that keeps it below prevailing winds.

By that time, Kominos Wines had already been established in the Granite Belt, first with vine planting and winemaking for the family following their return from Greece and then as a commercial venture from 1985. Comino's vineyards include chardonnay, shiraz, sauvignon blanc and cabernet, but he would like to add some Greek varieties to produce the kind of wines he sampled overseas in 1993:

They make some full-bodied red styles that would go well here in Australia, so we hope to import cuttings of some of those varieties. Greece has a great genetic pool of varieties, but it has never really been exploited. We think some of those would certainly have a niche for us here.

Denis Parsons, owner and vigneron of the award-winning Bald Mountain, was looking for a site to establish a vineyard in the early 1980s and settled for one that was famous for its shiraz. He didn't realise how good it was until he worked it: how the soil was deep enough to retain moisture after summer rains to get through the severe droughts of the 1990s and how the climatic conditions nurture the grapes.

When you get to over 30 degrees here, we complain bitterly about how hot it is — and then it cools down at night. It might be 28, 29 degrees during the day and 14, 15 overnight. We always have to have the blankets pulled up at night. So that gives you a longer maturation period for the grapes and they tend to perform better under those conditions, as distinct from being in very, very hot conditions where they ripen quickly. Our shiraz hangs until April and our chardonnay comes off at the end of March. They just sit there and ripen up slowly and they get some lovely characteristics.

Bald Mountain wine is not made on site. At first, it was sent to Cassegrain and now to Simon Gilbert at Muswellbrook. 'We ship the grapes out of here on a semi-trailer at about six or seven at night, and they're at the winery by about one or two in the morning and in the tank by breakfast. Then several months later, after the winemaker has finished — could be a couple of years later — it all comes back as bottled wine.'

Parsons has been working with a style of lyre trellising developed in Bordeaux in which the canopy is on an incline:

The grapes get a lot of sunlight and so do the leaves, and the leaves are separated nicely so the whole vine performs better. The fruit is of a much improved quality. We had trials in the shiraz: one row was on the lyre trellis for several years and its neighbouring vines were not. Anybody could taste the difference in the grapes in the field, and these characteristics flow through to the wine. You get different wines altogether. So we're quite confident that it's a good system and it suits the sort of wines we're trying to make.

This configuration that we've done retraining the chardonnay … these were previously just a single vine and we push one vine one way and one vine the other to train them into this configuration where they get a floating canopy towards the sun. You can see how the sun is interacting with the canopy almost all day and the shoots are spaced so that there's a clear separation of leaf for good photosynthesis. And where the bunches are, you're getting sunlight on the bunches. If you've got too much of the bunch in the shade, you'll get a certain flavour, too much of the bunch in the sun and you'll get a different flavour. The trick is to get the right balance of sunny grapes and un-sunny grapes, if that's the right way of saying it.

You can get a bunch of sauvignon blanc and the sunny side will be the melons and gooseberries, the shady side will be like asparagus and capsicum, and around the edges you'll get passionfruit sorts of flavours. In the case of chardonnay, the sunny ones will have more peachy, honey sort of characters and the shady ones will be limes and lemons, maybe even Granny Smith apples. So getting that balance of the sort of lemon versus the sort of honey is one of the tricks of producing good chardonnay.

While chardonnay grabs the white market headlines, semi
that many connoisseurs put at the head of their list of win

Semillon

It doesn't appeal to everyone and one semillon

A major reason for the v

Semillon

being one of the few optimum spots in the world for a

Semillon

Semillon

sits back quietly, maturing into a honeyed, golden wine

watch and try.

't necessarily taste like another.

on in flavour arises from the area where the grapes are

grown—the Hunter Valley in New South Wa

Semillon

lon that will age with distinction.

Semillon

*W*hile chardonnay grabs the white wine market headlines, semillon sits back quietly, maturing into a honeyed, golden wine that many connoisseurs put at the head of their list of wines to watch and try. It doesn't appeal to everyone and one semillon doesn't necessarily taste like another. A major reason for the variation in flavour arises from the area where the grapes are grown — the Hunter Valley in New South Wales being one of the few optimum spots in the world for a semillon that will age with distinction.

Karl Stockhausen, who started his winemaking career with Lindemans in the Hunter Valley in the mid-1950s, has watched the development of sophisticated technology from relatively primitive times:

> In the 1960s, there was simply no refrigeration. You walk into any winery today in Australia, and they all have some form of refrigeration — in most cases to the point where they can totally regulate the temperatures during fermentation. Whereas, in the days of the 1960s, we simply had open fermenters and were crossing our fingers that the temperature wouldn't come up too high.

He has also seen semillon go through a long identity crisis that started about a century before his time when one of Australia's first viticulturalists, Thomas Shepherd, brought vine cuttings into the Hunter Valley that he thought were riesling. Shepherd's riesling, as it was known, turned out to be semillon. Even in recent years, however, semillon wasn't a grape that stood alone as a known variety overseas or in Australia. People knew their styles of wine and bought their Hunter River riesling, chablis and white burgundy — all made from semillon. In the 1970s, one company put semillon on the label, but sales fell so they went back to the tried and true riesling.

Now semillon has its own identity and a growing band of fans. One of them is wine writer and judge Jancis Robinson, who heaps praises on it in her book *Vines, Grapes and Wines*. 'The one country which has really made something exciting from the semillon cuttings taken there by early settlers is Australia. Hunter Valley semillons may be great because of a conjunction of quirks of nature, but they do indisputably deserve a place in the wine world's top ranks.'

Phillip Ryan, winemaker for McWilliam's Mt Pleasant, which is famous for its aged semillons — not even released until they are five years old — describes the key to semillon success as the Hunter Valley equivalent of what the French call *terroir*: the combination of soil, climate, rainfall, humidity and temperature. Semillon, he says, loves the challenge of growing on ground where 'our old vignerons used to say that even the rabbits carry a lunch box'. And the weather conditions suit because they are warm without being so sunny that the vines are stressed:

> We're what we call a warm viticultural area. And that is very much part of the development of the flavours of shiraz and semillon that we get in our wines, and it is the warmth that we get during the summer period that is very important.
>
> We do have a crazy weather pattern here in the summertime where we get a lot of afternoon cloud, so we actually reduce sunlight hours. The photosynthesis slows down. There's still warmth, but the sunlight is reduced so the actual ripening slows. We pick semillons in mid-February and they normally budburst about the first week of September. So it's a normal growing season.

Pouring semillon

At McWilliam's, there is no machine harvesting of semillon for their premium wines:

> Machine harvesting is an absolute no-no with producing quality semillon in our philosophy. It's about protecting that juice. Protecting the flavours inside that berry and getting them to the crusher. It's a very thin-skinned variety and, under the stress of mechanical harvesting, you do get a lot of breakdown in skins and opening of the juice — and any delays in getting it to the winery, then you're losing flavour.

Ryan's description of semillon flavours makes your mouth water. 'As a young wine, it has very fresh, zesty, lemony characters, but as it matures in the bottle it develops all those lovely toasty, nutty characters which are the hallmark of great Hunter semillons. They're unique to Australia, unique to the world.'

Then there is the colour, starting with a young semillon that is almost transparent — a very pale yellow, lemon colour with a little bit of a green tinge. 'That's, to me, the most attractive part of the young semillon. It has to have that slight lemony, green tinge. This shows that the wine is certainly heading down the right track to developing lovely colours with maturity.' Semillon maturity is so golden that people often think it has been aged in wood, but this is not so — in the Hunter, at least:

> Picking semillon is about retaining acid to obtain that freshness. We pick semillon at fairly low sugar levels compared to chardonnay. These wines are 10.5 per cent alcohol, so you're looking at a wine that is virtually 25 per cent lower in alcohol. At that level, the acid is much higher. So you have this lovely natural acidity coming through, which is the factor that then ages the wine through a long period.

The wines are actually bone dry. There's no residual sugar in these wines. However, as they develop in the bottle, they become much more intense in flavour due to this slow aging process and it gives the impression of sweetness. But there's no sugar there. It's the fruit flavour changing from the lemon — the lemon zest — into this lovely nutty, honey flavour which gives the impression of sweetness. It's just complexity.

Not everyone wants to drink their semillon as mature wine. Karl Stockhausen had a case of the 1991 vintage returned only the week before.

Whatever the owner thought, to him the wine was no longer right. Something had gone off. 'You said it would last for ten years — now look at it.' Well, we opened a bottle and it was absolutely magnificent. So we were pleased to replace the seven-year-old wine with a two-year-old wine. It kept us both happy. We have something very pleasant, very good to drink — mature white wine that's kept fantastically well over seven years — and the owner's happy to have a much younger, fresher wine and drink that.

When you talk about wine generally, and it applies to semillon in particular, not everybody likes the same thing, and wines will age and change. I prefer to say change rather than improve or become better. The same as I don't see wines going over the hill. Over the hill, to me, means a wine has kept on improving and improving, and suddenly decided: 'I've reached the peak, now I must go downhill.' It's not what wines do.

Karl Stockhausen, winemaker

Semillons and shirazes from the Hunter will change and, let's say, they mature. They lose their primary flavours and develop more complexity, then reach a certain plateau. They reach a development at which they will stay. They won't just disappear. They'll hang in there for a long number of years. It's the preference of the consumer, the drinker, the wine connoisseur, how he feels and if he doesn't like that style, well then, so be it.

You must keep in mind that not every vintage is like the previous one. So you get some years that will not last as long as others. If you have great wines, great years, yes they will. There are great examples of wine that I made in the 1960s through the 1970s that have lasted and been acclaimed as excellent wines after they were 20 years old.

Not every winery or individual can afford the investment of keeping wine until it has reached maturity. At first, the relatively small winery of Brokenwood made only semillon to be sold young, and this is still its main style. In the early 1990s, however, it expanded its ambitions to an aged semillon as well — each of the wines made differently as winemaker Iain Riggs points out:

Stainless steel tanks at McWilliam's

Brokenwood style of semillon is a grassy, almost lemon grass, cut grass style of young semillon which has gained great acceptance in the market place. A little bit different to a lot of other Hunter semillons. We first started making it in 1983 and just protected the juice. High sulphur, high ascorbic acid, keeping the juice cold and semillon has quite a good varietal character. But in a warm area you really have to keep at it to protect it — which we did and still do — but now we also make another style.

Semillon in the Hunter occupies that unique position where it'll age extremely well into a glorious toasty, almond, honey-flavoured wine. But we did come to the realisation that, if you make it too grassy as a young wine and then you bottle-age it, you don't end up with those toast and honey and almond bread characters. So we now make two styles of semillon.

It involves different techniques because, no sooner do we look for grassy characters, upfront characters in a young, drink-now semillon, we don't want those in a semillon for bottle aging. So we use a lot less protection in the handling, and run the juice straight through so we have no skin contact — we don't get any phenolical grassy pick-up from the skins. Fermentation with a slow, neutral yeast. Clean it up, put it in the bottle and say goodnight to it for five to seven years basically.

We've tried to pinpoint the difference in the styles and, really, for a great aged Hunter semillon, they need to be lean as a young wine with the flavour on the back palate, so that as they age the flavour builds. We find that quite often with the grassy wines, the flavour is all upfront and, as it ages, this gets exaggerated into a sort of vegetable character. If you try to make a herbaceous wine, or if you're in a region where you have herbaceous characters, and you bottle-age it, you end up with this interesting flavoured compound similar to compost … because it does go very vegetable, and that's not a particularly enjoyable character.

Semillon is grown and made, unwooded or oaked, in other regions of Australia. In the Barossa Valley, South Australia, wineries make fuller flavoured, barrel-fermented styles, whereas in the Hunter, they use a stainless steel tank. The climate in Western Australia gives taste similarities with sauvignon blanc, very gooseberry in character. Semillon grapes from the Riverina are used in workhorse blends and, of course, there are wonderful sauternes for which semillon happily succumbs to the noble rot, botrytis cinerea.

But nothing is quite like the Hunter semillon. As Karl Stockhausen puts it:

> You look at Australia, in particular with semillon, go to other districts — and they wouldn't like me saying this — but go to the Barossa, go to South Australia, and you find they can make very nice semillon which is very acceptable and drinkable while it's young. But, once it comes to aging, these wines have a tendency (and this is my opinion) to become fatter, blowzier and prematurely aged within a few years. Whereas the semillons from the Hunter achieve something extra. Become more complex and high-class wines.

SEMILLON

Tetsuya Wakuda is one of Australia's greatest chefs, at the same time meticulous and creative. He is renowned for his ability to get the natural flavours out of raw ingredients, and always maintains a delicate touch. This is so important, whether it be fresh vegetables or seafood — and they are the best food matches with semillon.

Tetsuya explains his choice of dish to go with a young semillon as he prepares it in the kitchen of his Sydney restaurant. It's sauté asparagus with angel hair pasta and a touch of truffle oil, parsley and chives. Other ingredients — all added in small quantities, a dash of this and a pinch of that — are oil, chopped eschallots, salt, sugar, pepper, chicken stock (although it could be vegetable), sake, soy sauce and garlic.

'Just a little bit of basil. You don't taste the basil at all, but basil holds the flavour of the truffle. Drain and add the pasta — then just mix it all. Last the truffle oil, which is very dominating.

'Because the young semillon has beautiful fruit, but also has a big amount of acid in it, I used oil. The acid cuts the oil. So it's easy to eat pasta and lighten up the palate.'

To accompany a more mature, richer semillon that's 11 years old, Tetsuya chooses ravioli of lobster with tomato and basil vinaigrette, served on seaweed.

'This is the rice vinegar and tomato,' he says as he spoons it over. 'Old semillon hasn't got acid like the young ones, so I am adding acid.' A little basil goes in to lift the other flavours. 'And this is fish roe. Marsh lettuce cress. Again, this texture has a slight bitterness that gives the shellfish more sweetness.'

The finished dish brings the flavours of the wine alive.

Cellar Door Tasting

Tasting wines at the cellar door of the winery where they are made is one of the great pleasures offered in profusion in the wine regions of Australia. The sheer number of wineries can be quite daunting, so you want to make the most of your time. And with the range of wines on offer, three or four wineries is usually enough in one day.

It is best to arrive with a fresh palate — in other words, not to have any strong tasting drinks such as coffee or foods such as garlic on the way. If you cannot resist them, a glass of water will help cleanse your palate or you might like to nibble some plain, dry biscuits but try to avoid the cheese—it tends to coat your palate.

Smelling the wine is the start of the tasting process. And if you want to smell and taste wine properly, it is important to get oxygen through the wine. You do this by swirling the wine around in the glass and, when you have taken a mouthful, by sucking air through it. It does sound disgusting, but it is a great way to taste wine.

Of course, you don't have to swallow every mouthful. Don't feel embarrassed to use the spittoons that are provided in the tasting area of every cellar door outlet.

Many wineries now charge a small fee for tasting, which covers the sales tax they have to pay on any wine that is consumed. You often find, though, that the fee is refundable if you buy some of their wines at the cellar door.

There are small family run wineries in most regions, and they usually offer the special opportunity to talk to the winemaker, who is likely to be the person pouring your wine. It is a great chance to learn firsthand about the area, the wines and how they are made.

Most wineries have a range of wines to taste and it is best to do this in the order of sparkling wines, then whites and reds, moving from the lighter whites through to the heavier reds. Sweet and fortified wines should be left until last.

Some of the larger companies offer tours of the winery and a range of facilities for the family to picnic and the children to play. Others have you seated at tables and tasting wine paid for by the glass, with light and tasty snacks available. Do not hesitate to ask about any food matches they might suggest for the wines they make.

At the cellar door

You probably won't get any bargains at a cellar door, but you may track down wines that you won't find at your local bottle shop. And there is extra pleasure in buying and taking home wines associated with your cellar door tastings.

Phillip Kelly, Kellybrook Winery, talks to Maryann Egan

Choose some wines to drink straight away and others that will improve with time. If you find you want to buy more of them when you get home, most wineries provide mail order and internet facilities for home delivery — for which there will usually be a charge per case.

If you have bought a considerable amount of wine at the cellar door, home delivery may be the way to get it back anyway. In some regions, neighbouring wineries have an arrangement in which a few bottles from each can be combined as a mixed dozen to make up the minimum case for delivery.

If you do take your wine home by car, however, beware of leaving wine in the boot on a hot day because heat can affect the flavours of wine. It is best to travel with an Esky and store the wine in it as you move around the wineries. If you're travelling by plane, do not forget that altitude may affect the wine, so leave it a month or so before opening after you get home. If you can resist the temptation.

*Michiji and Tomiko Yamanaka, owners/vignerons,
Barossa Valley*

Tomiko and Michiji Yamanaka

Tomiko Yamanaka and her husband Michiji
really enjoyed the chance to taste wine
amongst the vineyards on a trip to France
in 1985. Five years later, they had migrated
to Australia and bought a vineyard in South
Australia's Barossa Valley, where they grow
grapes and make wine with no background
other than what they have read in books
and experienced as consumers — unusually
experienced consumers admittedly, as
Tomiko had qualified as a sommelier in
Japan and they sold wine in their restaurant
there.

> Because we were serving European food,
> we naturally had wine with it. We were
> having wine instead of miso soup for our
> health. I used not to be able to eat
> meat — I got a reaction similar to food
> poisoning. But when we travelled in
> France in 1985, drinking wine with food,
> I never fell sick. When I went back to
> Japan, I heard that there was an exam for
> a sommelier's qualification. I applied and
> passed it, though I wasn't really interested
> in becoming a sommelier. Rather, I
> wanted to gain more information about

> wine. Living in Nagano, there was hardly
> any information about wine. Even in
> bookshops, there was no book on wine.
>   I could drink wine without thinking
> anything difficult about it, but, in those
> days, for average people in Japan, wine
> was expensive and something difficult.
> Instead of being formal about being a
> sommelier, I like people who want to
> become familiar with wine to be
> introduced to it casually and as something
> which is fun.

On their first trip to Australia in 1987, the
Yamanakas were 'utterly delighted' by the
people, the food and the wine. 'Until then,
we thought we'd like to import wines from
Australia,' says Michiji. 'But we felt we'd
rather export wines from Australia to Japan.
Hardly anyone knew about Australian
wines in those days. So, we felt we wanted
to migrate with the intention of increasing
awareness of Australian wines back home.
That was our initial motivation.' Tomiko
underlines their reaction: 'We felt it was
such a wonderful country that we wanted to
live here — live in a wine region and

export Australian wines back to Japan.'

After visiting McLaren Vale and Coonawarra, they settled in the Barossa Valley, where they particularly liked the wines and the people:

We had a language problem, but that didn't matter. We have great neighbours. Most of them are grape growers — third, fourth and fifth generation — so they have plenty of experience and give us advice. From the first day, Lyle Gerlach has looked after us, not just in the vineyard, but giving us advice about many aspects of life. We are lucky.

The neighbours are working on vineyards because they love it. The people who don't necessarily appreciate city life are dealing with earth. So we could become a part of it very easily. Even now, we have many things we don't know. So whenever we have questions, we go to ask many different people. The Australians give us different advice, but they all say the final decision is up to us. It was easy for us to be told that if we thought the suggestion was good, apply it, but if we didn't think it was a good idea we could use other methods.

The Yamanakas sell grapes to another neighbour, Peter Lehmann, who also bought them from the previous owners:

We went to him to ask and were told: 'That's no problem. We will be buying your grapes.' It was in the recession and we were very worried — but they really bought our grapes. Since then, the market has gone up and we are where we are today. So we are very thankful to Peter Lehmann. He not only gave us advice, he gave us culturally rich experiences. He has given us a good time.

They keep some grapes to make their own wine — at first pretty awful, according to their brutally honest neighbour Lyle, but now quite a tasty drop:

We make our own wine as a way to help us think about wine in general. We are not making wine which needs to taste good. Our purpose of making wine is different. It's for our study to learn more about wine. We are looking for winemakers who can produce consistent wine year after year, and we'd like to introduce it to Japan. Not the wine we made, but the wine we found and chose. Not the wines which are influenced by fashion. We like to meet people who make wines according to their own philosophy.

We only knew about how to drink wines. So we depended on that. Our knowledge of growing grapes and making wines was solely from books. So it was best to live in a place like this to study it practically. Especially living in the vineyard, that is our best joy. By living in the vineyard, we learn about grapes and wines, and we want to inform people in Japan what we have learned about wines.

And not only about wines. Tomiko wanted to eat the wine offshoots which they prune to prevent the loss of nutrients, but she was cautious:

We thought the leaves were too good to waste. We wondered if we could use them for tempura, but we weren't sure if they were poisonous. Grape leaves are used in Lebanese cooking, they wrap food in them. These leaves are still young and free from chemical spray and rabbits eat them. They eat young shoots, which they know taste best. As it doesn't kill rabbits, we decided it'd be OK for us.

What is good about coming here is that we have great neighbours in the Barossa. It is country, but you can have cultural experiences. There are always music concerts somewhere. There are many wine and food events. We are really enjoying the life here.

Characters of the Industry

Dr John Middleton, owner/winemaker, Mount Mary
OPPOSITE: *Yarra Valley*

Dr John Middleton

Mount Mary wines are considered by some people to be up there with Grange and Hill of Grace. You do not, however, see this small winery in Victoria's Yarra Valley, just outside Melbourne, promoted in the same manner or even written about very much. That's because its owner, a family doctor turned winemaker, Dr John Middleton, has never believed in marketing his wines. Yet he can scarcely keep up with demand. So how has this come about?

The fact that I've never advertised means it has to be the wines that have spoken for themselves. We could see from the very first releases in '76 and '77— just the appreciation when we sold them to restaurants. The way in which people rang up and said 'Oh, can I have some more of that wine? Everybody raves about it.' They just like the flavour of our wines.

And it's continued. And we've just continued to make the wine in the same way from the same grapes. We don't buy grapes from outside. We've got a very traditional, Francophile way of making

wine. I stick to Bordeaux methods for Bordeaux varieties and Burgundian methods for chardonnay and pinot, and I'm extremely careful in the winery. It's a surgical operation, a clinical procedure. I'm quite obsessive about cleanliness and transmitting infection. The wine's always clean. It's topped up regularly. I think that's the most important thing in winemaking — regularly topping up. And when they're bottled, the wines just taste good. There's market hype now, but prior to that, there was none. It was just people's acceptance of it.

I like to see my wine in restaurants because I like to see it drunk with food. It's not for quaffing. And that is a great shop window, as good a marketing as you need. You don't need gold medals stuck all over the bottle, you don't need to be crowing to the rooftops, you don't need television ads. I was taught as a child by my father that bragging was vulgar. But bragging has become the catchword of this century. It's quite shameful.

Dr Middleton has seen huge changes in public enjoyment of wine since he grew up in a family where his father, also a medico, was a teetotaller. 'He used to entertain the bishop occasionally and they would have sherry and stuff — I remember the Seppelts Imperial Reserve Claret for the bishop.' It wasn't until the young John Middleton joined the Air Force that he did a crash course in beer drinking — 'as most people do' — and then, when posted to a southern training station near Mt Gambier, on the edge of one of South Australia's most famous wine regions, he discovered the joys of that town's Gen's Hotel:

> It had the most fantastic cellar of early Coonawarras from the 1920s, and I learned wine drinking there. Marli and I were married at the end of 1947 and we lived in East Melbourne, and wine with food was part of our life, and has been ever since. And then, when we came up here, with its history of winemaking, it was pretty natural that I got interested in the old vineyards.

Dr Middleton had been invited to join a medical practice in the Yarra Valley town of Lilydale, but he had already been inducted into the fascinating business of making wine. He and his wife used to stay in the Great Western wine district with friends who were, in turn, friendly with the Seppelt manager of the time, Colin Preece and his wife, Dorothy.

> Colin really fired me on winemaking because I was interested in the techniques. I'd spend the morning in the laboratory, or whatever Colin was doing — racking or fining or blending. He did a lot of blending and he had a very good palate.

He would put out twenty wines and say 'I'll give you two hours and I'll come back and I want to hear all about them.' So he was really good, and I learned a lot.

I probably had a natural palate, an appreciation of flavours and tastes and smells. But he was the guy that formalised it in my brain, saying: 'Now this is tannin and this is oak and that's American oak and that's French oak and de-da-de-da. And so that's really where it started.

When Dr Middleton and his wife moved to Lilydale, some of their patients worked in the vineyards and farming people were buying grapes from the market to make wine on a small scale. 'One of my medical partners used to ferment his in a barrel. I can still see him stuffing those bunches through the bung hole of the barrel to ferment them. That was about 1953.'

Dr Middleton got some planting material from Colin Preece, planted out a small plot, learning from experience how to prune and combat fungus diseases. He began to make wine in one-gallon and five-gallon glass jars that he bought in secondhand shops, blowing up a couple of them that he had corked tightly, thinking they had finished fermenting. 'In one of the children's bedrooms there were curtains that went down to the floor, and of course the red wine spilled on the floor and went up the curtain. I wasn't very popular. But I really learned how to make wine, because the microbiological problems are amplified if you are making a small volume. It stood me in good stead when I started to make stuff in higher volumes.' He also made his own crusher and press.

As well as learning from hands-on experience, Dr Middleton and his wife travelled in France and California, talking to the winemakers. His scientific background in training to become a doctor also informs his approach.

I think intelligent use of systems and technologies eventually follows the empiricism of the past when there wasn't this investigative science and we didn't understand biochemical pathways. There were a lot of people who, obviously, discovered the ways in which wine was made so it was palatable and didn't deteriorate. In time, people have researched those processes and now we are learning the scientific reasons. I think that's great. You can change your techniques, you can do all sorts of different things as a result ... once you understand the pathways.

He is impressed by the research into flavours and aromas, and the benefits of drinking wine. 'There seem to be benefits in some of the substances in wine and there's a lot of research going on there to find out. Are they meaningful? Is it worth telling people that wine is safe to drink? Also, what are the safe limits?' Dr Middleton is concerned by consumer abuse of wine and worries that the wine industry is not sufficiently caring about this:

Cheap wine, particularly wine in casks, constitutes a substance which is being used in the community in abusing fashion. Maybe we shouldn't have it in casks, we should have it in bottles.
I'm not convinced that the wine industry has done much to adopt the Southern European ethic of wine and vinegar and oil and bread as part of living, part of dining. It's become some secretive sort of thing and this, I think, has encouraged binge drinking, it's encouraged teenage drinking. All sorts of things that are really foreign to a sensible consumer ethic in the place of wine in the community. It ought to be part of our food, but it's now considered a drug. The wine industry's got itself an awful lot of adverse criticism. The spirit industry's got the same problem, so has the beer industry, and their advertising of consumption of alcohol at other times besides food times — we really have turned the ethic upside down. It's a sort of anglicised attitude to drinking and it's time we adopted a more sane European approach.

It was the migration of Europeans to Australia who helped expand public interest in the first place. There is a lot more wine around — and an accompanying information industry that Dr Middleton is not so sure about.

In my day, if you wanted to find out about wine you went and bought the books and you read about it. Or you went and found a winemaker and you talked to him. And this is the way I learned. If you wanted to know what a wine tasted like, you went and bought the bottle and you took it home and tasted it. But nowadays you have people — as a result of this nanny generation created by wine journalism and books and things — who don't seem to have the initiative to go and get a bottle of wine and taste it. They have to go and read about it ... Everybody has to be taught how to think, how to do things. I feel that's a pity. I think it's sad.

New Regions

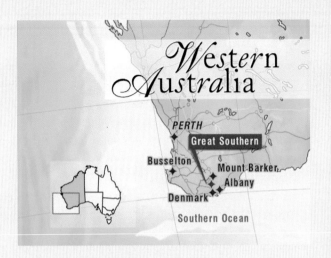

Great Southern Region

The Great Southern Region in Western Australia is further south than the State's more famous wine region, Margaret River — it's four and a half hours by car from Perth, an hour by plane from Albany — and many people find it more beautiful, with its majestic stands of trees such as karri and red gum. Winemaker John Wade appreciates its visual appeal, but he chose to settle here in 1986 because he believed it would be a good place to grow his two favourite grapes, riesling and cabernet.

He has not only been proved right about that on his own behalf, but he is also celebrated for his chardonnay and pinot noir as a contract winemaker in a large region that starts at Kojonup and focuses wine activity around the towns of Denmark and Mt Barker. 'The region is about 150 kilometres by 100 kilometres, which gives the area diversity, though the vineyards are on fairly similar soils, mostly gravelly loam. And we've got the temperate climate of the coast — cold nights and not so hot days.'

When Wade arrived in this unproven wine area, he had faith and talent, but not a great deal else. He launched his own label — Howard Park, named after his father — while working as winemaker to Alkoomi, Goundrey Wines and Plantagenet, each of which allowed him to make a small amount of wine for himself. For a decade, he was a winemaker with neither a winery nor a vineyard, producing his wines in a former butter factory, converted apple packing shed and a mechanics shed. In 1997, he got a state-of-the-art winery near Denmark where the individuality of his winemaking in small quantities promises to be maintained as he expands. Since 1992, he has had a second label, Madfish, for a range that is competitively priced and styled to match popular contemporary cuisine. And he continues to work under contract for other producers:

We don't make as many contract wines now as we used to, since Howard Park and Madfish have expanded. We still do some and I'm very glad we do because we get to see fruit in different places and differences in trellising techniques, management techniques and varieties. In some years since I've been in the West, I've made something like 12 or 15 rieslings in one year, or ten or 12 cabernets in one year, and so on. It's amazing to see how much influence that soil, site and management in the vineyard do have on the wine style.

Karriview vineyard

Some of the vineyards around the area have excellent fruit that we like to have some of, and the owners don't have the capital to invest in putting up a winery themselves, so we can help them out by making their product and also source fruit for ourselves. The learning curve of looking at different varieties, techniques, subregions and vineyards comes into it as well. We're still a very young area, there's a lot of things to learn, whether it be trellising, irrigation techniques, soil types, whatever. And I suppose the biggest question for all vineyards is clones, so we always tend to look at whatever we can to try and learn.

I see a difference in clones as subtleties in that variety or in that wine, but there are other points that come out of it from the vineyard point of view. Whether a subtlety is suitable to your region is another thing again.

There are so many variables that happen every vintage. In all the vintages I've ever done, I've never had two the same. So it's just this ongoing learning and adapting — and I suppose the most obvious thing is having an open mind each vintage. I think the satisfaction you gain — or I certainly gain — from making wine for myself and for other people is just not replaceable.

With the input of industrial manufacturer and wine lover Jeff Burch coming into Howard Park as principal co-owner, Wade now has his winery with a capacity of 1,000 tonnes, but he continues his practice of buying grapes from growers not only in this large region, but beyond it as well:

Coastline near Albany, Western Australia

Usually in the growing months — particularly close to vintage around December, January, February — I'm in the car most of the time, looking at vineyards and tasting the fruit, working out when we're going to pick. All our decisions are made on taste, whether they're out in the vineyard or inside the winery. We use analysis as a backup, and good housekeeping, but every decision is based on palate. I cover about 20,000 kilometres each vintage, just in visiting vineyards.

Wade has a particularly strong association with local grape growers Bruce Day and his wife Mary with their Karriview chardonnay and pinot noir:

John's a contract winemaker and we use his expertise by taking our fruit to the Howard Park winery for him to make it for us. I'm the vigneron who operates the vineyard. We overlap through the fact that I go to the winery and discuss the oak components and all the winemaking things. John leaves me to my own devices out here with a little bit of input, but mainly we keep apart until it's the time to make decisions.

When the grapes are ripening, we have to work in with the winery. We check flavours and the sugar levels to make sure of the peak ripeness and he has to keep a check on it to see how we're going. We've been in the industry a few years, we've got certain clientele and we have to produce wines in the Karriview style, and I think John's aware of this. He's trying to work in with Karriview and not trying to make something that's totally different.

Wade steps in:

I probably should add at this point that Bruce has already made the wine by his vineyard work. As a winemaker, the best I can do is keep it as Bruce grew it. I suppose my main job is not to wreck it. No matter what anyone says, grapes come in at a certain value — you can't improve on it. One of the things we try to do is keep oak in the background so that the fruit has the bigger say. The oak is there as an adjunct to that, to balance out — the same as the acid and the alcohol level. Hopefully, you get everything right and compliment the flavours that Bruce has spent 12 months in the vineyard producing.

Day continues:

Without John in the area, we don't have a winemaker, and that would disjoint the region. Western Australia is a big, big place and all the other wineries are so far away that he's created the infrastructure for Denmark.

We get John to come out to address the wine group that we have in this area. He comes with a sample of wines that show problems that have happened in the vineyard, not winemaking problems, so we can get it correct next time around. We'll all sit around tasting these wines and he'll explain what the problems are and what he has to do to overcome them, which is sometimes detrimental to the wine. And it's quite amazing to us growers to see the end product because, quite often, it's forgotten about once you pick it.

Winemakers with their own labels have to take their product almost to the consumer's table. According to Wade, most of the West Australian wine that is produced is probably sold in its home State:

> When I look at my own market, we sell a third of our wine to the UK, a third to Sydney and the other third is for everywhere else. So it's quite diverse. Western Australia, even though we're the largest State in Australia, does only 1.5 per cent of the national production of wine. The good thing about it is that we take up about 20 per cent of the premium area. I'm sure there are a lot of people who would like to be in there with us and it's an area we guard jealously. We'll do anything we can in the way of production, making good wines, to stay there.

These days, West Australians are producing greater quantities of less expensive wines as well:

> There are cheaper wines coming through now. We're usually criticised for having nothing but expensive wines. I think part of the reason was that it was such a small winery production area — that all the places were family owned with very low production, so the cost of growing and making was much higher and this came through in the price. Now the West is expanding and we're getting up some decent volumes, the cost of production does go down.

Wade, whose winemaking background includes vintage experience in Australia, France and Tuscany, and seven years as manager/winemaker of Wynns Coonawarra Estate before moving to Western Australia, is confident about the future.

> I think there's an enormous potential for the region. The main reason that it hasn't gone ahead as quickly as Margaret River is that there hasn't been the professional money invested down this way. It's starting to happen around here and the wine sales are specific to the region. When I came here in 1986 there were two small vineyards and that's now expanded to 17, with two more that I know are going in. Two wineries are being built, with another one coming up, so that's providing a lot of employment for the region.
>
> If you go back quite a few years, there was an active timber mill here. But that closed down since I've been here and employment around the area became scarce. The viticultural industry has grown up in the past 12 years and I think the long term future for the town is involved in tourism. Certainly, the wine industry is going to play a part, because at the moment that is the largest and fastest growing industry.

Riesling was Australia's most popular white wine variety in
the way. But it is said to be making a comeback, and there

behind that re-emergence of this cla

Riesling

Riesling

and there are people

Riesling

1960s and 1970s before chardonnay shouldered it out of

people putting their money and energy

German variety.

GRAPE VARIETIES AND WINE STYLES

Riesling

Riesling

ng their money and energy

behind that re-emergence of this classic German variety

Riesling

*R*iesling was Australia's most popular white wine variety in the 1960s and 1970s before chardonnay shouldered it out of the way. But it is said to be making a comeback, and there are people putting their money and energy behind that re-emergence of this classic German variety.

One of them is Jeff Grosset, who is finding new terrain to add to his domain in South Australia's Clare Valley, 136 kilometres north of Adelaide. One of the most unlikely of his vineyards is on a hilltop which almost needs the skill of a car rally driver to reach:

> I was chasing the altitude. To get a little bit better varietal definition, that little bit better concentration of fruit. Put it up as high as we can — this is the highest part of the Clare Valley where you could plant a vineyard. Facing east so you get the morning sun. The kangaroos can be a bit of a worry, but they don't eat much. They're usually inquisitive. They'll just jump in and sometimes have a little nibble at the fruit, but that's about all really.
>
> What we're chasing are the really special sites to make, hopefully, great riesling. The fact that it's a pretty crazy place caused a few stirs and a few jokes when we were putting it in, but I think it's proved to be worthwhile.

Riesling is, more than most wines, the product of its fruit, and Grosset is acutely conscious of that:

> What I'm trying to do is get pure expression of the fruit. You're trying to convert it in its purest form into the wine. And what most writers and experts in the world now agree is that riesling is, arguably, the finest white grape on the basis of expressing the vineyard and keeping its own character — you know, varietal characteristics.
>
> That's why I think riesling making takes a lot of discipline. I think it's just as creative, but it's important that the winemaker is aware that he or she is trying to maintain that character and use some restraint rather than with others, like chardonnay and cabernet, you've got oak and malo. All these things that you can add to it and play around with. With riesling, you should really be pretty much leaving it alone. Show some restraint and, I think, some respect for the variety.
>
> To me, the Clare Valley is particularly suited for riesling because we've got great weather. It starts with a lot of sunshine, but then the elevation takes the edge off the temperature so it makes it a bit cooler than most parts of the Barossa, Southern Vales and Adelaide. Every 100 metres you go up, it's nearly a degree on a sunny day. And we're a fair way from the sea, so we tend to get pretty cold nights. The

combination means you retain acid and it seems to work pretty well.

Obviously, the warmer parts of the Clare Valley will give slightly fuller wines. The cooler parts will tend to be a little more lively on the palate, maybe a bit leaner, but there's more zing to it. So it sounds like a bit of a trade-off, but both can be lovely. It depends on what you want. Some, particularly the finer ones, will often age very well, too. So if you are chasing that, there would probably be a preference for them.

And the effect of the soil?

Polish Hill, Clare Valley

In Watervale, which was originally believed to be the best and is probably still the most famous subregion, there's limestone underneath and clay loam on top. The limestone gives great resistance to drought, the roots can get down and you get quite generous flavours — lime and citrus, very mouth filling and satisfying flavours. In my case, I've made Watervale since 1981 and Polish Hill as well from a lesser known part of the valley at the same time, and it's really fine. It's a little bit leaner, but still very powerful and has a longer palate. So the profile is different. If you were to draw it, Watervale's up front, the Polish Hill is finer and longer and just keeps going. We can't explain all the reasons why, but clearly it's on different soils in a different part of the valley. And all these things add up to quite a different flavour.

Riesling is on a bit of a roll at the moment. There is obviously strength in the market, particularly in the premium end, and what we should be doing as an industry is putting out as many premium rieslings as we can. There's some great riesling in Australia that is probably underrated in the world. When we send it away overseas, people are going to acknowledge that it's pretty good, but what's really going to top it off in terms of our reputation is to have some stunning rieslings from individual sites. You know, wines that are really special. That's what I'm trying to do.

It is an ambition that has crystallised for Grosset since he established his winery in 1981:

I was very keen on making a number of wines, but riesling in particular, and I'd been keeping my eye on what was happening up here in the Clare Valley. There'd been some pretty exceptional wines already made out of the valley, quite a few of them by John Vickery. So I was pretty convinced that there was a lot of potential here for the variety. I moved in and started thinking about the long term and not really thinking about the short term trends. To be honest, probably not that aware of the trends and not really thinking about any international considerations either. I was just thinking about the local market and the fact that I could make a go of it.

Over that time, chardonnay has been jostling for space:

Jeffrey Grosset, winemaker

Even here in the Clare Valley, there's quite a lot of chardonnay grown — nearly as much as riesling, which is quite surprising because most people would know it as the area for riesling and not for chardonnay. The production of chardonnay in this area when I started was tiny and I probably crushed half of it. There was about 10 tonnes or something. Now it's nearly 4,000 and, in Australia, the production of chardonnay has gone from something like 10,000 tonnes in the 1980s to 170,000, while riesling has just stayed on a similar level of say 30,000 in the 1980s to 35,000 now. The other premiums have moved in a curve with the industry. So riesling's the odd one out in that respect.

Part of the difficulty riesling has in raising its profile is confusion amongst consumers as to what riesling actually means, the difference between the variety and the style:

Well, riesling is a grape variety and, in Australia, riesling has also been used for many years to indicate a style. Where most people know about that is riesling on a cask. The point of this is that riesling-the-cask is not made out of riesling-the-grape. Or if there is some in there, there would be very little. It will be made out of lesser varieties. The most common one that people would know would be sultana. So what they're getting in a cask is an easy drinking wine that is not like riesling the variety at all. It was just used in the past to indicate a style, and by now it should be gone because it's causing confusion in the market.

We thought when the label integrity program came in, that this would all be attended to and that riesling on the cask would disappear in as long as it took for the larger companies to think up another name for the wine. Unfortunately, that was in 1993, and the cask producers are forever wanting more time, now to the end of 2000, to think up something else. In the meantime, there's confusion because someone buys a cask for $10, and they don't understand that this riesling is actually lesser varieties. It doesn't taste anything like the bottle of riesling that they might be paying $10 for, and I think that is causing confusion.

One thing that's so good about the Australian industry is that our label integrity program — which means that what's on the label is what you get — is acknowledged internationally. It's one of the best in the world. So why riesling should be on casks is something that the majority of riesling producers can't understand, and it's really something we have to address because from an international point of view we have a great reputation. It would be silly to risk all of that if people in, say, Japan or the United States were to get the wrong story and suggest that we're perhaps misrepresenting things. That we're not telling the truth. All because cask producers can't think of another name to call their white wine that they've been calling this name of a grape variety.

One of Jeffrey Grosset's winery buildings

Moving on from the labelling problem, Grosset looks to the future:

I'm looking forward to seeing different rieslings coming out of different regions. It's pretty exciting, what's happening nationally and internationally, so there's plenty of room for new players. The Clare Valley produces just on ten per cent of the total production in Australia. Nearly 80 per cent of all the riesling grown in Australia is grown in South Australia — but that doesn't tell you about premium rieslings.

So, say, in Tasmania, Andrew Pirie from Pipers Brook planted a few acres a few years ago and managed to get the one per cent for Tasmania. A lot of people know about the winery. In Western Australia, the production is tiny and yet you hear about the names, like Howard Park and others. What's happening is that they're making a mark in the premium market … and they're pretty interesting wines. Quite different to what we're doing here and we welcome that. I look forward to the spread of the style — not so much style, but to the expression of that region and, in some cases, of the vineyard. And that's what riesling does so well.

John Vickery, renowned for his riesling over five decades, is winemaker for Richmond Grove in South Australia's Barossa Valley, which lies halfway between the Clare Valley and Adelaide, but a little further east. He has made red wines as well, but it is the riesling that he is best known for and he says it has given him great rewards, 'particularly seeing some of the old ones now that are still very drinkable and still alive. Unlike some other white varieties, its simplicity when it's young develops into a complex, flavoursome style with a few years' age. Some of the early 70s were classics, certainly the late 60s, 1969. Unfortunately a lot of those wines haven't lived. Corks have let them down.'

John Vickery, winemaker, Richmond Grove in the Barossa Valley

Does he make riesling for now or later?

We try to do both. Riesling is attractive when it's young and fresh and vibrant. It's got all those lovely fresh, citrusy flavours. So we certainly make the wine to be drinkable and palatable when it's young, but make sure that there's sufficient acidity and that the wine will also live. Acidity's not a prerequisite, but you need balance. If you're going to develop a lovely honeyed, toasty flavour with age, you need a certain amount of acid to balance those flavours as they develop. But the style we market these days, as was back in the 70s, is certainly one where the wines are consumable as soon as they're bottled.

Wine & Wherefore

SENDING BACK A BOTTLE

Tasting a bottle of wine at a restaurant is a ritual we are all familiar with. Is it really necessary? Yes. The reason we do it is to make sure that we receive a bottle of wine in good condition. Restaurants charge hefty mark-ups for the wine they serve and patrons are entitled to enjoy what they have paid for.

The main offender in spoiling wine in an unopened bottle is the cork. Cork is the product of bark off a tree — an organic substance subject to bacteria. A microscopic bacteria known as trichloroanisole, thankfully abbreviated to TCA, is often present in corks. And research has shown that five per cent of all corks have cork taint, where the flavour of the wine has been altered.

Two glasses of the same wine from different bottles could taste utterly unlike each other. One might have a lovely, fresh, plummy sort of fruit flavour. The other might taste of wet cardboard or wet hessian bags — particularly unpleasant — which means it has cork taint. It is corked. You would send it back and ask for a replacement bottle.

This type of cork taint is obvious and once you've tasted it you won't forget. But a lot of cork taint is more subtle, and if you are not familiar with a particular type of wine you may not be sure if it has cork taint or not.

So, in these circumstances, ask the wine waiter, who may go under the French name sommelier. Most good restaurants these days employ sommeliers and it is their job to compile the wine list and know what all the wines taste like. They will give you an honest opinion as to whether the wine is in good condition or not because it is their main role to make sure you enjoy the wine and the experience.

Another circumstance in which people can send wine back in a restaurant is when you have asked the sommelier to select the wine for you and given specifications as to what you want, and the bottle of wine is shown to you before being opened — but it doesn't taste as you have requested. Under these circumstances you are entitled to send the wine back, and should do so.

But if you have selected the wine yourself, without assistance, and when you taste it you don't like it … sorry, you're not entitled to ask for a replacement. You can choose to drink it or select another bottle and allow the sommelier and staff to enjoy the wine that wasn't to your taste.

The marvellous thing about the riesling vineyards we have today is that they have been there for a long time. There's been virtually no planting done in the past 15 years, so we've still got the same resource. We're drawing fruit from the same vineyards that we made our wines in the 70s. So assuming the quality is there, the inherent grape quality, theoretically those wines should be as good. Grape yields are much the same. Basically, the winemaking process is the same. I guess we've got a few more toys to play with, but we always took a great deal of care in making the wines. And those principles are still applied today.

Vickery's winemaking career has spanned highs and lows in the industry:

I guess the greatest low was in the mid-80s, when all companies had surplus stocks, surplus inventories of bottled wine. Grape growers were not being paid. We had a minimum pricing scheme in those days, a government-controlled grape price scheme. But the industry was on its knees. I remember one year, I think it was 1982, there was something like 50,000 tonnes of shiraz and cabernet and grenache left on the vine. Just in this State alone. So it was very disappointing to see those growers left with fruit and it was a very difficult time for our grape growers and for the industry as a whole. As a result, some companies went under …

Riesling was pulled out during the South Australian government vine pull scheme, which was designed to assist growers to get out of the industry or take out some of the varieties which the industry was not interested in. So we lost some fruit in the Clare Valley, Watervale, Eden Valley, Barossa, Southern Vales. We hope that some of those vineyards have been replanted — they were certainly valuable vineyard sites — and that we'll probably continue to see some of those vineyards replanted with riesling in the future.

And the future, like the present, looks like a complete turnaround from those bad times:

It's really fantastic. The growers are receiving marvellous payments for their fruit. We're exporting and competing overseas and doing well. And the quality of the wines is marvellous. The new districts that are being planted throughout Australia, the new resources we're having and will continue to have from these new areas, are going to be a wonderful boon for the winemakers as well as the consumers of the future. So it's all very exciting, both for the makers and the consumers, what's coming on board in the next two or three years.

Characters of the Industry

Mick Morris, left, and Bill Chambers, winemakers

Bill Chambers and Mick Morris

Rutherglen, in Ned Kelly country up in northeastern Victoria, was one of Australia's flourishing grape-growing areas when phylloxera ravaged the vines at the turn of the 19th century. But this did not stop the growers who knew it was a valuable site for growing grapes and making wine. Some wines in particular, as it turns out.

'The Chambers came here in 1858 and we've just been here ever since,' says Bill Chambers, fifth generation of the family winemakers at Chambers Rosewood.

Phylloxera hit the area in 1899 and this vineyard was replanted in 1907, and it's just about on its last legs. I'm going to let some of it go. It's a hard decision. We've been making muscat, sweet whites, sweet reds and dry reds pretty well from the start — since the 1870s anyway.

Some patches of ground make nice wine and others, not quite as good. Why is the ground different? I don't know. I don't think anybody knows. Everybody talks learnedly about it, but it's a bit of trial and error. You put vines in a patch of ground and, even in this area, some places are good and some are not so good — but the muscat and tokay, that's another thing.

The fortified wines of liqueur muscat and tokay, singled out for praise in the *Oxford Companion to Wine* as 'two of Australia's greatest gifts to the world', are at their very best in the Rutherglen area. Why? 'It's pretty difficult to say why Bordeaux makes great clarets. It just does. Why does Burgundy make great pinots? They just do.'

Not far from Chambers Rosewood, Mick Morris is another famous maker of these rich, sweet wines — along with a limited range of table wines including the rare red durif — with a label that carries his family name. His great-grandfather had established the winery Fairfield in 1859, building it into the biggest vineyard and cellars in Australia at that time. His grandfather decided to start on his own a few kilometres away in 1897. Mick Morris, who has that vineyard today, expands:

There were a few vines here, but they were wiped out with phylloxera. Then he replanted in 1920, just after the war years, with grafted root stocks and, of course, they're immune to phylloxera. The phylloxera can live on them and it doesn't hurt the vines, so all the vines in this Rutherglen area have been grafted.

You know, I don't think anyone makes tokay or muscat in the world as well as the Rutherglen area. There's something unique about them. You get the wine writers, English wine writers who tend to be more open minded about the different wines … whereas, you know, if you're a French producer, you tend to look at the French or the American, where the English don't grow many grapes, so I think they're the best judges because they haven't got preconceived prejudices. Let's put it that way.'

The point is, English wine writers have particularly praised the tokay and muscat from Rutherglen.

We've been very fortunate that our ancestors have put wines away and they've matured, and we've got the basis of blending with those old wines and young wines to freshen them up. Dad took over from his father and I took over from my father and I've handed it over to my son David. So we've made sure that we've had supplies of these old wines and we virtually say that we're the caretaker, and we make sure that we try to improve the quality and the quantity of wines that are left for the next generation.

Morris describes the qualities of his premium fortified wines:

Tokay is made out of a white grape called muscadelle. This is the top of the range … an old wine freshened with the young wine to get the balance and flavour. It's got that toffee-like character — malty, but it jumps up and hits you. Old rancio characters. Sweet, but not cloying. Finishes dry. The rancio, the age, the oxidation and the wood that it's picked up give it that dry finish. Very clean and mouth filling … I think they go best with things like custards and bread and butter pudding.

The muscat is made out of what we call a brown frontignac. The true name is *muscat a petits grains rouge*, which is muscat with the small, red berries. It makes a brownish pinky wine, not a red wine because there is not a lot of colour. But there again, it's the aging and the youth and the complexity of the old wine marrying together to make it a good wine. Very typical of raisins because we sun-ripen on the vine and the grapes get that raisiny character. They go well with plum pudding or if you're having a pick of nuts and raisins.

Both wines are made the same way with fruit that is given maximum ripening on the vine, up to the point of cutting them so they start to dry on the vine. Annual vintages become the basis of a delicate process of blending that creates their richness and intensity. David Morris, now the Morris winemaker, demonstrates with vintages as much as three decades apart:

It's the art of getting the young and the old, and keeping it fresh and keeping it on the palate. It's got to be round and smooth and luscious. We've got to be patient for the wines to mature so, when we blend, we like to do justice to the style of wine that evolves over a long time.

I've got a range of muscats here. There's a '97 — you'll see it's young in colour, a bit pale … it hasn't started to fill out and get richness in it. It's too young to use. We've got to let it sit for a couple of years in wood to mature and fill out, so that's still a baby.

The '95 is showing a little more raisiny character. The 1990 is starting to gain a bit more viscosity. The colour's starting to change from the red, going a bit darker. It is more complex and it's got some age characters. This one is a 1982. You can see that the colour's getting a lot more dense. It's getting more complex, a richer raisin character and on the palate it's starting to get extremely concentrated, luscious, intense and a lot more viscous.

And then the last one — this is a wine a little over 30 years old. It's very heavy, very treacle in colour, very dense, lost a lot of its muscat aromas but the palate makes up for it. It's the essence that we would use in a blend. A few per cent will add extra dimensions to the wine in complexity and concentration. The middle vintage years will add the weight of flavour. They fill it out and they'll have some intensity. But we need to use some of the younger material to freshen it, to give it that nice muscaty lift on the nose. It's all come together … you can see the four components showing. The freshness of fruit, some maturity in the character and let's have a look at the palate … youth, age, maturity, rolls over on the tongue and yes, it's got persistence. Must have a good length of flavour, linger on for a long time.

Using wines made over three decades to make a premium blend demands a special kind of attitude:

You've just got to be patient. Put the wine into casks and, while keeping an eye on it, just allow it to mature … which is the reaction with the air breathing through the cask and also the evaporation. You've probably heard of the angels' share — well, that's the evaporation and that's what is also concentrating it. If we put a wine away and left it for 20 years, you'd only end up with half the quantity … so the angels have done quite well out of it and we end up with a pretty good wine which will be rich, concentrated and the essence for the young wines to blend in. So that's the difference between table wines and fortified wines, where we're blending for complexity with various components and we've just got to be patient. With the table wines, 18 months in and out of casks and you can bottle them and they're right. Yeah.

What about alcohol content? 'We fortify it at vintage time up to about 18 per cent and theoretically, with the aging process, the alcohol should increase because the angels' share is more of the water solution. It can only go up to a certain percentage — I think the highest one would be up to about 20 per cent and, by the time you put it together as a blend, it might come out at about 19 per cent alcohol.'

Getting the Morris and Chambers clans together is no problem, and that's indicative of the Rutherglen area according to Wendy Chambers, wife of Bill:

Rutherglen is a very interesting area because the winemakers do get on together and they do share ideas — I think it comes from being a farming community. It seems to have taken a long while for big winery consortiums to start to put feelers into the area and it's remained a small, interesting sort of area in which the men can all converse very freely. And it is unusual. Very unusual.

I think they get enormous camaraderie from this. They have a winemakers' evening once a month. They have all their wines masked and they say whatever they feel about other people's wines and nobody takes great offence. Hopefully they learn from it. It's very interesting. They don't only taste local wines, I might add, they taste anything, everything, and it's a very open collection of people that can discuss it freely. I think it's a wonderful thing. Probably a great deal to do with the district's attraction is the fact that these men are farmers and they are able to be friends as well.

We've got to talk. We've got to push everybody up and striving for quality and we've got to talk that way. It's no good keeping secrets and saying, 'I'm not going to talk … I've had some very bad wines this year.' You've got to say: 'Look, I've made some crook wines this year, fellas. Has anybody else?' And you find out that way. (Bill Chambers)

You can't do much about it in hindsight. You always aim to make your best wine. You always hope it's good, but, at the end of the day, you can really only talk about what you made. You've got to be honest enough about it and say: 'Well, it was a pretty average year, wasn't it?' or 'Very good year, I thought.' And someone else's vineyard will maybe give some different results and they think differently. But you're always honest with your neighbours and tell them what you thought of the season and how yours worked out. (David Morris)

It would be nice to make the best wines every year, but unfortunately season conditions dictate what sort of a wine you're going to make. So we're always striving to make the epitome of a great wine, but it only happens once or twice in ten years. Would you agree with that? (Chambers)

We're pretty lucky with the climate here. We have very few poor vintages. It's either got to be severe drought or a very wet season so that the grapes rot. I think that only happens every seven, eight, nine years. Otherwise they're generally fair, average quality. But every three years or so the quality is exceptional. The climatic conditions and everything seems to fall into place. (Mick Morris)

I still reckon it's only about two or three years in ten that we make the great wines that we want to prop up our old wines with. Would you agree with that? (Chambers)

Yes, mmmm. (Morris)

Technology means, hopefully, that we're not making as many crook wines as we used to. They still happen, unfortunately, because when you play around with bacteria and yeast they don't always do what you want them to do. So not all our products are as perfect as we'd like them to be, but we're trying very hard. (Chambers)

And succeeding, judging by the demand. As are their colleagues in the Rutherglen area. And it might not only be the soil and climate that makes the region's tokay and muscat so special. It may also have something to do with the rough diamond modesty, directness and fellowship of these farmers of grapes and makers of wine to be sipped and relished by people who value its unique Australian character.

Phylloxera

Phylloxera is a tiny killer — an aphid that makes its home in the roots of a vine and saps its energy. It's a slow death: over three or even five years before you see a reduction of vigour in the vine. In the meantime, phylloxera could have spread to other vineyards. The potential of destruction to the Australian wine industry — already experienced in Europe in the 19th century and more recently in California — is terrifying.

Prue Henschke, of South Australia's Eden Valley, describes the aphid:

Phylloxera

It's quite a bright yellow, a tiny speck of flesh without much shape. In most cases, you can see them clearly in the late summer, close to the soil surface. That is when they're starting to come up the trunk. They will lay their eggs first in the galls that form on the leaves and then they develop a winged form which can be dispersed by the wind to new sites.

The way they damage the roots is that they suck the sap out of the root, and by penetrating the root they form a lesion. The root then makes quite a kink, so if you are looking for phylloxera you can see these really right-angled roots and the little bugs are nestled in that inner part of the right angle where they are working away at absorbing the sugars and the sap out of the roots. And with that injury, the vine root slowly dies away.

Phylloxera was first discovered in Australia in the 1870s, in Victoria. After the turn of the century, there were no more major outbreaks until the 1960s, when several areas in Victoria were infested, causing substantial losses to growers. Quarantine restrictions have so far confined the insect to small areas in New South Wales and Victoria, making Australia almost the only grape-growing country in the world that is still predominantly free of phylloxera. But three outbreaks in Victoria's King Valley in the 1990s have been a warning. And the risk is increasing as the industry expands and there is greater movement of people, grape vine material and machinery between the wine-growing regions.

While Henschke is primarily concerned with prevention in phylloxera-free South Australia, where she has been a member of the Phylloxera and Grape Industry Board, Mark Walpole has to face the threat of disease on a daily basis at Brown Brothers, where he is chief viticulturist. He and the company work pragmatically, vigilantly and constantly at the winery's Victorian base in Milawa to make sure that the phylloxera aphid has as little chance as possible to move around.

There are probably a number of different ways it could be shifted. Soil is probably the most likely because they live in the ground. So — on car tyres, on people's boots, those sort of things. On vines which have still got soil on the roots. During the summer, when the numbers are at their greatest, the insects crawl up on to the vines to the leaves, so people working in the vineyards can actually have them on their clothing, and if they went from one vineyard to another, phylloxera could be spread on their clothes.

Rebecca Dunstone, research officer, showing Grant Van Every a vine root infested with phylloxera

Brown Brothers have made sure there are no susceptible vines in the public area so that there is no risk of visitors making contact and spreading the disease. When staff are employed, they are given a copy of the company's phylloxera protocols and they need to sign a document saying they have read and will abide by them — basically, that they are fully aware of which vineyards have phylloxera, how it can be spread and how not to do so.

Sharing of equipment with other wineries is another danger:

We have a process whereby the equipment is steam cleaned. It goes into a room where all the vine material and mud is removed. It then goes into a heat treatment room where the temperature is maintained at 45°C for at least two hours, and that would dislocate any other insects that might have been on the machine, that hadn't been removed by the hot water washing.

When grapes are brought from another part of the State, all the fruit bins are dipped in hot water at 70°C and there is a wash-down pen for truck wheels to be cleaned before they leave the site.

So far, no way has been found to eradicate phylloxera other than pulling out the vines. In Europe, people tried chemical treatments and flooding vineyards. In Victoria — as in France and California — research continues on ways to combat it through resistant rootstock. Rebecca Dunstone, a research officer with Agriculture Victoria–Rutherglen, is examining the behavioural characteristics of the phylloxera populations in Australia. This is similar to work being done with American infestations where researchers have identified how a particular biotype of phylloxera overcame what was thought to be a resistant rootstock: how they behaved differently in that rootstock compared to others.

Mark Walpole, chief viticulturist, Brown Brothers, with grafted root stock

You start off by identifying strains. You have, for example, different strains of the flu virus that develop every year. They're all the same species, but the various strains behave differently. The word biotype means biological type — the biology of the insect, how it behaves on the vine. In Australia, we've identified (so far) two separate biotypes.

Ironically, one comes from Rutherglen and establishes only on the fibrous roots, where you don't see any decline on the plant as you do with infestations on the main root. 'So we have vines in Rutherglen that have been infested with phylloxera on their own roots for well over 20 or 30 years.'

Most Australian vineyards — 95 per cent of them — are planted on their own roots, which is considered by many people to be less expensive and offers more durability. It is said that vines planted with grafted rootstocks often show some weakening and a lower yield after 30 years or so, compared with very much older vineyards that produce some of Australia's best wine. Prue Henschke, a vigorous campaigner for protective action in South Australia (which began its preventive measures with the first Australian outbreak in the 1870s), puts forward a terrible scenario for their most treasured vines, more than 130 years old: 'If Hill of Grace vineyard got phylloxera, it would be just dreadful. It would be a loss of a lot of tradition and a wonderful gene source of a prime variety like shiraz.'

Conversely, there are other advantages of using rootstocks such as vigour control or increasing particular nutrients in vines. They also offer protection against nematodes, a microscopic worm which attacks vine roots, though with less devastating effects. Dunstone has another reason for recommending the use of rootstocks:

The way I see it is 'insurance'. There's been figures done that, if you have a vineyard that is only on own-rooted vines and it got infested with phylloxera, it would cost you $22,000 a hectare or even higher, depending on methods you used to replant your entire vineyard. That's not only based upon the cost of your new vines. That's the cost of losing production.

Practically all vineyards in Europe and California are being planted on resistant varieties because phylloxera is prolific over there. There's no distance between vineyards of, say, one or two kilometres like there may be in Australia. It has spread very rapidly over there, whereas in this country it's been quarantined to specific areas, so there's been less emphasis put on rootstock here.

The resistant rootstocks come originally, like the phylloxera, from

North America. The aphids live in harmony with native grapevines from that part of the world, although they are not totally resistant. It was only when North American vine roots were brought to Europe in the 1850s to help in research on powdery mildew that the phylloxera moved in on the unresisting vine varieties of France and their catastrophic effects were revealed.

Mark Walpole is reassuring in his experience of living with phylloxera at Milawa, where it has no effect on the grapes or wine of the grafted vines:

> A grafted vine that has phylloxera on its roots — you really would not know that the phylloxera were actually present at all because phylloxera just do not like living on roots of the American vines. They do live there, but the actual effect on that vine is negligible. So you don't see any reduction in vigour or crop at all. Or any change in quality of the fruit or the resultant wine.

New Regions

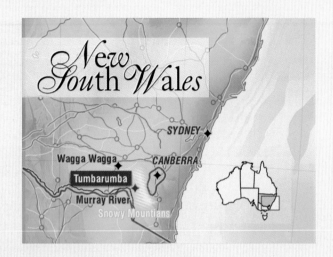

Tumbarumba

Tumbarumba is one of Australia's new cool climate regions for growing grapes. It is in New South Wales, a six-hour drive southwest from Sydney, where the Snowy Mountains begin to form rare cold peaks on this hot, flat continent. Until relatively recently, no one even attempted growing grapes here at an altitude of around 600 metres, but once the idea took hold and good results could be seen, the numbers grew.

Frank Minutello and his wife, Christine, and Juliet Cullen and her former partner, Ian Cowell, landed in Tumbarumba from different paths in 1980. Their aims, however, turned out to be the same. Juliet says:

> I got interested in the wine industry in my early 20s. I went to France and fell in love with Burgundy. I came back here with information about the climate you needed to grow good pinot noir and realised that nowhere in Australia at that time was pinot noir being grown in the right place. In order to start a top quality vineyard, I'd have to go to somewhere new. I went off to the bureau of meteorology looking for places that matched the temperatures of Dijon in northern Burgundy, and Tumbarumba's fit was uncanny. I'd never been here, but my family comes from the southern tablelands of New South Wales, so I felt at home immediately. I was young and foolish, and I had a vision.

Frank relates the story of his conversion to grape growing:

> We were involved in the family business in the northeast of Victoria, growing tobacco. Basically we could see that the days were numbered for the tobacco industry — obviously the consumption of it is becoming very anti-social — and we were looking to diversify. We had three

family members obtaining a living from a fairly small farm and we thought, it's time to make a change, time to see what else we can do. We started investigating where we could set up a horticultural enterprise.

Tumbarumba trellises

We were looking for an area that was climatically fairly safe in the sense that it had abundant water, the soil was reasonably fertile and it had scope for development because you're flushed with a lot of energy — perhaps not flushed with the wherewithal. We wanted to find a place that we could put in the hard work and develop something, and we came to Tumbarumba. We moved up in 1980 with two young children. The place was totally undeveloped. No house on it, no buildings and in the first years we rented a house lower down in the valley and commuted here to do the work, virtually living out of the Esky for a few years, didn't we Christine?

'Yeah. Our children said they didn't really want to go on picnics any more after three of four years of living out of an Esky.' Their initial plans included growing blueberries or grapes; data put out by the CSIRO and the encouragement of Italian friends triggered their plunge into grapes. In 1982 they secured an undertaking from Rosemount to take their fruit, so they planted vines and developed a vineyard essentially on that fast learning curve of trial and error — since grapes had mostly not been grown in such a cool climate in Australia, definitive information was not available. 'We were very isolated from other viticultural areas, so this was a fly-by-the-seat-of-your-pants thing. Although we had information from experts in the Hunter Valley and down towards Adelaide, and a lot of the practical things applied, cool climate viticulture was in its infancy, so there were a lot of things that you just had to make up your own mind about.'
Frank continues:

This area traditionally was sheep and cattle grazing. There was a little bit of home fruit development within Tumbarumba and, of course, Batlow, which is famous for its apples, is not far away. But it was very much a new industry and, as always with a new industry, the subject of a lot of scrutiny, a lot of negatives at times. And the more negative comments that came through, the more determined you were that this was going to work.

Christine and Frank Minutello with Juliet Cullen (right), Tumbarumba

Juliet had similar experiences:

Establishing a wine label is a lot more than just business. You've got to have it in your heart, you've got to have passion. When you've got to fight frost and drought and the financial stress of it, and coming to a new area where they've never even seen a small tractor before, where it's sheep and cattle country and you start growing vines ... I mean, somebody told me that I just ploughed up the best hay paddock in the district, as if I'd committed a mortal sin. And I said, well, it's going to be the best sauvignon blanc paddock in the district — and it is.

We subscribed to American journals of oenology and viticulture so we could find out what they were doing in Oregon, which has got a climate like Tumbarumba, and in New Zealand because they're very advanced viticulturally. So you read as widely as you could ... but most of the time, Frank and I talked to each other because we were the only two people with the problem. So I'd say, Frank, I'm a bit worried about the trellis design. Or, I think my vines are not looking green enough, what do you think? And he'd come to our place and I'd come to his place and we'd have a look around the vineyard and then we'd go and discuss it over a bottle of wine.

Frank concurs:

That's right. Or you'd come to a patch and say, 'Gee, you know this looks a bit different to the rest and it's looking very good — what have you done here?' And from that situation, we'd do the same practice on ours and vice versa. So you shared your problems. I think where you learn is from people sharing their problems. Success doesn't really teach you anything, it's the surmounting of problems that we used to discuss over bottles of wine and lots of good food.

From the problems of the vigneron pioneers at the start of the 1980s, the area has boomed. In 1989, there were still only the original two vineyards; by 1992, there were eight, the following year an astonishing increase to 14. In 1998, there were 30, planted between 350 and 800 metres above sea level. Southcorp, which is the chief buyer of grapes, now has its own vineyard as well — the one that Juliet planted originally, while she has established another. The 1997 statistics record plantings of 154 hectares of chardonnay, 87 hectares of pinot noir — the two grape varieties most likely to excel in the area — and 14 hectares of sauvignon blanc. There were also small plantings of merlot, pinot gris, pinot meunier, shiraz, verdelho, riesling and sangoviese, plus a large and surprising 24 hectares of cabernet sauvignon to test its possibilities.

There are more grape growers waiting in the wings for a decision to be made on water usage, in which new balances are being worked out between ecological protection of the river systems and increasing demands on them for grape growing in established new vineyards and as insurance for dry years. Frank explains:

We formed an association about five years back. Since so many potential new players were coming into the industry, we thought it would be foolish for them to necessarily go through the same mistakes as we made. The association was instrumental in steering these intending growers to expert information so that they had the groundwork to make a decision themselves. It wasn't an ABC primer of 'This is what you do' because that doesn't help anyone. It's basically knowing the basis for what you're doing. We undertook a fairly extensive program with the involvement of all the membership to bring to this area the various experts in their field to talk to us here specifically, to do the vineyard visits and see what problems they find.

Basically, we've had all the top people here. Back ten, 12 years ago, there was the two of us and we couldn't afford to fly them over, but now that we've got 30 members of the association, you can spread the cost. We're still learning, as well as the newer people, and it's really gratifying that a lot of those people are now telling us that we have some of the best viticulture practices in Australia. That puts a smile on your face after all these years. We've really achieved something and the whole district is being recognised as a premium grower of wine grapes. It's come a long way. (Juliet)

The new growers are no longer novices, they can be teaching you something now. They've gone through various experiences, so the experience pool is enlarging. And while we are bouncing problems and ideas amongst each other, it helps us solve them, it helps us maintain the quality edge we have. It also fosters some friendly competition, and friendly competition is terrific because it urges everyone else to do a bit better. We work very well together, a very vibrant group.

One of the highest risks is the climatic problem — I wouldn't say problem, but rather events that can happen in Tumbarumba. Being so high in the mountains, there is always the situation that you can get frost. I suppose the thing we dread most is to listen to the weather report saying it's a great ski season because that means a lot of snow on the mountains. It takes a long time to melt and potentially it's a cool spring. The mitigating factors are site selection — to have good air drainage — or mechanical means of frost protection such as the wind machine that we have down here. It works on the principal of bringing down warmer air from an inversion layer and mixing it, displacing the colder air at the bottom. (Frank)

We do things like they do in Europe, where this happens regularly, like burning hay. And you can look at overhead sprinkling systems. But it comes with growing on the edge. If you look at where the great wines come from in the world, they're always on the edge of 'it can be great or you can have a natural disaster'. You just have to take that into account in your planning: that one year in seven you might have a severely reduced crop. You have to learn to live with it. In our household, there is complete silence while the weather is on every night. I open the newspaper and go to the weather forecast every day, and that becomes critical in the frost season.

Tumbarumba vineyards

Up in these high elevation areas that suit pinot noir in particular, it's a double-edged sword. In order to get the cooler springs and get away from the extremes of heat, the other side of the coin is this ever present fear of frost in the spring and late autumn. Site selection for air drainage — so that the cold air flows off the ridges and down into the valleys — is really important. The soil is important, but you can modify soil. We have to lime every three years and you can add nutrients — but you can't warm up a night.

If you've got a cold site, you're going to be hammered by frost, so when I came looking for a second vineyard and found this site where I was told that my nearest neighbour can grow things in her garden that other people can't and doesn't get the frost, I knew I was onto something good. The rows are planted due north–south to maximise the sunlight penetration up the rows, and you've got the western sun coming in the afternoon and warming them. The granite soils here also tend to warm up in the daytime, then give their heat off in the night. The other important thing is you've got to keep the grass really short between the rows, you've got to keep the weeds down. Sometimes we cultivate between the rows and you spend a lot of time sitting on a tractor with a slasher mowing it really short so that the earth stays nice and warm. (Juliet)

And the hardest decision to be made in the year? Frank responds:

I suppose the most critical decision you make is at pruning time when you set the crop levels for the following season. You are in winter, trying to predict what the climate is going to be for the next 12 months. So you take a bit of a gamble and use the criteria from your record keeping of past years and set your pruning levels, perhaps, to those criteria. But there can be other vagaries during the season and you may have to take more fruit off — you obviously can't put it back on — or perhaps thin leaves. Certainly, for your next vintage, pruning is the most difficult decision that you make.

I'd agree. But also, from early September through to almost the end of April, you make hundreds of decisions about the vine from when it starts to move in the springtime budburst: when to put on fertiliser, when to spray, do the vines need some supplementary irrigation, have I got the weeds under control, is it going to frost tonight, when should we pick, are birds going to be a problem. It's decisions, decisions. But that's the fun and the challenge of it. And it's lovely to produce a product that you can taste in the bottle at the end. And the excitement when the pickers come in and those bins start to fill and you see the truck laden, and you say, 'There's my year's work going off to the winery. Well it makes all that decision making worthwhile.' (Juliet)

And that you know you get the feedback then from the winemakers and they say 'Gee, Frank, you know your vintage this year has been excellent. We made a lovely wine out of it, a great wine out of it.' You're obviously uplifted, you're ready to say: 'Yeah, I can tackle another season now.' (Frank)

You could say Frank has had a lifetime of vintage experiences. One of the earliest memories as a child in Italy before he came to Australia with his family aged four and a half, was to do with winemaking.

I was hoisted by my father into a stomping tub filled with ladies that were tramping the red grapes, and I had great fun hanging on to people's skirts and plunging down to my waist in these red grapes. Now it could be that's how it got into my blood … But my father also developed some quite extensive vineyards in the northern part of Italy.

In recent years, Frank has been involved in establishing a new consortium vineyard and in wine industry matters, so his wife Christine has been supervising the casual labour force that they value so much, as she points out. 'We've been very fortunate. We've had a very reliable core of workers. You can trust these people to do their job and now I think we're going to run into short supply because as the vineyards develop and everyone expands, we'll probably have to import labour.' Her contribution to their venture is obviously a major part of its success, but she is modest about it. 'There are many skills that Frank would have that I don't. I think the important thing, if you're committed to an enterprise such as this, is that you really have to complement each other in what you are doing.'

These original Tumbarumba growers are now producing wine under their own labels, as well as selling grapes. The winery at Charles Sturt University, 100 kilometres away with its national wine research centre, has been doing their winemaking for them — to their great satisfaction. Juliet emphasises the importance of that final stage in her summing up of the highs and lows of being a pioneer winemaker in Tumbarumba:

You have to have the courage of your convictions, you have to have the support of people like Frank and Chris, and the other growers in the area because there are times when you wonder why the hell you're doing it. But I love farming, I love the four seasons we get in Tumbarumba. I love at the end of the year being able to see my handiwork, to be able to open a bottle of your own wine, to drink that, to have other people praise it, to see it in a five-star hotel in Sydney, to see it on a restaurant table ... It's such a buzz. I don't know of any other industry where you'd get such a kick, such satisfaction out of your work — and that sees you through the cold days, the hard days, the frost and the droughts. It's a passion. You've really got to love your vineyard and stick with it. It's part of the family.

Riesling Food Match

RIESLING

Stephanie Toole is a winemaker and an extremely good cook. She is also the partner of winemaker Jeffrey Grosset, whose speciality is riesling … and that's a wine she knows how to match with recipes developed to complement its fine flavours.

For a young riesling, she chooses scallops with lime, fresh coriander and a chilli sauce to reflect the fresh, lively flavours of the wine — 'the youth and the vibrance from the scallops and the lime as well as the wine.'

An aged riesling, 14 years old which has 'toast and honey' flavours but is still showing zesty, limey fruit characters on the palate is matched with marinated quail. 'You are getting this really lively combination of rich intense flavours from the quail. Chilli and garlic are enemies of many wines but riesling, of all the varieties, can take really bold flavours.'

For a dessert wine, her first recommendation is a fresh lemon tart. She also suggests pannacotta, fresh strawberries, a fresh fruit salad … or the increasingly popular partner for sweet wines, cheese.

Scallops

Allow 4 to 6 scallops in the shell per person. Wash scallops and remove any sand or grit, then pat dry.

Heat non-stick frying pan until very hot and add a small amount of olive oil. Quickly seal scallops on both sides — allow 1 to 2 minutes each side.

Place the scallops back in rinsed shells and squeeze over fresh lime. Top with chopped coriander, julienne spring onions and freshly ground black pepper.

Serve with a sweet chilli sauce.

Marinated Quail

quail
1 clove garlic, finely chopped
3 cm piece of ginger, finely chopped
1 small red chilli, finely chopped
1 to 2 tablespoons soy sauce
1 tablespoon honey
juice of ½ to 1 lime
freshly ground black pepper
mixed salad greens to serve

Spatchcock quail and remove breast bone. Marinate in the garlic, ginger, chilli, soy sauce, honey, lime juice and pepper. Preheat the oven to 220°C. Cook the quail skin side up for 10 to 12 minutes or until nicely browned. Rest for 5 minutes skin side down, then serve on a platter of the mixed salad greens, including rocket and fresh asparagus spears. Drizzle any juices over top of quail.

In one of those fascinating and intriguing elements of win

terra rossa—in the Coonawarra district of South Australia

Cabernet

Cabernet

happens to produce exceptional grapes. It is jus

kilometres wide, and tr

bernet Sauvigno

to the region's success, especially with cabernet sauv

Cabernet

GRAPE VARIETIES AND WINE STYLES

Sauvignon

Cabernet Sauvignon

*I*n one of those fascinating and intriguing elements of winemaking, there is a cigar-shaped island of red soil — terra rossa — in the Coonawarra district of South Australia that happens to produce exceptional grapes. It is just 12 to 13 kilometres long and two to three kilometres wide, and treasured by those who have vineyards planted on it. Or rather, in it. Because the soil is the key to the region's success, especially with cabernet sauvignon.

Around 385 kilometres southeast of Adelaide, not far from the Victorian border, Coonawarra has only relatively recently been given celebrity status in the wine industry after being used for producing workhorse grapes since the 19th century. In the 1890s, there was pinot noir and shiraz and varieties that suited fortified wines. Gradually people realised the area was too cool for the grapes that made their port, sherry and brandy, so these varieties gave way to riesling and shiraz, which were the main grapes right into the 1970s. And for half the 20th century, most of the grapes were sold in bulk to big wineries headquartered elsewhere. Coonawarra didn't even have a label of its own until 1950.

Bruce Redman, who, with his brother Malcolm, is the third generation of his family to make wine in Coonawarra, says of the district:

> Now the rush is on to have Coonawarra on the label — in those days, the rush was to leave it off. The first Coonawarra wine was bottled and released through the Wynn family, and Rouge Homme was also labelled in 1950. Ever since then, Coonawarra has crept into people's psyche. So it's become very famous nationally and internationally.
>
> There's no doubt that the terra rossa soil is crucial to the style and contributes greatly to the flavours of the Coonawarra. I don't think there's any doubt about that. Obviously soil doesn't follow a nice, neat paddock and there are vines planted on black soil, so you can see the difference between the quality of the grapes from the red soil and the quality of the grapes from the black soil. And I don't think there is too much argument that the red soil produces consistently better grapes than the darker soils, the more marginal soils.
>
> Basically, the thing about terra rossa soil is that it's a red-brown earth over limestone. The top soil varies from a few centimetres up to a metre thick. So then you go into limestone, which obviously hasn't got a lot of fertility. What the terra rossa soil does is act as growth regulator — it regulates the level of your crops — whereas the dark soil is really a bottomless clay and it's very fertile. So what happens with the dark soil is the vines grow very rapidly vegetatively and produce very large crops which, in an area that is pretty cool, have difficulty ripening. So you

tend to get greener, more herbaceous flavours than with grapes off a terra rossa, where you have much warmer, richer flavours in the wines. And that's basically the difference — the level of fertility of the soils.

The rise of cabernet sauvignon with consistency and depth of flavour has been the key to Coonawarra's fame, although it also produces a range of red and white varieties that go to make some of Australia's better known premium wines. The Redman family came into the industry by chance, through Bruce Redman's grandfather:

He was born on a dairy farm not very far from here. He was one of a number of children, and there wasn't enough work for him on the dairy farm. So he came to Coonawarra to work at the vintage, grape picking, in what is now Wynns, which was the original Coonawarra winery. That was in 1901.

Bruce Redman, winemaker

Because he was relatively small and could get in and out of barrels, they said, 'Well, look, you'd better come and work in the winery. You can clean some of the big vats.' And he stayed, basically. So, from 1901 to 1907, he worked at Wynns winery as a cellar hand and learned how to make wine. In 1907, he bought his own vineyard; in 1908, he made the first wine. He then continued on, acquired more land and gradually built up contracts to sell wine and so on. Through the 20s, 30s, 40s and 50s, he sold wine to other wine companies. He was known as the person who was almost the keeper of Coonawarra. At that stage, it was really maintaining and sustaining the vineyards that were left — quite a lot were being pulled out through that era. There was really only the Redman family that continued making wine in Coonawarra.

As the wine became more popular and more revered, the demand grew — and outgrew some of the sources. There were more vineyards being planted and he kept buying more and more fruit. In 1950, we released our first wine under the Rouge Homme label. My father came into the business at that time, and my uncle. And they continued on in Rouge Homme until the mid-60s, when we sold out to Lindemans and my grandfather retired. My father started the current Redman wine.

I've been pretty fortunate because my father and grandfather showed a great deal of foresight in producing mainly red wines. So we're in an enviable position of actually growing the right grapes in the right area, which takes a lot of the pressure off. I guess there's an historical pressure to keep producing high-quality red table wines, but, apart from that, we're really starting with a pretty fair jump on everybody else.

We've made a few refinements, but no changes. After the technocrats ruling through the 70s and perhaps into the early 80s, there's a much more traditional view of winemaking now. A lot of people are reverting to traditional ways with refinements, rather than changing the whole way that we've made wines. I think it's interesting that we're following much more traditional patterns now in making wines — with some technological refinements.

Doug Balnaves,
owner/vigneron

Doug Balnaves, vigneron, is another who came into the wine industry by chance:

I started off on a small family property and we ran sheep, fat lambs and a few cattle. By a lucky set of circumstances, I stumbled into the wine industry in 1970. We had bought another property along the main road towards Coonawarra, and Hungerford Hill came along and bought that to plant a vineyard, and offered me the job of developing the vineyard — which seemed a strange thing to do because I didn't know one end of a grapevine from another. But I took the job … to think about it … and here we are in 1998. I think we're going to stay in the wine industry.

These days, Balnaves has his own vineyard and winery with cellar door sales. He employs a winemaker and he has two children involved in the business:

We were never going to do any of those things. But we made our first wine in 1990 and established the cellar door sales in '91. Then we had the opportunity to build a winery and that was done in 1996, and we were very fortunate that Peter Bissell came along to join us as a winemaker and it's going very well. But ten years ago, I wouldn't have ever dreamt that we'd be in this situation.

Grape growing remains Balnaves' pivotal contribution to the business and he has observed tremendous change in that area:

The technology that's coming at us is mind boggling. The degree that we go to, for example, to manage soil moisture is quite incredible. We've got gypsum blocks through the whole vineyard which give us daily readings — or however often we want to read them — down to a metre so we know exactly what's going on down in the root zone, and with that information we can manage the vine much more effectively. In fact, I think this technology is the biggest step we've taken since the introduction of mechanical harvesting in the vineyards all those years ago.

You've got to have good soil to start with and everybody's got little patches in their vineyard that perhaps they'd rather not have. It's a small percentage, but we can see even clearer that our best grapes come from our best soil. The most important thing, I think, is that it has good drainage. And the soil around here that's got good drainage has quite often got limestone underneath it. Depth of soil can vary and we're getting some confusing pictures about the ideal depth, but first and foremost good drainage — and we see the good drainage on the good red soil.

We're keen on mechanical pruning as an aid to spur pruning. By that, I mean that the machine goes through and prunes the vine down to a series of spurs, and then we feel it's most important that you have a follow-up team of people who clean that out and make a spur pruning job of it. Some people still rely on cane pruning and I think that's interesting. They feel that they get a slightly different characteristic into their wines and that makes the whole diversity of the area just that bit more interesting. There are different styles of trellis being used. I think everybody's just trying for that extra quality that we all need to have.

On the subject of difference, are the wines different or better than they were?

Well, I'm not a winemaker, so it's very much a layman's opinion, but I would feel — and I'm probably repeating other people's judgments — that they're more consistently better. We're getting more consistently good wines in Coonawarra, without perhaps the highs and lows that we might have had 20 years ago. I think the wines that are coming out now seem to be extremely good and the exciting thing is that they'll get better. They will get better because there's more and more assistance coming in decision-making — in vineyards in particular. I'd like to be 25 and starting again because I think there's a terribly exciting world in viticulture in this area still to be explored.

Doug Bowen, winemaker

One of the reasons for the flavour in Coonawarra grapes is the length of the ripening period:

We have budburst in early September, about the same time as a lot of other areas in Australia, but some of them are picking in January and February, and we're picking in April, May — and my understanding is that's where the depth of flavour comes from. The latest we've picked is the 17th of May. Now that is getting alarmingly late, but we did get some outstandingly good grapes by doing that. We would like to finish by Anzac Day, the 25th of April, and very rarely do. But that would be the perfect year. Usually we drift into May.

Sometimes it's a bit of a rush to get them in, but the mechanical harvesters enable us to leave the grapes until the optimum period of ripening and then we can go out if the weather's changing. We can pick them very quickly. I think that's a tremendous help to Coonawarra because you can wait until they're really ripe.

Coonawarra is an interesting mix of big companies and small producers:

It works extremely well, and the whole community here works very closely together in everything we do. I think we're very lucky to have the big corporate groups here, and I think the smaller ones just add a nice balance to the whole area. It's a great area to be in for cooperation and working together.

In fact, there are others who would like to be in it as well, and want to extend the boundaries of the region described, labelled and marketed as Coonawarra. Expansion would bring in soil types other than terra rossa, which has sparked controversy and the need for an independent committee to make a decision which hadn't been finalised at the time of writing.

Meanwhile, the Coonawarra grape growers and winemakers on a smaller scale are a convivial bunch. When Doug Balnaves, Doug Bowen, Ian Hollick and Bruce Redman get together, as they tend to do, for a game of petanque and a round-table discussion, all manner of topics are batted about — including this matter of the Coonawarra boundary.

At the end of the day, there will probably be a bigger line around the district. But if you can make as good a wine outside that old cigar shape as we can inside it, well good luck to you. My bet would be they won't — or not as consistently as we can on the cigar shape. (Hollick)

I think that's the real point. In years to come, people are going to have to be a little bit more discerning about the Coonawarra labels. They won't be able, like today, to just go ahead and be guaranteed of absolutely top quality in the wine. They're going to have to be more picky and choosy between the labels. (Bowen)

I think you'll find there will be a subregion formed within the larger area of Coonawarra. It may not be a subregion according to the Geographical Indications Committee, but it will be a trademark or a club or something that represents the better growers. (Hollick)

So would it be fair to say there is Coonawarra as a wine style because of that particular dirt and the grapes that are grown there? 'There's more than one style in Coonawarra, but there is regionality that is common to us all. There are various styles around the regionality,' says Hollick. Redman continues:

But if you look at wines over the past 20 years … go back 50 years, when there was still a lot of Coonawarra cabernet … the styles have changed dramatically. If you go back to the 1950s, the wines were quite light and very elegant styles. Now they're much fuller and richer. Certainly not as herbaceous as some of the older Coonawarra styles which were, as I said, much lighter and more elegant without the tannin and richness and depth. And that's probably a positive for the area. So it's going to be interesting to see where we go from here with an expanded base. Because when we were talking in the 50s, we were only talking 200 acres of vineyard compared to six, seven or eight thousand acres now. The area, in 30-odd years, has grown enormously. And in that era, there was not that much cabernet planted at all. Whereas today, a third of that area is probably cabernet, or even a bit more.

Going back to your father's day, everything was handpicked, and people started early because we were always worried about the rain. These days, we're not so concerned about that because of the advent of viticultural techniques, particularly harvesters. We don't need to start picking grapes early. We can wait for the grapes to be fully ripe. And I think that's seen a big change in the style of wine. (Bowen)

That's right. And the use of oak — I mean, oak was used sparingly in those days, so the wines are pretty austere. As they've got older, the aging has produced a lot more positive influences than, perhaps, the wines of today. We'll still see them age nicely, but whether there is as dramatic a difference in a 20-year-old wine … (Redman)

Playing petanque,
Coonawarra

I think if we could go back to those days and taste those wines as young wines, we would, by today's standards, find them undrinkable. And it's taken them many years — you know, 10, 15, 20 years — to come into the realms of what we perceive to be really nice drinking wines. Whereas the wine styles we're making today, they are much more approachable as young wines. I think we are crossing over that area of making wines which are better drinking wines at an earlier age and, hopefully, they are having longevity as well. (Bowen)

One of the things that has frustrated me over the years has been to try to convince a customer that you can actually drink this wine in its third year, but it is going to actually last for ten. And they look at you with wide eyes of disbelief. (Hollick)

Coonawarra vineyard

I think the really true inherent character of Coonawarra is flavour and soft tannins. That's the real key to any good Coonawarra cabernet. With the soft tannins, the wine can be appreciated as a young wine. But the tannins, even though they are soft, still have that ability to give longevity and wines can be appreciated at a later date. It doesn't mean it's just a soft, early drinking wine. (Bowen)

That seems to be one of the problems inherent in the wine industry at the moment: making wines of huge alcohol and huge tannins. Everybody is looking for really big wines, mistaking that for flavour. Whereas, Coonawarra has got elegant wines with intense flavours, but without huge tannins and huge alcohol. So it's the flavour that's carrying the wine through, and that flavour's maturing and changing. You go from the berry fruits in the chocolatey and cigar-boxy sort of characters you get in the beautiful aged Coonawarra cabernet. (Redman)

Show Judging

Competitions are always controversial. Wine competitions are more controversial than most. People challenge the way that prizes are awarded and judging is done, the judges' approach and attitudes to style, the sheer quantity of wines in any one competition, the youth of the wine and the marketing advantage that gold, silver and bronze medals give to the wines and companies so honoured.

The first thing to know about the Australian judging system, which is different from those in other countries, is that it is not a first-past-the-post system like a race. Gold, silver and bronze medals do not indicate wines chosen by the judges to be the best, second-best and third-best in their class. These medals are awarded on a points system, so there can be many medal winners or none at all in any one class.

Points are awarded out of 20, a total arrived at through the maximum of three for colour, seven for smell and ten for taste. A gold medal means 18.5 to 20 points, a silver medal 17 to 18.4 points and a bronze medal 15.5 to 16.9 points. They are assessed on factors such as technical quality, style, flavour, aroma, balance, structure, complexity and length of palate. The wines are judged against standards, rather than being set in competition with each other.

At a recent wine show in Brisbane organised by the Royal National Agricultural and Industrial Association of Queensland, there was a record number of entries — more than 2,500. Panels of three judges were sampling up to 200 wines a day — sniffing, sipping and spitting, of course, not swallowing each sample. A certain amount of alcohol is inevitably absorbed, however, and the process of evaluating so many wines is a testing process for the judges themselves.

Brisbane Wine Show 1998

None of the wines is identified. Even the label and code that organisers use are changed from show to show. Judges are mostly experts from the industry — winemakers judging the product of other winemakers — in a panel which does not discuss opinions until everyone has finished judging and their scores are written down. If they then disagree, the chairman or chief judge may be brought in as arbitrator.

John Stanford, chief judge of the Brisbane wine show with the record number of entries, is not surprisingly an advocate of the Australian wine show system. At the end of a week when he calculates that he personally 'had a good look at' 1,500 to 2,000 of the entries, he talked about Australian wine shows and their competitors.

They are not only seeking recognition, but also comparison with their peers in the industry. That's how the show was developed and it's unique. Other countries like France don't show their best wines to their competitors three years before they put them on the market. Very few industries do, actually. But it's been of enormous value to the Australian wine industry because the process of bringing in their best wines to compete with their peer winemakers, and then the awards and showing the results at the end, means that every winemaker knows every advance that every other winemaker in the country is making. That has helped to tune up our winemaking technique and we are regarded as technically the most advanced winemaking country in the world. Our winemakers fly overseas to make wines, even in France.

It has raised the quality of Australian wines and it's allowed the winemakers to develop the most attractive characters in their wines. One of the main advantages that we have here in this country is our climate, but it's been regarded as a handicap for a number of years because we always had ripe grapes and we couldn't make light, skinny, elegant wines like the French. But now we've discovered that the world winemakers, especially in Europe, didn't particularly like those French wines and they like ours better. So now we're making better wines with more depth of flavour, and that is the 'flavour of the month' at the moment.

Does palate fatigue play a part in judging?

Yes it does towards the end of the day. We've worked out that somewhere around 200 wines a day begins to fatigue even a good judge. Some will go further, but some will fall off at an earlier stage. This is quite different to international judging where, in France for instance, there are some types of judging where they may sit down to a category of 10 to 15 wines, and then continue on to lunch with them. That's another style of life. Here we work hard to clearly determine the basic characteristics of wine in 15 seconds per wine as we go past it. We'll go backwards and forwards past the wine, taking a decision every 15 seconds. So it's not the alcohol intake that makes judges fatigued, it's the sheer brainwork of taking all those decisions continuously all day.

All these judges are experienced and most of them are graduates of one of the two colleges here in Australia or an overseas college. They've learned all the details and the background, the organic materials that make up wine. They have learned to recognised them in a flash as they're tasting the wines, and they can all do that to a large number of wines. The three judges in any particular class may come from entirely different districts but they all have the same basic training and experiences, and they tend to average out the final result which comes out of that class. They're remarkably consistent. You find that there's only half a point difference between the judging. There's rarely an argument about the differences — and these are mainly on style and the approach to the style of wine.

And does the show system set benchmarks for the Australian wine industry? 'Very definitely it does, and this being the first of the series of shows around Australia — immediately after the bottling of the first wines for last vintage — all the winemakers come up here to see what has happened in the other districts. And this is the best way to see it because this is an exhibition of wines from every district in Australia, from Western Australia right up to central Queensland.'

It's not too early to judge those wines? 'As a consumer, you would find some of them a bit hard to drink at the moment, but most of these people are, or have been, senior winemakers in their wineries and they're accustomed to tasting young wines and looking through the structure of the wine to find out how its going to turn out. They've cut their teeth on tasting wines as they come out of the vintage tank and following right through until they're about 20 years old.'

Lined up for judging

But does the consumer understand the medal system? 'No, because essentially it's not designed for the consumer. It's designed to train and activate the winemaker towards a higher level of quality and finesse in the winemaking that he's doing. That's the original idea.' Yet the wine companies use the results to sell their wines. 'Anything that encourages people to have a close look at the wines — as distinct from one wine opposed to another — they regard as good marketing. But that is not the objective of national shows. They are quality control exercised by winemakers on themselves.'

Wine writer and judge Huon Hooke would agree that the wine show system has improved the quality of Australian wine, but he has strong and differing views on some other points made by Stanford:

There are too many wine shows in Australia where wine is judged and given an award when it is yet to be finished and finally put in the bottle and sealed up. In shows such as Brisbane, it's very soon after vintage and most of the wines are not yet in the bottle. That show is terrifically valuable for the industry because it gives them a yardstick of how they're going in the latest vintage. But I don't really think those awards should be commercialised because the wine that the public is going to buy later on, with the sticker on the label, is not the same wine that the judges saw. Simply because they saw a cask or a tank sample. By the time it gets to the consumer, it's been blended. It may have been a much bigger blend than originally intended and you end up with a different product altogether. So I think it's deceptive to put those medals on labels.

Different companies use the show system with different effect. The big companies are by far the most expert at using the show results to their benefit. I've spoken to a lot of winemakers in big companies and they admit to me quite candidly that they would not bother entering a wine in a show if they could not use the result on the label. So if the wine has been bottled, labelled and is in the market place, there's no opportunity for them to attach medals to that package. So they wouldn't bother. That, to me, is a confession that basically the number one role for shows — as far as that company is concerned — is generating awards which they can help use to sell the wine.

Fiona Donald, winemaker and associate judge, Brisbane Wine Show

Jimmy Watson was a guy who sold very young, very raw, unfinished barrel wines over the counter and his friends wanted to make an award which perpetuated his memory and traditions. But that was a long time ago and things change. Consumers are now far more aware, more knowledgeable and educated, and much more able to judge quality for themselves. So I think the industry has to get real about things like the Jimmy Watson and say: 'This is silly. This is deceptive. It's misleading. We should not be giving awards to wines which are not finished.' The Jimmy Watson Trophy winner is invariably a cask sample of an unfinished wine. It's the finished product which is important. That's what people buy, that's what people relate to. So if the industry is going to commercialise results, it must only do it for finished wines. I refuse to judge in shows now where unfinished wines are given awards because I feel that strongly about it.

Hooke admires aspects of the Australian judging system and the judges' speedy skills:

The Australian system is very consultative. You'll judge the wines in total isolation. But after you've judged them and made your comments and your scores, you'll then discuss the wines amongst your panel. And if you've overlooked something or if you've been too harsh on something, you can reassess the wine and modify your opinion on it. Whereas in the international system, there is no consultation. You judge in total isolation. You arrive at your scores and the scores go into a computer. And that's that. So, if you've missed a good wine — and we all have aberrations now and then — that goes into the system and wrecks the average when you add up the scores. The Australian system, which involves consultation, gives you the opportunity to find consensus among the judges. And you end up with a much more meaningful result that way.

As an international wine judge, he has experienced the two systems. He also prefers Australian efforts to segment show classes according to style — for instance, full-bodied dry white or medium-bodied dry red, soft finish classes — as well as varietal classes. He believes it would benefit, however, from changes such as judging, but not giving awards to unfinished wines; not inviting winemakers to judge in shows where they are also competitors; expanding the pool of judges and taking a fresh look at the system's administration.

> The wine show system in Australia was originally set up more than a hundred years ago by the Royal Agricultural Societies attached to the capital cities. They judge produce of all types, and wine was regarded as a type of agricultural produce and judged accordingly. I think perhaps the days when the RASs were important have probably passed. They are not as good at coping with change as perhaps they could be, and I think we're now seeing the growth of a lot of other shows that are not run by agricultural societies for that reason.

Winemaker and judge Tim Knappstein observes the Australian wine show system from both points of view:

> I think the show system has made Australian wine what it is in the international scene because there's always this undercurrent of competition. The shows are set up so that makers can compare their wines with those of their peers, and it's this constant exposure to your peers and, secondly, to the public that makes people more and more determined to improve. I think that's done wonderful things for Australia's reputation. We found at this show that the average standard is going up — nearly 50 per cent of the wines are bronze level.
>
>
>
> *Brisbane Wine Show*
>
> We've judged some very big classes this week. Chardonnay had nearly 140 wines. Some lucky panel judged 150 shirazes one day and that's seriously hard work. A class that long would probably take more than three hours. In our panel, we start people at different wine numbers so we'll get someone to start on wine number one, the next guy will start on 50 and and the last guy will start on 100. That's so we have a fresh palate on every section of the class. And then we get together and compare our results. The panel system is really the only safe way you can do it. One person's concentration could waver. The concept of wine quality tends to be very individual, too. So having three people, there are checks and balances built in.

And are winemakers the best people to judge wines?

I think in the Australian context, where we put a lot of emphasis on wine quality and freedom from faults, it's good to have a reasonable number of winemakers. My ideal panel would probably have two winemakers and someone who is either an enthusiastic amateur or a retailer or someone who has had wider experience in the industry and is not actually involved in the technical side. Winemakers tend to ride their own hobby horses a bit.

Shouldn't wines be judged in relation to food?

It's very difficult to know what you could do in a context like this, with this huge number of wines. But there's no doubt that this particular system tends to throw up very big, bold wines which might be a bit over the top when you have them with food. If you look at a class of 100, judges will get used to a background level of fruit, tannin and oak, and it's only the wines that are big enough and bold enough to stand out that really get noticed. So there's no doubt that in the red classes — or probably any big class — the bolder wines are the ones that are going to win.

Prizewinning medal stickers on the label

Does the collective opinion of show judges, expressed by their choice of winning wines, shape the way people make their wines? Angelo Puglisi, of Ballandean Estate in Queensland's Granite Belt, says:

It sure does. I mean, you go and have a look at some of the wines that are being judged and you think, well, why can't I do that. And you go home and try very hard to copy that.

We're quite happy today. We've picked up two bronze medals. We've always got to remember that this is a national show, we're competing against wineries from all over Australia — the big companies, not just the small wineries. And it's great to have a few bronze medals in amongst all the big guys. A big company might have 25 or 45 tanks to choose from or to mix and match with. The small winery, which has one tank of a particular wine, hasn't got much choice of blending and matching so his efforts have to be a lot more spot-on to pick up a medal.

A representative of the big companies, Orlando Wyndham's chief winemaker Philip Laffer, who has enjoyed success at the show, talks pragmatically about the system's power to influence:

It provides an independent review. You don't necessarily change the direction you're going based on the show, because quite often you have a style in mind and it might be different from the judges. On other occasions, you might take notice of what the judges are doing because they might say: 'Well, that's the style, you're moving a little bit this way and you should make some fine adjustment.' But if you think you're on the right track, you've got to stick with what your heart tells you and stay that way. Maybe you don't win all the awards and the like, but if you think that's what you want to do …

Kathleen Quealy of Mornington Peninsula's T'Gallant Wines is both critical and appreciative of the system:

You get to compare your wines against other people's, you get your own personal view and you also see what other people think, which is really important. If you win a trophy, it's all you want. It's very good for business — you sell a lot more wine more easily, you make money and you can make more wine, so that's pretty important.

I think show judging tends to fit wines in a category and you might not know the pedigree. We've been putting pinot gris in wine shows for the past six or seven years, but there really is no category for pinot gris or pinot grigio in Australian wine tasting at the moment.

She goes into a thoroughly confusing list of category possibilities in which the comparison is like apples with oranges. 'There will be classes for those wines as more and more people make them.'

I think the show system, through its trophies and results, puts enormous pressure on us to make certain styles. You can resist that and people do. But, without question, it does shape the sorts of wines that we make in Australia, especially commercial wines. I suppose I'm known as a person who doesn't think that premium wines have to taste like new French oak, and I've noticed over the past ten years that any chardonnay or pinot noir that's won a trophy has enormous amounts of French oak in it. I don't know if that's really going to contribute to the style that cool climate Australia is going to make. I don't think our style of pinot noir is going to be this wine that tastes like new French oak. It's going to be wine that tastes like the fruit and soil.

If you talk to the wine judges in the show system, they have this amazing way of saying 'We judge them as we see them' or 'We judge them as they are' — which I've always thought was a pointless thing to say. They don't go 'Oh, this is a beautiful example of Coonawarra Cabernet' and therefore give it a trophy. They go 'Oh, this wine looks good in the line-up.' The show system has done nothing to help with a regional style, it's done a lot to develop the varietal styles. You know, chardonnay is meant to smell like this or pinot noir is meant to smell like that. At T'Gallant, we're interested in making and developing a regional style. We're saying, this is how we think chardonnay should smell when it comes from the Mornington Peninsula and this is how we think pinot gris should smell when it comes from the Mornington Peninsula. So it's as if we're at loggerheads, really.

Pam Dunsford, winemaker for South Australia's Chapel Hill, is a trophy winner in Brisbane, but that doesn't stop her questioning the direction the system is taking:

The Australian wine show system has been marvellous for the wine industry because it's been a training ground for palates. But as people have been able to get medals and trophies, and use those in a marketing sense, I think there's too much focus now on making wines that are going to achieve those marketing results. Maybe the show system has to be revamped and moved away from this set style tendency that we've created for ourselves. I mean, we've created a monster in a sense.

When I've been judging, I've found that it's difficult to pick out the elegant wines against the over-concentrated, over-oaked wines. Even though you plan to pick out the more elegant, drinkable wines, by the time you've judged 100 cabernets that are only one or two years old, you find that you've chosen wines that are really exaggerations of what you have hoped to select. It's inevitable. You're going to get fatigued and, as much as you concentrate, your palate is still adjusting to those very high levels of flavour and the elegant wines often get missed. I think, probably, the elegant wines are what the public wants to drink.

One of the risks of the wine show results being used on commercial wines is that people would choose a gold medal wine, not understanding that it might have won an award in a class that is not appropriate to their palate. It might, for example, be five or six years old, but it might have won the award when it was only one year old. Or it might be a big oaky wine that's won for that reason, and the person drinking the wine might not appreciate it. I mean, what people don't understand, I suppose, is that there's something like 70 different classes of wine in six wine shows around Australia. So there's an opportunity for a lot of wines to get a lot of accolades and they may not necessarily be the types of wines that those people want to drink.

Vanya and Di Cullen, owners/winemakers

Di and Vanya Cullen

Di and Vanya Cullen are a mother and daughter team producing some of Western Australia's leading wines at Margaret River under their Cullen label. Vanya is the winemaker these days, but in the pioneering years of the Cullen winery, Di made the wine in a venture that she and her general practitioner husband, the late Dr Kevin Cullen, went into almost by chance, as Di relates:

> The farm was sheep and cattle. We still have cattle because we've got 2,000 acres that we don't intend to put under vines. The reason we started was because a man called Dr John Gladstones recommended this area as being one of the three best for growing cabernet, which my husband really liked. He said, 'Oh, you're mad growing sheep and cattle, why don't you plant vines?' So we did. And that was 1966, when we first planted.

Considering their reason for contacting Dr Gladstones, an agriculture department scientist, was to consult him on growing lupins, it is not surprising to find they had absolutely no experience of growing grapes or making wine. Dr Cullen had gone to work as a general practitioner in Busselton in 1948 and they bought their first land in the district three years later as a coastal getaway. Help came to their viticultural efforts in the guise of the only person in the goverment's viticulture department, Bill Jamieson, who used to travel the 280 kilometres from Perth at weekends because he was not allowed to go on week days. 'He's never had enough credit really for all the things he's done.'

Di Cullen had drunk wine with meals since she was a child and had a well-developed palate. In addition to enjoying wine, Dr Cullen could call on family tradition, as his teetotaller grandfather, Ephraim Mayo Clarke, had planted a vineyard on sandy soil in the Bunbury township of 1890. The Cullen vineyard began serious development in 1971:

> Our first wine was a disaster. It was something terrible. We gave it to all our friends. I just hope there's none of it

around any more. But the '75 was quite good. The '76 won several golds and so did Vasse Felix and Moss Wood. That was in the Royal Melbourne Show and there were only three of us then, so people wondered, where in the dickens is Margaret River?

It was a very different place from the thriving centre for wine and tourism that it is today:

It was poverty stricken down here when we came. This was a little dairy farm. They had sixty cattle on it, I think, and nine children. The man cleared it all by hand with ringbarking. It was terribly, terribly hard. I really admire the people who set up here when I think about it. I don't know how they did it. Gravel roads and no doctor's service. And people talked about how many children they reared, not how many they had. It was depressed and people had a depressed outlook, really. That's totally changed now. People are proud of the area.

Has it, perhaps, changed too much?

As long as it keeps its character and they don't allow total development, particularly along the coastline, I don't think it will matter. The coastline is wild and rugged, and that's what attracts people here — and the wildflowers in spring and things like that. One of the great attractions of Margaret River is that it's got things that are fairly unique. If they allow development it would be really sad.

I think it's important, too, that they plant grapes in the right soils, and don't get carried away with the commercial side

of it. It's taken 25 years to build up the reputation of Margaret River, which it has now all over the world, and it would be tragic if they let that go for the sake of commercialism and chasing money.

So what is there in the region that makes it distinctive?

I think probably the maritime climate as much as anything. And the old, granitey sort of soils. All this building is made from the granite off the vineyard, and it's very old soil over clay. The clay is quite deep so the roots go down, but I think that the climate is terribly important. It's pollution-free, too, coming straight off the sea. We're only a kilometre from the ocean so it's very clean air.

I think the combination gives quite a unique flavour. It gives very good flavour in the fruit so we have good fruit to work with. There's something about the granitey soils that seems to impart concentrated flavour, as well as small tonnages. Because we dry farm, we don't get large crops and that also concentrates the fruit. But it's a very even climate. We get a lot of rain in winter, then we have pretty dry summers. Slow summers. We don't have hot weather — usually 35°C is our maximum — and it's always cool at night from the sea breezes.

At wine shows, Cullen Wines made West Australian industry history in a couple of areas, winning the first trophy for Margaret River in Canberra and a trophy at the Perth show, which was the first to be won by a woman winemaker. Did the male domination of the industry provide any problems?

When I started I remember going to one of the wine colleges — I won't mention names — and asking questions … and my husband being given the answers. Which was very funny. But on the whole men have been very helpful to me. I don't have any complexes about that at all.

Vanya Cullen loves to surf, just as she loves music, which may have turned out to be her career if her father had not suggested she learn winemaking.

I was born in the area. I lived away while I was studying science and music and wine for ten years, then I came back. I've been back here working since 1983. I believe it's one of the most beautiful areas in the world to live, in terms of quality of life. Wine is about people and about life, and we're very fortunate to be in Margaret River where you can enjoy the wine and the ocean. I do surf, though not as often as I would like.

I've put 15 years of my life into Cullen Wines and I'd like to see it continue as a family operation. I enjoy working with my mother and emotionally it's very important to me. It would be fun to work in another country or to try different things in the short term, but, in the long term, my family and life is here. It's a different sort of a life — very demanding, especially being in a small business, a family business. It takes up a lot of your life and your time.

Vanya Cullen's wines have already won high commendations. Her 1996 chardonnay was the most popular current-release wine in *The Wine Magazine*'s top 20 chardonnay tasting and her cabernet merlot was ranked in the top five in that magazine's top 20 cabernet tasting. She is much admired for her palate and in demand on the show judging circuit:

I have to readjust my culture clock and put on my wine-judging cap. It's a very different world. Wine judging is very intense and it requires a lot of concentration, but it's a great thing to do if you enjoy it. I don't think everyone would enjoy tasting 150, 200 wines a day, but, you know, I really love it. But you couldn't do it all the time and it's always nice to come home to this wonderful place.

Bush Liqueur

Bill and Lyn Lark, makers of bush liqueur

Tasmanian Bush Liqueur lives up to its name in that its chief ingredient is collected from the bush in Tasmania — *Lanceolata winteracia* or mountain sugar plum or pepper berry. Just take your pick.

I think the old bush people used it as a spice in their food, but most newcomers to Tasmania get caught — we did when we first came — because it looks little and round and, as you're walking along, a local will say, 'Try one of these, they're a little sugar plum.' And you put it in your mouth and the skin is quite sweet. But as soon as you bite into it, it gets quite hot and then it gets hotter and hotter and hotter … but they're nice little berries.

Lyn Lark, the newcomer who innocently bit on the pepper berry, runs the Lark distillery with her husband Bill in partnership with Paul Boland. Bill says:

It's a bit like the juniper berry, isn't it? It's herbal and aromatic … and we were actually trying to find the juniper berry to make gin. We're fairly sure we're the first ones to have made a liqueur out of pepper berries. We were trying to make gin, but there was a food specialist in Hobart, Catherine Brys, who kept persisting because she knew we had the distillery and the distilling licence. She finally thrust some at us at the opening of a restaurant one night and said to Lyn, 'Take them home, for goodness sake. Put them in the still and tell me what you think.'

And that's what Lyn did. She took them home and put them in the still … and rang me up at work and I came racing home and we were very excited. There were these lovely flavours just exploding from the still and we knew straight away this was very special. Not a gin type drink, but one that people would describe as being like a Drambuie with a bush flavour or something like that: a distinctive and unique drink.

On a hot day, over crushed ice with lemon juice, it makes a lovely drink. The lemon enhances the flavour and softens it a little bit because the pepper berry has that lovely hot, spicy bit in the middle. A good strong black coffee with nice, thick fresh cream and the liqueur poured through the cream makes a wonderful drink that is now becoming very popular in restaurants where they're finally able to talk about having an Australian liqueur coffee. It works with tonic, like a gin and tonic. And we've got a wonderful ginger beer in Tasmania that people are drinking it with — ginger and spice, we're calling it. We even had a lady in the shop this morning who said that, in winter, she heats it up and drinks it like a mulled wine.

These berries are fairly prolific all over Tasmania. They like the regrowth forest areas. They grow in the wetter forest parts on the coast and, of course, in the highland areas. There are some good areas we found on the west coast, in the northeast and down south of Hobart in the forestry areas where we get a permit from the Forestry Commission to go and collect them from the regrowth forestry areas.

The bush comes in flower about November and the berries start to form around Christmas time. By Easter, they blacken up and are nice and juicy and plump, and ready for picking. And they pick right through until it is just about to snow. Then they drop off and that'll be the end of it for the year. Nice intense flavour in these alpine berries. In the higher altitudes, the berries are smaller, but they have a good strong flavour, so we can use less of them. Down on the coast, the berries are probably twice the size and plump, but not as good a flavour.

We bring them back to the distillery and it's a bit like making London gin or something like that. We collect the berries and crush them and steep them in a strong neutral alcohol. Just a sugar-fermented alcohol, it has no flavour. So when the flavour of the pepper berries has really been taken up in the alcohol, we then add water to that and do the distilling. Lyn's the distiller, she does that next part.

Pepper berry

'It usually takes abut ten to 12 hours to make a run through,' Lyn says. 'I just keep the best of the run and use that to make up the liqueur to my secret recipe and we bottle it and label it and sell it.' Passing tourists buy it as well as locals, and increasingly it is being used in Tasmanian cuisine. 'A lot of restaurants are using it in different sauce mixes and in gravies in game foods. There is a company, Tasmanian Fine Ice Cream, that makes a pepper berry ice cream of all things — and that's exciting. It's a nice warm, spicy ice cream.'

Food Match

CABERNET SAUVIGNON

Leading restaurateur Cheong Liew was invited to choose some dishes to go with cabernet sauvignon at his restaurant in the Adelaide Hilton, the Grange Restaurant.

First he talked about a seafood dish that he described as 'more or less like a laksa or a bouillabaisse in a white curry sauce — but the idea is purely a laksa.' It's a mixture of seafoods, noodles and quite spicy, and it goes well with a lighter style of cabernet, a rosé style that can be drunk cold, quite fruity and soft to the finish.

Next is a young cabernet, very robust with lots of tannin. 'I chose the pork hock because of the rich, gelatinous, caramelised skin style of meat. It is braised in a sauce of a bit of hoisin and a bit of tahini for the nuttiness, a bit of chilli … and it is slightly sweet to combat some of the young tannin and fruitiness of the wine. And the fungus really helps us soak up all the flavour that has been put out by the hog. I think it's a perfect match!'

Then a mature cabernet, mellow at the finish, not as fruity, but with more earthy characters. 'I've got Kangaroo Island lamb — to me it is one of the best lambs in Australia. This is cooked with a little bit of garlic and buttermilk sauce with some lamb's kidney and some steamed eggplant. The buttermilk is not going to be too heavy, it's got a slight tang that cuts the heaviness of it. And just on the outside of the dish are chopped olives and parsley and spice of Sichuan pepper and buttermilk chillies.

'The reason I picked this is because of the delicateness of the lamb will really suit the soft, mellow, aged cabernet — which complements the earthiness of the cabernet. You'll find that roast garlic will suit this really well. And a little bit of lamb fat really sets off the pleasure of the lamb and the wine. That's what I like about it.'

Loin of Lamb with Sichuan Pepper, Buttermilk Chillies, Steamed Eggplant, Lamb Kidneys and Garlic Sauce

1 loin of lamb
5 lamb kidneys
salt, pepper
chicken stock for poaching
3 slices fresh ginger

Steamed Eggplant
2 eggplants, seeded and cut into batons, lightly salted and rubbed with lemon
4 cloves of garlic, crushed and roughly chopped
a little dark soy sauce

Vegetable Julienne
250 g in total of snow peas, red and yellow capsicum, whites of leek, garlic chive flowers, cloud ear fungus
10 g shallots, finely chopped
a little butter

Garlic Sauce
250 ml brown lamb stock
3 cloves of garlic, roasted
30 ml buttermilk

Garnish
freshly chopped parsley
chopped black olives
deep-fried lightly battered basil leaves

Sichuan Spice Mix

20 g buttermilk chillies, deep-fried until crisp
10 g Sichuan pepper, ground with chillies

Preheat the oven to 100°C.

Bone lamb, trimming loin to leave a 3 mm layer of fat on top. Season with salt and pepper, sear and slow cook in the oven for 1 hour or until medium-rare.

Clean lamb kidneys and cut each one into six. Poach in chicken stock with the ginger until tender.

Steam eggplant with garlic until soft. Toss in a little dark soy sauce to season.

Julienne the snow peas, capsicum, leek, garlic chive flowers, cloud ear fungus and sauté with shallots in butter until just tender.

Scatter the vegetables on the plate. Place the eggplant in the centre, carve lamb and lay on top.

To make the garlic sauce, reduce the brown lamb stock, then add kidneys and roast garlic. Finish the sauce with buttermilk to taste and spoon around the lamb.

Garnish with parsley, black olives and basil leaves. Sprinkle with the Sichuan spice mix.

New Regions

Mornington Peninsula

Mornington Peninsula, an hour's drive southeast of the heart of Melbourne, is best known as a holiday destination for sailing, surfing and summer nightlife. Although it has a brief history of grape growing in the 19th century, its rise to prominence as a wine region is recent and sudden. After a small-scale return dating from the 1960s, there were 40 hectares of grapes owned by 15 growers in 1988; by 1995, this had risen to 420 hectares and 122 growers. And it's still expanding.

Even more significant, perhaps, is the increase in the number of winemakers living on the peninsula: from one to eight over the same period. And among the people the region is attracting are newcomers keen to introduce innovation into Australian winemaking — not only to grow and make traditional varieties and styles in ways that reflect the region, but also to introduce less familiar grapes and wines.

Garry Crittenden was a horticulturalist with a plant nursery business when a family holiday to Tasmania alerted him to the quality and potential of Australian wine. He decided to switch to growing grapes and spent two years finding a property that was on the Australian mainland, but would give him something close to the Tasmanian climate. After studying historical data from the meteorological bureau in Melbourne so he would have a good understanding of the celebrated climatic vagaries of this maritime area, he opted for the lower part of the peninsula 'where the climate is just that tad warmer — a little more reliable in summer, not greatly different in winter.'

The dangers of frosts are usually out of the way by September budburst, but there are fresh threats during shoot elongation and flowering in November:

PREVIOUS PAGE:
*Dromana Estate vineyard,
Mornington Peninsula*

That's a very critical time in the vine's annual development and it's also the time when we get the equinoctial gales — that is, major weather patterns moving across from the Bass Strait. The weather can transform from being a mild, benign, sunny day. Ten minutes later, it will be bitterly cold with strong winds, hail and rain. Now that sort of weather poses the possibility of severe interference with flowering.

He explains how, in cold and wet conditions, the pollen cannot drift around: it simply turns into sludge on the flower. 'Pollination doesn't take place or the flower aborts and you get what are known as shock bunches or shock berries so you get a diminished crop. It is not uncommon here to have crops diminished by 50 per cent.'

Since planting his first vines at his Dromana Estate in 1982, Garry has gained a reputation for a meticulously tended vineyard and an attitude of careful experimentation. He is not only using the lyre system of trellising — splitting the leaf canopy in two directions so that it makes a U-shape above the trunk — but also pulling the traditionally trellised vines high above their usual heights to capture extra sun, which produces more fruit-bearing buds. He has also developed a way of propagating vines which he says will delay budburst beyond the frost danger period when you plant them out and produce a crop within a year — and a big crop in two years, and for every year after that.

The French have a fairly rigid approach in that in many areas the fruit is required to be de-classified until the vines are about seven years old. Here, we start to pick our crops off three-year-old vines. My own experience is that, now that our vines are somewhere between 12 and 15 years old, we are beginning to see a transition in concentration. That's not to say we can crop them up to any level — we still have to watch that — but, yes, the structure of our wines is changing. I guess that simply demonstrates in an empirical way what the French have been telling us forever: that you can't get good crops off young vines.

The industry here is so young and vineyard practices in particular are still unformed — I mean, no one could give you the definitive answer of the best trellising system, the best cropping levels — and I'm happy to say that the growers down here seem to be pretty open-minded. They employ consultants or professional viticulturists or qualified winemakers, and that's been a great advantage to us as a region: that people have been prepared to pay for expertise. We never give up — I mean, we've always got something going on here in the vineyard. I've just embarked on a new program with the department of agriculture here in Victoria to look at a better way of forecasting cropping levels earlier rather than later in the season. You must constantly experiment.

While Crittenden grows pinot noir, chardonnay, cabernet sauvignon and merlot on Mornington Peninsula to make around 3,500 cases each year for Dromana Estate, he also produces a range of Italian style wines with grapes grown in the warmer areas of Victoria. Having initially wondered what all the fuss was about when he sampled Italian wines, Crittenden was introduced by friends to the better quality product. His enthusiasm is such that, since he entered the field in 1992, he has built up his Italian wine range to single varietal reds made from sangiovese, barbera, nebbiolo and dolcetto, a rosé, a Piedmont-style riserva, a dry white and an Italian style grenache.

> When we first started making these Italian varieties, in the absence of any better knowledge, we treated them as if they were French … and this is definitely not the right way to make them. Since then, I've been to Italy during vintage, had a look at what they do, read more widely, opened up a dialogue with a lot of Italian grape growers and winemakers — and I think we're far better informed now as to how we should be dealing with these varieties. So our technical approach to the winemaking has changed, and it's just appropriate for Italian varieties. Some of the best compliments we've heard about these wines is not so much that they're great wines, but more that they express the typical characteristics of the varieties that you would expect to see if they were made in Italy.

Port Phillip Bay and Mornington Beach

While Crittenden is only one of a number of pioneers in making Italian wine in this country, the average Australian consumer doesn't know much about them:

> It's not in the drinking lexicon. They don't have an understanding of the names, the styles — and, in many cases, it's a little bit of a shock the first time you taste them, as it was for me. It's really just a matter of education. After five or six years, we're starting to see a breakthrough. People are now coming back and wanting the new releases, asking questions, seeking more information. Whereas four years ago, it was 'No, I've never heard of it' and 'No thanks, I don't particularly want to try it'. Now things are changing.

One of the stars of individuality from Mornington Peninsula happens to have an Italian inflection in its name — a pinot grigio made by T'Gallant — although wine writer Huon Hooke has described it as 'opulent and decidedly un-Italian'. Its makers, husband and wife team Kevin McCarthy and Kathleen Quealy, use the pinot gris grape, a pink-skinned relative of pinot noir, for this and another style of wine.

We make a very big, rich, late-picked style and we call that pinot gris. With other grapes from other vineyards we make a more savoury style which really has that hallmark — or watermark — of salt-air aroma and a palate that's very savoury, and we call that pinot grigio. We've borrowed a little bit from how the French and Italians divvy up their styles. And it gives you a bit of an indication of what sort of food you serve it with as well: the pinot gris, as they do in France, with big, rich food, and the pinot grigio you have with food from pizza up to spaghetti through to … any food.

Garry Crittenden, winemaker, taking wine from the barrel for Grant Van Every to taste

We introduced pinot gris on to the Mornington Peninsula. It's a cool climate grape variety, so it's the first time it's really been showcased in the kind of climate where it can perform. We started our business in 1990 with leasing one small vineyard. We've got 12 vineyards that we make pinot gris with now.

That's a mix of their own, leased and managed vineyards. 'And then we buy grapes from what we think are some of the finest vineyards in Mornington Peninsula — it's very important that they are Mornington Peninsula grapes and that we have access to so many high quality vineyards down here.'

Quealy and McCarthy came to Mornington Peninsula as winemakers wanting to look beyond the making of 'white and red, Burgundy style'. Having decided unwooded white was the way to go, and chosen a region where they would get high quality white grapes, they really only had chardonnay to work with. Although they produce a changing range of strikingly designed labels that include unwooded chardonnays and pinot noir, it's their planting of pinot gris which is giving them the regional individuality they were after.

When we started T'Gallant, the idea was to make regional wine, which was something we saw the Australian wine industry moving away from. Although Australia had a great history of making beautiful regional wines, people were saying, 'You know, we can make wines just like Burgundy or Bordeaux,' and we thought, we don't want to do that with the rest of our lives. We want to make wines that taste like they come from a region. We wanted to come to a cool region to explore making new sorts of table wines, which meant you were looking at new regions because winemaking in Australia until a decade ago was in much warmer areas.

So we had a bit of a look around for a couple of years and, in the end, we settled on the Mornington Peninsula. We see the regional style down here being a white wine that uses the flavours from the region —

OPPOSITE:
Mornington Peninsula

which means that you're not looking at wines that taste like French oak or American oak. You're looking at wines that taste like the grape variety, the pinot gris or chardonnay; that taste like the soil they're grown in; like the yeast that is on the grape even before it ferments; and that taste like the year tastes — whether you've had a hot year or a cooler year.

Blending wine from different vineyards is offering a variety of choices that are building into a pattern after nine vintages for T'Gallant:

Kevin McCarthy and Kathleen Quealy, winemakers, T'Gallant, in their laboratory

With chardonnay, if you put more vineyards into the wine, you actually get shoulders on the wine. It will give the wine a fatness which makes it far more attractive. The pinot gris seems to be going the other way, where the wine seems to look better as a single vineyard wine. Pinot gris and pinot noir don't lend themselves to blending, they've got so much character individuality in that single vineyard. Chardonnay, in our experience, looks better when it's a blend of many vineyards.

The sites of the vineyards make their own stamp on the wine:

The pinot gris style is inevitably from the deeper red soil, and these are the sites that ripen latest as the elevation is higher. The pinot grigio has to come from the lower vineyards, closer to sea level, where the grapes are picked earlier because they're warmer sites. And it just happens that the soil down there is different. It's a much thinner soil which doesn't sustain the whole vine into the end of autumn, so the grapes do demand earlier picking.

As a variety, pinot gris doesn't have the sort of tendency to get negative — the tiredness you get from something like semillon, which is a fairly big berry and thin skinned. It's a very small berry: a pinot gris bunch down here would be as big as my fist, with very small berries and very thick skinned so they're naturally pretty resistant to botrytis. If you have a good site, they will hang pretty relaxed to the end of April, and if it's a very good site they'll hang there until the middle of May.

T'Gallant takes its name most obviously from maritime references. It is an abbreviation of topgallant, the top sail of a square-rigger sailing ship. It implies the peak, the best — and this is how Shakespeare used it when he gave the line to Romeo:

Which to the high topgallant of my joy
Must be my convoy in the secret night.

You'll find this inscribed on every T'Gallant cork you pull
from the bottle.

Twenty years ago, you had to search for a bottle of shiraz t[...]
top-selling Australian red wines in its own right.

Shiraz

South Australian winemakers have had a lot to d[...]
especially in McLaren V[...]

Shiraz

wines in Australia, Penfolds Grange and Henschke [...]

Shiraz

GRAPE VARIETIES AND WINE STYLES

Shiraz

*T*wenty years ago, you had to search for a bottle of shiraz that wasn't blended with another variety. Now it's one of the top-selling Australian red wines in its own right. South Australian winemakers have had a lot to do with its success, especially in McLaren Vale and the Barossa Valley. That State and the shiraz grape also happen to be the source of the two top-priced wines in Australia, Penfolds Grange and Henschke Hill of Grace.

In McLaren Vale, an hour down the coast south of Adelaide, the third winemaking generation of the Osborn family — named Francis, but always called d'Arry in an echo of the family's d'Arenberg winery — extols the qualities of shiraz from years of experience:

> The magnificent fruity flavour of shiraz, the tannin finish and the acid in the finish … it's just so satisfying. I think McLaren Vale shiraz is the epitome of shiraz. It's really as good as you'll get anywhere in the world and it's creating a lot of interest around the world. Shiraz from Australia, and particularly in this area, is really getting people fired up to try again to make shiraz in other parts of the world. It's a great complement to red meat, there's no doubt about that. Shiraz, particularly from this area with its spicy, peppery characters, really goes well with red meat.

The d'Arenberg winery makes more than one shiraz, but its most prized is the Dead Arm Shiraz, whose name is the clue to the age of the vines it comes from. Chester Osborn, now the family firm's chief winemaker, offers a tour with his father of a shiraz vineyard, planted around 1912:

d'Arry and Chester Osborn, winemakers, with Grant Van Every in the d'Arenberg vineyard

> It's still very vigorous growing, but if you have a look at the butts you can see that it's starting to look very old … This is a dead arm. There's another one over that side. You can see the cracks where the major cuts were made and the fungus gets in through these cracks. Eventually, it kills the arm off and it stops growing. It can travel through and kill the whole vine off.
>
> But what happens, of course, is instead of growing that way, the vine starts growing out another way, so it actually hasn't made that much of an impact on the crop level or the flavour of the grapes. If you were to cut the butt, you'd find it would be dead two parts of the way though. There'd be just one-third of it or so that's growing green still. And all the sap's going up there. It's just amazing how tough vines are. You can actually cut these old ones off and they'll probably start to shoot from the bottom and start again.
>
> The roots completely cover the area under the ground. Anywhere you dig you'll find vine roots, so they have a very tenacious root

system. That's why they keep growing. We've got quite a few blocks of very old shiraz and it depends on the year as to which block we gather it from for Dead Arm Shiraz. If it's a cold year or a hot year, the different soils are better under different circumstances. But this one, in some years, makes it into the Dead Arm for sure. The way we came up with that name is that it's another way of saying 'old vines', basically because the older the vines, the more dead arms you've got on them.

Dead arm vine

When it gets this dead arm developing, the butt is half dead and the vine struggles for its sap to come up, so it's not as lush in its production of grapes and it makes better quality fruit because it is struggling to produce the fruit. If you had a young vine, it would be full of great big bunches and juicy berries. These tend to struggle and are usually smaller and more flavoursome as a result, and we encourage that of course.

Generally speaking, though, what makes the McLaren Vale shiraz so good?

It comes down to the terroir, the French term for the climate and the soil, and the region as a whole. The climate is affected by the sea. Two miles to our right we have the sea and three miles to the left we have the Mt Lofty Ranges. It's a nice warm spot. It's dry — six months without any rainfall, basically all the way through summer. We get the cool sea breezes at three o'clock and we get the cold air drainage at night time off the hills, which can make the temperature down in the gullies ten degrees colder than it is up here. So often it might be 30 degrees during the day and, say, 12 degrees at night down there. So we get this little bit of stress and then cool nights to retain acidity, and that's the ideal thing for shiraz. It's got power and finesse. The structure of the acid and the vibrant fruit characters, along with huge amounts of rich flavour, are what shiraz is all about.

The Osborns, father and son, mix old and new technology in their winemaking. Father says: 'When I think of all the wasted time we did with hand pruning — three or four months of the year, half the time with overcoats standing in the rain — when nowadays we run a machine over them and clean up afterwards. So much easier and the fruit is even better.'

Son says:

Most people think that we're pretty crazy doing 2,000 tonnes through these two old basket presses. Yet the labour cost for two months of vintage is not that big compared to buying a big modern tank press of $150,000 and it sits there idle for ten months of the year. You're actually ahead with the old basket press, both in quality and in cost effectiveness. It's very, very gentle. If you imagine a grape sitting in an alcohol solvent for ten days, it's a very fragile thing.

Elva and Ron Laughton, Jasper Hill

He describes the 'extremely gentle' process of the century old basket press and compares it with the modern tank press with its stainless steel slotted screens. 'In pushing the skins and seeds against those little knife edges, you get the bad tannins and bitterness. From this, you get very soft, rich tannins and you still get all the juice out as well. They're now producing this type of press again because, for best practice in winemaking, I think the basket press takes a lot of beating.'

It's only a little more than ten years ago, in 1985, that South Australia introduced a vine pull scheme because of surplus shiraz grapes in particular, as well as some other red varieties:

A lot of the vineyards were very unproductive. The growers couldn't make a living out of them, and the idea was to try to help them be viable again, so they were paid money to pull them out. They weren't allowed to replant for another five years. I think probably, in hindsight, it was a pity that they grubbed them out because a lot of Grange material went for a start and this upset Penfolds, but I think if you weren't paying enough for it you couldn't blame growers for seizing upon the opportunity. I remember grape prices in the 1980s — $275 a tonne for shiraz around 1987 and now it's more than $2,000 a tonne. So it's changed dramatically.

Ron Laughton always had faith in shiraz. He began planting vines for his Jasper Hill winery in the mid-1970s in Heathcote, 116 kilometres north of Melbourne in central Victoria:

My simple belief was that there was more to shiraz than was being offered in Australia at that stage. Now, don't forget, 20 years ago, cabernet was the rising star, pinot hadn't even surfaced. I did have a strong belief that shiraz wasn't being planted in the right spots. That it could produce not necessarily better, but different wines. Slightly cooler probably than most areas that were already planted with shiraz, but not too cold that I was going to get unripe flavours. So that's what led us to this broad climate.

The inland slopes of the Great Dividing Range of Victoria all have a similar climate, similar sun exposure etc. And then the final clincher came when we found this little strip of soil here in Heathcote that we believed would enable us to grow shiraz grapes not only in the right climate, but also without irrigation. Since then, Heathcote shiraz has become a recognisable style.

Obviously, when I started, I didn't know what those flavours were going to be, but, as it's turned out, this sort of soil and this climate yield generous wines that are fully flavour ripe because of the climate, but very rich in all the spicy, berry, earthy characters and a generally very well balanced wine. Others are producing it and you can recognise that this wine has come from Heathcote. And wines from this area, even though it's small, are going around the world — in small quantities, I must add. But people recognise Heathcote as a district now.

The soil that Laughton prizes is red and deep, 'very, very deep':

Here you can see the Cambrian soil — five to six hundred million-year-old soil that's basically been pulverised into gravel — and you can see a layer coming through here, a coloured layer, where the Cambrian soil is sitting on top. So we have a soil that ranges between two and four metres.

The little green bits are copper ore — it's very high in copper — but the red bits are probably the most important. They're the iron ore components — lots of iron in the soil. But more important than all the nutrients is its structure. Physically, it's very gravelly and very open, so it can drain well, but it can also hold moisture. So I can get away with growing grapes without irrigation because of the depth of soil for the vine roots to explore and it's neither waterlogged nor too dry.

Here in Heathcote, we've had this happy position that there are a couple of north–south faults … running like this for 500 million years and they've pulverised the bedrock and also fortunately lifted and exposed this red soil in pockets along this valley between the two faults. And that's the whole key to the Heathcote terroir. It's not continuous as in Coonawarra, where it's a continuous cigar-shaped strip. These are little pockets up the valley. And the vines are on those pockets.

If you plant vines on the other soil, you will succeed in growing grapes. The flavours are, in my opinion, different. Sure, it expresses the climate, but it doesn't express the soil. But more to the point, you can't grow grapes without water on these other soils. It's just too dry and you must irrigate them. And once you irrigate, you're introducing a totally different variable and that was outside my range of variables. I wished to do it without irrigation. It might sound ridiculous, but basically the rose bush and the gum tree and every other member of the plant

Food Match

SHIRAZ
It is hard to pinpoint the typical Australian shiraz because it is so widely planted. Flavours range from pepper and spice in our cooler climates to sweet raspberries, plums and leather characters in our warmer areas, and there are plenty in between.

Luckily shiraz is versatile when it comes to matching with food. One of the best choices is a simple meal that will highlight the flavour burst of a top quality shiraz — like a porterhouse steak, simply barbecued and not overcooked. It should be juicy, and the meat juices will soften the tannins in the wine.

If you are looking for a vegetable alternative to red meat, try a vegetable stew like ratatouille. The juicy nature of the stew will blend superbly with a fruit driven shiraz.

kingdom evolved without man throwing a bucket of water on them. So if you're technically trying to find the best place to plant a shiraz grape you shouldn't need to put water on it.

I'm not the first to say that wines are made in the vineyard. I'm a technician when it comes to making the wine, but the flavours are created in the vineyard. We have very low vigour vineyards. Every bunch, every leaf is exposed to the sun. From that exposure, we end up with fully flavoured grapes. I've been called a lazy winemaker. This is really an easy way of saying I'm a low or non-interventionist winemaker. In other words, I let the wine make itself in effect — just purely conserve as much flavour as possible. And, fortunately, I think the wine does have some longevity using that technique.

Though they haven't bothered to seek official organic status, Ron and his wife Elva are proud that they have been able to grow their grapes organically. 'We don't spray with any chemicals and that's because, basically, we are purists,' says Elva. And is the fruit any better as a result? 'To be honest, we don't know. But it's very nice to see a ladybird in your vineyard. Many of them.'

Nature hasn't always been kind to them. In 1987, they were caught in a bushfire that nearly finished the business. As Ron explains:

The bushfire was a turning point in Jasper Hill's life — and in our life, I suppose, because you can't plan for that sort of thing. Apart from the trauma, it did prove that human values do come to light and so we were overwhelmed by the response that we had from other grape growers that obviously still had their minds working right. After the bushfire, ours were a little bit screwed up, I suppose, and they suggested that if you don't have a crop, you don't have a business. But the others were right, so we did accept the purchase of grapes from outside the region, purely to stay in business, and the wine was called Friend Shiraz. It was a good story, I suppose, from a human value point of view and many people learnt about Jasper Hill because of that wine. And it still drinks very well, too.

In turn, grapes from Jasper Hill were among those that went to Bannockburn ten years later when its crop was wiped out by a freak hailstorm. 'Once again, you'll find that everybody has helped as an industry because the unique thing about the wine industry is that no one can ever duplicate your wine,' says Elva. 'Whilst there will be other shiraz producers in Heathcote, they will never produce a Georgia's Paddock or an Emily's Paddock, regardless of how close the vines might be. You really are on your own and you don't have competitors. You're complementary. It is a complementary industry. Because no one can ever quite make the wine the same way that you make your wine or grow it or have the site.' Ron has his own thoughts on the subject: 'I think there is a national spirit.'

Speaking of Georgia's Paddock and Emily's Paddock, named after their daughters, Ron says:

Ron Laughton, viticulturist and winemaker, Jasper Hill, showing Grant Van Every the Cambrian soil

They are only one kilometre apart, the two individual vineyards. Same clone of shiraz, same age vineyard, same row orientation, same winemaker, same grape grower, same everything, right? And yet the wines can turn out like chalk and cheese. Why is it so? Sure, the Emily's Paddock has a touch of cabernet franc in there, but that doesn't make it a different wine.

The wines are different basically because the sites are different in that one is slightly warmer, one has slightly shallower soil and the net result is two totally different wines. The Georgia's Paddock vineyard produces more sweet red berries and spice and the Emily's Paddock has an extra degree of complexity about it, with a touch more earthy character. So if you compare that difference to another region, it's logical you're going to have totally different styles. That's what wine is all about. Difference.

Characters of the Industry

John Charles Brown, patriarch of Brown Brothers, in his personal cellar

Brown Brothers

John Charles Brown is the patriarch of Brown Brothers, the family wine business founded in 1885 by his father, John Francis Brown, who began planting vines when he was 18 and made his first vintage four years later. John Charles is now well into his 80s and has handed over leadership of the company to his son, John Graham Brown — but his life still revolves around wine, as a visit to his personal cellar reveals.

This little cellar was built about 1962. We were starting to put a few wines down in bottles for longer bottle aging, and we needed something to keep them in. When we built this, we thought it was going to last us forever. I think in about ten years it was full. So, we built another one of these and I put my name on this one. This is my private cellar now, where I store some bottles to try to get a bit of bottle age on — to prove that wines do actually get better as they get older. And also prove, maybe, that they can get too old and you'd rather you had drunk them off earlier.

He believes that passion is important in winemaking:

It's like an artist who's a painter — he has to be passionate about his art and what he does. I think wine is a form of art because it involves colour to meet the requirements of your eye. It's got a perfume to smell, a taste to please the palate. I think it's really an art form — and it's got to a really commercial art form nowadays, of course. Just the same, it's a great pleasure to make good wines and see your friends enjoying them and see them becoming popular in the market place.

It sounds like a satisfying lifestyle, but had he ever wanted to do anything else?

Oh no, not really. Not once I joined my father. When I left school, I was at matriculation stage and could have gone on to university, but at that time it was at the height of the 1930s depression and you couldn't get a job. My father at that stage needed someone to come and help him. He had had a manager looking after the farm and the vineyard operation, but he had just left my father to buy a little property on his own. My father was fairly elderly — I was an afterthought in the family — and I think he was rather pleased that I decided to come and help him out. And I have been here ever since — since 1934.

Back in the middle 60s, there were twenty of us left making wine in the whole of Victoria. Last count I heard, there are something like 250. Every time you drive along any road now, you'll run across a winery or a vineyard somewhere, and I think that's good. It's reinstating some of the old winemaking districts that were making good wine 100 years ago and went out of production. It's bringing them back to life again, letting people see the great scope we have in Victoria for winemaking. We haven't touched the smallest part of winemaking in Victoria yet. There are lots of areas, hill country and along the river valleys, that haven't been tried out yet. Beautiful soil for growing grapes, plenty of water, good rainfall, good seasonal conditions. So that's something for the future.

Brown Brothers have steadily moved themselves into the future as one of Australia's leading winemakers with a huge array of wines — more than 40 varieties and styles, the largest single selection in the world from a family operation. Crop setbacks that began with phylloxera striking Milawa in this northeastern area of Victoria in 1915, and more recently frost destroying the 1968 vintage and a mini cyclone virtually wiping out the vintage in 1977, helped to trigger the company's expansion into a variety of areas. First it

was a frost-free vineyard in the Murray Valley. Further vineyard plantings and purchases in the immediate vicinity of the King Valley were followed by the development of the Whitlands vineyard, which is one of the highest in Australia.

Ross Brown, another of the third-generation wine producers and brother of John Graham, describes it:

Whitlands is a very unusual vineyard site. It's tucked right up in the Victorian Alps between Mansfield and Whitfield. Looking out, we can see Mount Buffalo and Mount Hotham. With most of the vineyards in Australia at a high level, all the good soil has been washed down in the valleys, but here we have a volcanic cap sitting right on top of the range that allows some really deep soil and gives a chance to grow a very fertile vineyard at very high elevation.

Having a vineyard at high elevation allows a very slow ripening and we have found this our best site for making our premium sparkling wine. The best wine is made when the grapes take longest to ripen, and here we go right through to May, which is very late to get the grapes fully ripe. This has been an absolutely new development for us and really pioneering this sort of cold climate, high altitude viticulture. We don't get frost because, sitting right on top of the ridge, the air drains down into the valleys and in that way we're able to have a frost-free location even though it's a cold climate vineyard.

Another of the company's more recent developments, celebrating its 100th year of winemaking at Milawa in 1989, was a new, mini kindergarten winery to produce smaller lots of wine for cellar door releases, fortified wines, sparkling wine and the Whitlands range. By keeping to small quantities, this winery allows experimental winemaking to be undertaken, while pursuing the established winemaking processes as usual elsewhere. Ross Brown was recently awarded a Churchill Fellowship to study family wine companies in other parts of the world and he is acutely aware of the pressures of running a family company these days:

They're pretty serious. I look back and almost call it 'the good old days' when I remember we just used to make little decisions. But the decisions got bigger and these days, with a couple of hundred staff and all those responsibilities, it's quite demanding. We have to see ourselves as being a very properly run business with good systems, and see ourselves benchmarking against the very best in the world because we really are now wanting to be an international company.

I had a fantastic opportunity to go and spend some time with other family wine companies in different parts of the world, and understand what their aspirations are and how they might get their businesses to operate in the future. The values of their family business are really to make sure they succeed for the next generation.

I think the common thing that makes the family company successful is passion. You know, somebody has to really love the business, love wine and love being in that sort of operation, and really excite the next generation to be involved. But if you don't have passion, I think the place will fall apart. You have to have a good company, you have to run it well, but if there's not that love and long term vision

for the company, it really won't succeed.

Gatherings of the family take place every day at morning tea time. Whoever is available turns up at the main house where Patricia Brown, wife of John Charles and dubbed the chief executive by her family, keeps an eye on everything that is happening. It's a good chance for each family worker to talk informally about what is going on in their area and catch up with everyone else's happenings — such as the news that a new vineyard about to be developed is to be named Patricia. It came as an exciting surprise to its namesake: 'I was completely overwhelmed to think my name will be on the bottle for many, many years. It really is very thrilling.'

The family member who announced it was Cynthia Brown, daughter of John Graham and, with her brother John Andrew, the fourth generation to join the company. She talks enthusiastically about the Brown Brothers Epicurean Centre:

It's a forum for people to experiment with wine and food. Essentially, we're creating meals with flavours and colours and textures to match certain wines that we have at the cellar door. For example, this is a goat curry. Goat's meat is very full textured and strong flavoured, and we've made it with lots of Asian type spices which gives it a really robust flavour, and it's on a bed of rice which has turmeric and other aromatic spices in it also.

What we're doing is matching it up with our graciano, which is a Spanish grape variety that makes wines of very big, spicy flavours with lots of mouth feel. So we're matching the mouth feel of the goat meat to the mouth feel of the wine, the spices with the spiciness of the wine.

Something else to have a look at is one of our local regional trout. It has been prepared in paperbark and has some lemon juice and citrusy kind of flavours with it. We're matching that with our Whitlands Riesling, which is a vineyard that is very high, so it tends to be quite acidic, almost a little bit green in character. So it matches the acidity of the citrusy characters that we have in the trout here.

When we're matching the foods and wines, we'll put all the foods out and all the wines out and play with the flavours. We'll mix different wines with foods as we taste them and experiment with them. There is no rule about how you do it and we're learning every day as we're putting different combinations of wines and food together. Asian foods are becoming very, very popular in Australia and there are some fantastic flavours and things happening with them. The challenge is on us to create wines that can match them.

John Charles Brown has the final word — characteristically talking about the future and the enormous range of wines that Brown Brothers continues to produce:

I'd hate to be making three wines, because wines can become trendy, then people don't want them any more and you're landed with a whole lot of vineyard that nobody wants the wines from. So, with our big range of varieties, we can just about cope with any change in demand. Most vintages now, we put in as many as 40 varieties of grapes through our vineyards — some obviously in pretty small quantities.

We have an experimental planting in our Whitlands vineyard. I'll tell you a secret — we've got another 50 up there we haven't tried yet, but we bring them in from time to time. For instance, if we want to bring new ones in and make a smaller quantity of wine from them and try those wines out with our cellar door customers, use them for guinea pigs, as a market survey. If they say, 'Oh yuck, we don't like that very much,' you can throw it away. But if their eyes light up and they say 'That's terrific,' you can take that to the next commercial stage. So, it works out very well and makes the winemaking game tremendously more interesting to have that range of wines.

Characters of the Industry

Peter Lehmann, winemaker

Peter Lehmann

The continuity of winemaking in South Australia's Barossa Valley, 70 kilometres northeast of Adelaide, means that it has seen the highs and lows of the industry in this country. And Peter Lehmann, fifth-generation Australian and the fourth generation of his family Barossan-born, has been a part of those developments for more than 50 vintages. His tenacity was a pivot for the Barossa Valley grape growers and winemakers in the last nationwide slump and now he is celebrating as one of a close community that is walking proud, as he puts it.

The past few years, it's been absolutely tremendous to see the whole district revitalised. Until about ten years ago, the Barossa was in the glooms because we had fairly long periods of surplus fruit. There is nothing more depressing for a grape grower or farmer to grow a crop and then find it's unsaleable. Just to see it rot or wither on the ground. So we went through this period until suddenly … it seemed to coincide with Chernobyl. [This was the nuclear power station that exploded in what was then the Soviet Union, spreading radioactive contamination on the wind through Europe.]

Scandinavian countries would not buy wines from anywhere near-east of them. And they turned to Australia because they knew it was a clean country, and what we thought was a lake was depleted very quickly. At the same time, the wine writers and the Masters of Wine in the UK suddenly gave their blessing. 'You know, this stuff from the colonies is not too bad. You have our permission to drink it.' Our wines were accepted in the UK, which is now by far the biggest export country for Australian wines. And the growers are getting a really good return on their investment, on their crops. They're walking proud. The whole area looks once again a really proud district. Such as it should. It's been great to see this.

Many people in the Barossa think of Peter Lehmann as something of a saviour in those bad times, as he stood up for the growers against his employers who had decided not to buy from Barossa growers, which would have been disastrous for many of the region's grape-growing families. This was the trigger for establishing his own company in 1979, with international and local backing — and all local produce. Initially, it supplied the bulk wine market, but in 1982, it began bottling wine. An investment crisis for a partner born of another company takeover led to Lehmann making a bid for the winery, which was floated on the Australian Stock Exchange in 1993 and is these days part-owned through shareholdings by many of the vignerons that Lehmann helped in the first place.

I think it was a little bit of the old stubborn Prussian heritage. I'd given my word and, my God, I was going to do everything possible to honour it. And this company I was working for at the time, they were owned by an English company. They reneged on their word with the growers and I was blowed if I was going to. So that's where it all started. Them reneging and me just being stubborn — and also, I did have an ultimate belief, which has been justified and vindicated, in the Barossa and particularly with our shiraz.

Lehmann's shiraz, especially the Stonewell, is his greatest pride, although he is also admired for his premium riesling, semillon, chardonnay, grenache and a cabernet blend, as well as his commercial flair for less expensive wines. Despite public ownership, Peter Lehmann Wines retains its family links through his son Doug, who is managing director, and his position on the winemaking team which includes Andrew Wigan, Peter Schulz and Leonie Lange. His entry into the wine industry was more by chance than a career choice,

but his family background in the settlement of the Barossa Valley gave him an ideal springboard.

The Barossa was free settled — as was all of South Australia, the only State in the Commonwealth settled without any convict labour. And this area in particular was an amalgam of British immigrants and German-speaking Lutherans who were looking for areas where they could practise Lutheranism — because their king in Prussia had said they should all follow the order of worship as laid down by Calvin. Thank goodness they didn't, because Calvinists don't drink very much and the Lutherans actually gave it their blessing. So there was a general exodus from Prussia to all parts of the world and a fair mob came to South Australia when that was being colonised in the late 1830s, early 1840s. And my family was among those early settlers who came to the Barossa.

Of course, there was no such country as Germany then. Bismarck hadn't unified the States. The settlers were German-speaking Lutherans from the kingdom of Prussia. The Lutheran dominance is still very strong in the Barossa. You drive around on a Sunday and you see quite a few churches. Sometimes in the little hamlets, the only things there are two churches. Both Lutheran. They have their little squabbles and say: 'I'll go and build my church next door.' They're still there, though a few years ago the United Evangelical and the Evangelical Lutheran Church split their differences and combined. So they're actually quite a strong voice.

I'm not as good a Lutheran as a lot of my growers are. But they have pride of their heritage, they have great faith. Which I think anyone should envy. They are believers and their pastors round them up, say, 'You come to church' whenever it is, and they are there. That's what I was about to say before: you drive around the Barossa on a Sunday and if you see a church with a hell of a crowd around it, you can bet your bottom dollar that's Lutheran. Catholics are not very strong, Church of England not all that strong, Uniting Church reasonable ... it's predominantly Lutheran.

My father was a Lutheran pastor. He trained in America because the time when he decided he wanted to be a theologian or a pastor, Australia had no seminaries so the would-be's had to go to Europe or to America for their studies in theology. Dad went to St Paul's, Minnesota, and, luckily for me, when he came back he took a parish in the Barossa which retained our Barossa identity. He died when I was only 14. I was actually, at one stage, going to be a parson. Following his death, I guess I would say in today's terminology that I was a drop-out. I would just take any job in the world to escape school and, as luck would have it, the local winery Yalumba was looking for a likely lad. Not that I really would have described myself thus. However, I wagged school, went up and had an interview and got the job. So in 1947 I started up there as an apprentice. Grew with the industry. It was obvious we were compatible. I enjoyed it and it's been kind to me. And following quite a few years' apprenticeship, I was let loose on the unsuspecting grape. Some years later, I left there and was winemaker at Saltram for 20 years.

Lehmann's association with the Barossa is reinforced by that of his wife Margaret, still regarded as an outsider from Adelaide but nonetheless topping the poll in a recent council election. She is a keen advocate of local produce, especially the delicious smoked smallgoods made by butchers in the area to recipes passed down through generations. She makes her own chutneys, lays down cucumbers with vine leaves, dill, salt and brine — kept in the refrigerator — and has become an expert at the traditional cucumber salad when fresh cucumber is sliced finely, salted, left to stand under a weighted plate, drained, then mixed with onion, cream, vinegar and white pepper.

'Australia is so lucky. It's got so many jewels in the crown. I think the Barossa might have a very slight edge on some of them, particularly with shiraz.' Peter Lehmann continues over lunch of the above, plus a range of local breads, and of course a glass of red.

One thing that's going for it, it's had 150 years of uninterrupted winemaking. South Australia's been fortunate, it's never had phylloxera like our American cousins, or war or prohibition, so we've just had uninterrupted winemaking. We've had the swings up and down, but the climate is ideal, we've got good soil, the right varieties and more importantly — these days in particular — the extra knowledge, plus all the latest technological equipment. So everything's there, the recipe's there to make really good, top grade wines.

Making wine is like raising children. You've got to collar them and cosset them when they're little babies. I mean, we still tuck our wine into bed every night. We check it night and morning. Not quite change its nappy but, you know, you sniff, you wait for the onset of H_2S [rotten egg gas, a by-product of an overactive ferment] and you take measures to eradicate that. It really is painstaking love, care and attention.

I think shiraz is the variety that's singularly going to make the Barossa more famous than it already is. I mean, we still do very well with riesling, semillon, cabernet, but shiraz is just that little bit special. It just seems to suit this area. The Barossa would have the oldest plantings of shiraz in the world. I can think of a dozen growers who've still got shiraz well over 100 years old. So it's a great source of original clones, which most probably came from Hermitage and the Busby collection that contributed to Australia's early viticultural history.

Characters of the Industry

Bill Moularadellis, winemaker, Kingston Estate
OPPOSITE: *Vineyard in the Riverland*

Bill Moularadellis

Talk about the major wine-growing areas of South Australia and you will hear names such as Barossa Valley, McLaren Vale, Coonawarra, Clare Valley and the Adelaide Hills. Yet people never mention the biggest area of them all — the Riverland. Tucked into the curves of the Murray River northeast of Adelaide between Renmark, Waikerie and Loxton, this is where the grapes are grown for 25 per cent of the wine consumed in Australia. The difference between it and the better known regions of South Australia is that the Riverland grew to prominence as a quantity grape supplier to the cask wine trade and no one ever considered it a premium wine area.

Now that is changing, and it has a lot to do with one new generation winemaker, Bill Moularadellis. When he was studying oenology at Roseworthy Agricultural College, he was told that you could not make good wine in the Riverland. He is pretty proud to have proved otherwise — and he has an impressive range of statistics to back him up. From his first crush of 60 tonnes at the family's Kingston Estate Wines in 1985, he has gone on to an annual crushing of more than 16,000 tonnes of grapes from the Riverland region. Export sales of premium wines from Kingston Estate rose from $600,000 in 1991 to more than $10 million in 1995.

It is an exciting success story, one that also provides an interesting view of Australian attitudes in local response to Moularadellis' starting point in selling his wine:

I remember my first foray into the retail world in Adelaide, Melbourne and Sydney, and I was literally thrown out of some liquor stores. This was in the height of the wine surplus, there was a lot more wine around than most people needed ... and the Riverland had the reputation for producing cask wine. It was not really recognised as a premium table wine producer.

So Moularadellis took his wines overseas, where buyers did not have those preconceptions and bought his wine at face value.

Historically, this region was much maligned by winemakers from other areas in that the quality of the grapes that were grown here were not recognised and the growers were not rewarded for the quality fruit that they were producing. So it was a downward spiral. I guess what we did differently was recognise that not all the grapes were the same, and we were able to pick the very best growers and the very best parts of their vineyards and that gave us a huge quality advantage — which we then marketed overseas. Those wines that we were offering were met with overwhelming success and response from buyers, particularly the major supermarket groups in the UK.

He has chardonnay going to the United Kingdom, red wine to China, and cabernet and merlot to the United States. When Australians saw the success of Kingston Estate overseas, they thought again.

I've actually been quite surprised at the rate the perception has changed. It was a huge brick wall in initial years, but I guess there was a lot of poor wine made from the area in the past. Now the pundits and the critics are prepared to give us a go and try the wines and judge them on their own individual merits. Over the past four or five years, I've been heartened that the quality wines we've been making — the ones that have been winning outstanding show success — that those wines and all our Estate range are being recognised for the value and quality they represent. And that's far in advance of the quality and value that some other regions or countries in the world are offering.

There has been a revolution in this region. Most of those cask wine varieties have been replaced by premium varieties like chardonnay, merlot, shiraz, cabernet sauvignon. We are doing that very efficiently, with the quality and richness that this region provides in that we have more sunshine hours in the Riverland than in most other grape-growing areas. That gives us an ability to ripen our fruit consistently, and this ripeness is the key. We have rich fruit flavours that come from the very rich grapes that we're able to produce.

Our philosophy is to provide better quality than our competitors, and that philosophy has worked for us internationally. Our thesis is that if you are selling wine at, say, $10 a bottle, but offering a quality of wine that your competitors are at, say, $15, then once you've had the opportunity of the consumers trying that wine, you'll win them forever. Because of the quality and the value that they are receiving, they will remember and they will come back. And for as long as we are continually improving our quality and offering exceptional value, I think our business and our wine sales will continue to grow.

It seems a very long way from the start made by Bill Moularadellis' parents, Sarantos and Constantina — Steve and Nina — who came to Australia from Greece. He had worked at his trade as a carpenter after arriving in Adelaide in 1955, but the following year he went grape picking in the Riverland. That's where he met his wife, who had migrated there as a 17-year-old. They settled in Kingston-on-Murray and grew fruit, which did well, enabling them to buy a second property which had grape vines on it. They came to be recognised as among the best grape producers in the Riverland, but only began to make their own wine in 1979 when grape prices fell.

That experience of grape growing for outside winemakers shaped son Bill's approach when he became winemaker:

> Growers were not appreciated for the quality of fruit. It was quite disheartening for them to see the extra effort that they went to to produce quality grapes being unrecognised by some of the major wine companies. How their fruit was tipped into the same receival hopper, into the same crusher as their neighbour's or perhaps someone down the road who wasn't giving as much care and attention. What we've done is to recognise those individual growers and keep their fruit separate, and reward them accordingly. That's given them extra motivation and a commitment to us.

Grower Sam Perry echoes his sentiments, pleased by the involvement that Kingston Estate offers its growers in inviting them to follow the wine through the various processes to the final product. Perry is one of the growers focusing on petit verdot, a relatively rare variety that the winery is developing as a speciality. As Moularadellis says:

> Australia has been at the forefront of innovation and that's been one of the major reasons why our wine sales have grown so very quickly internationally. We haven't been shackled by tradition. We don't do things the way our fathers did because that was the way things were done — we have basically a clean slate.
> We can improve quality continuously by making the changes through the

vineyards, in the management practices, in the irrigation, in trellising, right through to the winery with our state-of-the-art equipment and processors, in addition to the quite traditional methods that are used through oak maturation and so forth. So we have the double bonus of being able to use traditional techniques where it suits us, but also to adopt new techniques such as cold fermentation for white wines, which has given us a significant quality advantage.

With all his upbeat marketing talk, Moularadellis still has heart for the earth and sweat of grape growing. 'I was born in the vines. I mean, I was picking grapes before I could walk … All our after-school hours were spent in the vineyards … picking, pruning, doing all the jobs around the vineyard. Some of my earliest memories are steering the tractor for Dad when he was loading grapes with Mum.' His insights into the hands-on side of the business gave him a head start in combination with his Roseworthy science, especially in an irrigated area where the grower has the god-like power of controlling the vines' water intake.

> The vine is a pretty hardy sort of plant. In adversity it excels. As managers of the vineyards we can encourage the vine to grow, we can actually manipulate the amount of vigour and flavour by turning the water on and off. We get very little rain in the growing season, so we have total control of the vines' growing environment by drip irrigation. And that is an important tool that we use as viticulturists and winemakers to maximise the flavour and richness of our wines.

New Regions

Canberra District

Canberra District has been declared a formal wine-producing region defined by the Geographical Indications Committee and registered by the European Committee. But it is more District than Canberra in the sense that none of it is in the Australian Capital Territory, which was set aside for the establishment of the national capital. All the wineries are in surrounding areas of New South Wales.

And there is good reason for that, as David Carpenter of Lark Hill explains:

> We started in the mid-1970s with a group of people who bought land in New South Wales adjacent to Canberra, to the ACT. Because in the ACT it's leasehold. And if you buy a farm in the ACT and develop something, it's quite feasible that someone will want to put a road through it later. Bingo, you've done your dough. So everybody was in New South Wales. But obviously Canberra was the focus. So it was called the Canberra District.
>
> We first defined it as a circle — radius 50 miles around the GPO. That got everybody in. The trouble was that they moved the GPO. Then, of course, we had to metricate it, so it became 80 kilometres. And when you look at that, you notice this enormous amount of country over in the Brindabellas towards Tumut. In fact, 80 kilometres just about gets to Tumut. As the currawong flies.

Then the Geographical Indications Committee began its work and the local winemakers became involved in redefining the Canberra District, which now includes quite different country from the cool climate environment in which the development started:

The soils are different. It's lower, warmer. There's an enormous area there that's probably very good for grape growing, if anybody ever gets into it. But its focus is Canberra.

I think it's going to go ahead very well. We've got a good pool of small wineries that are building on their experience and getting better and bigger. And we've got BRL Hardy coming in. They'll certainly add to the focus and awareness of Canberra. [BRL Hardy will be the exception in that it plans to establish a winery, vineyards, cellar door sales and a tourism facility within ACT boundaries with encouragement from the ACT government.]

It's always going to be a quality area. If you want to make wine with other fruit, well and good, and those prices will come down. But I think there is going to be at least a good supply of Canberra fruit in the future, and I think the Canberra District will retain its identity in the same way that other small areas will. Like Mornington Peninsula and Yarra Valley. We'll just get better.

Canberra's climate is typified by extremes. We normally have a relatively dry summer. Certainly, evaporation exceeds precipitation throughout the growing season. We have frosts. Frost risk runs up to Christmas and starts again in New Year. That sort of thing. So, if you're in the wrong site, you'll just get frost, frost, frost. We can have a wet summer from storms. But even then, usually what happens is that, once the storm goes, things dry up quite quickly. So the climate is relatively benign for grape growing, although we really don't have enough water. That's partly because the soils are so poor. If the soils had better water-holding capacity, we wouldn't be so worried about it.

Sue Carpenter, winemaker, Lark Hill

Sue Carpenter, David's wife and the other half of this hardworking, complementary partnership in running every aspect of Lark Hill, comes into the conversation:

Because it's high altitude, you have cold nights and fierce, hot days in summer. So growth is restricted. Ripening happens in autumn, so you get fruit in good balance. But if you've had a late frost or you have a very cold position, you may not ripen things adequately. And I think the later autumn ripening is the one that gives the stunning fruit. Such good fruit that a lot of people, now that they have got to grips with the winemaking, they're making wines that win lots of awards. And that is what is attracting the big companies into the area.

The Carpenters were working in Canberra when they decided to take the plunge into winemaking — Sue as a consulting statistician with the

CSIRO and David as a research fellow at the Australian National University. David says:

> Early 70s was pretty exciting and we were enthusiastic about wine. It seemed like a really good idea to try to develop something like this. I suppose we saw other places, small ones, just getting off the ground and thought we could do it. We had lots of enthusiasm, lots of energy, and we loved this place — it's a beautiful location. It seemed like a challenging, interesting site to develop and make wine from.

Sue continues:

> We are the type of people who don't like spectator sports. We wanted to do it. We wanted to get in and develop our own place. When we started, people covered us with advice, most of it totally inappropriate. There was Dark Ages viticulture accompanied by Dark Ages winemaking. And after about three years of that, David and I essentially tossed a coin and I won. And I went off and, part-time, did the wine science degree at Charles Sturt University. And that was fantastic. I learned a lot. Winemaking is very technical, it's exciting, it's not fully understood.

So is the winemaking side of things her job? 'I think I'm the nose. I have a gift, actually, as well as a trained talent for smelling things and that is a big part of winemaking. To track wines during ferment and so on. But in terms of the day-to-day, hard yakka, that's Dave. In terms of scheduling and decisions about "What will we do with this fruit?" it's probably me.' And does Lark Hill have any favoured wine style? 'I think every year there's a wine that wins lots of awards and you get really focused on it, but at the moment we're very keen on pinot noir. Partly because of incredible success, partly because it's so suitable for this climate and with our vineyard.'

They have noticed a lot of changes in people coming into grape growing and winemaking, summarised by extremes of commercial and lifestyle advantages:

> When we started, the number of people who were involved in wine already was relatively small. And people who got involved in things like this were passionate about wine. Now, people are planting vineyards just because of the rationale of saying, 'Instead of having sheep die in the paddocks, I'll plant a vineyard.' They don't know anything about wine. They also say that it's a lifestyle, retirement project. Which is the most frightening concept of all. Because it is hard work and it is technical and expensive and scientific. But it still has that lovely

romance about it and integration of lots of things. Including lifestyle.

Tourism has its pros and cons at the cellar door, as Sue points out:

> It can be a problem for a small winery, but we find that a lot of our business is with people who come looking for our wines. And they are already alerted by journalists' articles or show awards or restaurants, and we love those people. They are very enthusiastic, very friendly and it's quite inspiring to get that feedback. But the public is more exploitative. They feel that they can come to a winery, take up your time, enjoy the ambience, enjoy the wines and go. And that can be demoralising, exhausting and expensive.

Over the past few years, Canberra District seems to have gone a long way in a short time. David responds:

> I think in outside awareness, yes, but internally it's just been a continual progression. I don't think there's been any sort of steepening of the curve. I think we've just had more and good enough wine that more people have taken heed of the fact that we're here and found the wines. Sydney now takes a lot of wine out of the Canberra District into restaurants. But then, it's a big market place — 40 per cent of Australia's wine drinking goes on in Sydney. So there has been a dramatic change in the external view of the Canberra District.

That's one result of entering wine shows and winning awards, according to Sue:

> In the New South Wales wine awards, our pinot noir was in the top 40, and our cabernet and merlot was voted Best Canberra District. This kind of feedback is wonderful for a winemaker. Makes you feel really great. But it's also very good for marketing — for the perception of wine and a wine area. People like to feel reassured that their choice has been approved by someone who's an expert in their field. And we win millions of medals. We do enter a lot of shows. And this is really our form of advertising. Word-of-mouth or show success.

Ken Helm wouldn't disagree, but he has added an individual touch to keep his winemaking business in the customer's mind. 'A good friend of mine is a little known winemaker called Wolf Blass. He's got a bow tie and so I thought, well, you've got to remember people with a bow tie. So, I've got a moustache — so people remember me. And that's all part of the game.'

Helm likes a bit of showbiz and humour about the place when he is introducing people to his wine, which he has been making in the Murrumbateman area around 40 kilometres north of Canberra for more than two decades. The vineyard and winery were established by Helm and his wife, Judith, in 1973 and 1977, respectively, initially as a weekend hobby and then a fulltime occupation. He is a fourth-generation descendant of German vine dressers from the Rhineland, who grew grapes in Albury and Rutherglen in the 1850s and 1880s. Their 12-year-old daughter Stephanie has already made three vintages and won a silver medal for her 1996 merlot.

They are only about 20 kilometres from the area around Yass where grapes were grown in the 19th century:

Yass was the great southern town back in the 1850s. They grew grapes there as they did wherever civilisation, as they called it, went from Sydney. And that wine industry excelled up until about the turn of the century. Unlike most other wine-growing districts in Australia, they disappeared through the temperance league, through lack of interest in wine and just generally Australia's isolation. The wine industry in Canberra was revived again nearly one hundred years later, in about 1971.

Before he took on winemaking fulltime in 1988, Helm worked for the CSIRO in the biological trial of insects, which took him into apple and stone fruit orchards, hop gardens and vineyards threatened by phylloxera. Was his scientific background a help when he moved into the wine industry?

Ken Helm, winemaker

In some ways. My philosophy about wine is that it's a bit like art. You can send 50 people to an art school and you may come out with one great artist. They had artistry. Its similar with wine. Anybody can make it. It's just a matter of crushing some grapes into a glass, allowing the wild yeast on the skin to ferment it and in ten, 15 days at 15 degrees, you've got wine. Drink it. It won't hurt you.

But to add the artistry into it, it needs the person who's got a bit of individuality. Who will question things and won't be dragged along by the show judges who tell you what you should drink. Or the wine writers or the television critics on wine. We need to have that artistry. And that will progress Australia's wines. That is one of my concerns at the moment with the show system. It tends to be giving awards to wines which are all pretty well the same. And we could perhaps be losing that artistry.

Riesling in this district is outstanding. I believe this is the 'Clare' of New South Wales. At the last Melbourne wine show, the trophy for the best white wine in the show went to a riesling. Riesling is on the way

OPPOSITE:
Lark Hill vineyard and winemaker Sue Carpenter

back, it is now a crackling, dry, aromatic wine. And we can produce that here, every year. It's very easy. And with the similarity in climate to Bordeaux, cabernet and merlot do very well. And that's what I'm now planting, and having people plant for me. But, of course, everybody wants a bit of shiraz. So, because money fouls our minds and I have a bank manager … I've got shiraz as well.

As well as his wine business, Helm is mayor of Yass Shire and does a lot of lobbying for the wine industry:

It does help. Walking through the cellar door here, I have politicians of all persuasions. I have permanent secretaries from different departments. When in Canberra, you tend to know people on a first name basis. And that's where I see an advantage. I think it's been the most ridiculous thing that the Wine Federation of Australia has been located in Adelaide. How can you lobby from that far away?

Every other group — wool, wheat, beef — has an office in Canberra, and they can walk up the hill there at any time and get their way. The wine industry, which is now regarded as one of the buoyant industries, really does have to start thinking a little bit more professionally on how it lobbies government. Otherwise, the taxation system which is crippling us at the moment, particularly the small growers — and the big companies are now also very concerned — will continue to cripple us. And may even push some of us out of business.

Over the past five years, the district has received recognition in the quality of its wines. People are having no difficulty in selling their wines. They just sell so quickly, we can't produce enough. And that has brought extra money into the area which has allowed for more technology. People started using better packaging and information tools, and the area of course grows from there. We have more and more people coming in. Our single biggest problem will continue to be … can we produce enough?

Cork

Demonstrating the way to remove bark for cork

It was Walter Burley Griffin who decided that Canberra, the capital city of Australia which he was designing, should have a cork industry. There was a worldwide cork shortage at the time and Canberra needed to be more than the seat of federal government.

In 1916, the first acorns for planting were acquired from trees found in Canberra itself at Duntroon. The first consignment of a larger supply from Spain was torpedoed as it travelled by ship to Australia in 1917, an unlikely victim of World War I. The second arrived safely. By 1920, more than 9,500 cork trees were planted in the Green Hills plantation within the Stromlo Forest in the Australian Capital Territory. Cork harvesting or stripping of these trees did not begin until the late 1940s. It turned out to be high quality cork and commercially valuable.

Today, the Glenloch Cork Oak Plantation is on the register of the National Estate and the ACT Sites of Significance register. It is managed by ACT Forests — although harvesting of the cork ceased in 1981 — and maintained for its heritage value, its landscape setting and character.

At a time when research is intensifying to replace the cork seal of a wine bottle with something less likely to give a taint to the wine or loosen under pressure from extremes of temperature, it is not surprising that high quality cork is in short supply. Spain and Portugal are still the chief suppliers of cork around the world, but each tree can be harvested only once in ten years. Carefully cut away like a tall bark tube with a slit down one side, the cork's removal does not damage the tree, which gradually grows new layers of cork to replace it.

While cork has been used to seal containers by every generation since the Ancient Greeks and Romans, it is under threat from wine lovers in the 21st century. When a bottle of wine is opened and smells mouldy, musty or like wet hessian, it is suffering from cork taint and will taste as bad as it smells. It is corked and, in a licensed restaurant, it should be returned and replaced.

Bottles of wine are already being sealed with screwtop lids, and plastic corks have been given wideranging trials. One way or another, the long relationship between the bark of the cork oak tree and wine appears to be coming to an end. Walter Burley Griffin's vision of a cork industry for Canberra will be even more of a distant dream.

Pinot noir is not a grape variety or a wine style to be pinne

enjoy it ... differently. And that's the challenge it throws o

Pinot Noir

the imagination of wine lovers—that it requires

make, but rewards t

*P*inot

Pinot Noir

Pinot noir can have so many styles. There is no benc

Pinot Noir

vn. This is one of its joys. People grow it, see it, make it,

capture

GRAPE VARIETIES AND WINE STYLES

special attention to grow

nsitive grower and winemaker, as well as the patient

wine drinker, with an explosion of complex f

Pinot Noir

Noir

x pinot noir.

Pinot Noir

*P*inot noir is not a grape variety or a wine style to be pinned down. This is one of its joys. People grow it, see it, make it, enjoy it … differently. And that's the challenge it throws out to capture the imagination of wine lovers — that it requires extra special attention to grow and make, but rewards the sensitive grower and winemaker, as well as the patient wine drinker, with an explosion of complex flavours. And these are likely to be diverse.

Phillip Jones is the owner and winemaker of the Bass Phillip winery in Victoria's Gippsland, where winemaking follows the coast east towards the New South Wales border. As he says:

Pinot noir can have so many styles. There is no benchmark pinot noir. If you look at the Old World in France, there are styles attributed to different districts in Burgundy and they are regularly, reproducibly, of a particular style. I think there are probably ten to 15 styles of pinot.

Phillip Jones, owner/ winemaker, Bass Phillip

For us here, amongst the wines we're familiar with in Australia … there are the early, easy drinking styles. There are styles that have more body and more richness. There are styles with more finesse. There are styles with great power. But the determinants of style are not only those personality type of factors. It's the flavour characteristics that are peculiar to certain vineyards or districts. So there are particularly strong fruit characters in certain regions and we know them as plums, cherries, strawberries and related things. But there is also the spiciness, the earth and mushroomy flavours, the forest floor smells and flavours … all of these things which contribute to extra complex and enticing, exciting flavours.

One of the most important features of pinot for me is texture, the mouth feel which is not just the grittiness of tannins, albeit they are very soft, but there's almost a viscous chewiness about some great pinot noirs. Another great attribute of pinot noir is the length of flavour, which is not just extended length as a result of fruit tannins or oak flavours. There's almost a hidden power in some pinots that's often described as the peacock's tail of flavour, an explosion of flavour in the back of your mouth which becomes more apparent in great pinot noirs when they have some age on them. Many of us have had those really exciting experiences at the dinner table with great old burgundies, and they're memorable.

Of course, the great French burgundies have been my inspiration. I guess I have tried to do things here in my own way, and experimented and fumbled my way through some of that. But there's no doubt that the greatest pinot noir wines in the world are French, and the great diversity of flavours and the power and intensity of these wines is far beyond anything we've achieved in this country. So they're the icons I look up to. In terms of techniques, my approach has been trying to keep my hands off the process to the degree that I can get some kind of harmonious result. That means using some techniques that I've read about — I've never worked in France — and using techniques that are inexpensive because that's been a factor for me in building the business. Gradually, I'm trying to refine those as each vintage goes past.

I love nature and I love the process to be natural. I am a technologist, but I use very little in the winery and there are some very specific reasons why, say, in the winery I refrain from using certain technologies like pumping — reasons that are scientific or engineering based. I love being outdoors. I love to see the plants grow in the way they want to grow and my outlook isn't really strongly commercial. I really just want to enjoy what I'm doing and improve on it as the years go through.

Bannockburn vineyards

Not that he doesn't use fungicides (although he avoids systemic fungicides) and herbicides:

I started by being very organic and ended up one spring with four-foot high weeds here. It's just unbelievable, the growth. So we do use herbicides a couple of times during the season and we scarify down the rows.

We have five soil types here, which made life quite an experiment for a few years. I guess I'm looking for a reasonaby low cropping level, between one and two tonnes to the acre. And small berried bunches so I can get intense flavour. My reasoning is very simplistic: small apples from small apple trees are the most flavoursome, so a small number of grape bunches from a small vine, I figure, will have a similar effect. The soils here are very deep and fertile. The rainfall's quite high, there's no lack of humidity. So I want to control vigour by having root competition with vines closer together and to push the roots deep down because, as far as I'm concerned, deep roots and a stable moisture environment for the root zone as so important for pinot. We hedge the vines often during the growing season because it's such a vigorous region. Otherwise I don't manipulate the vines, apart from leaf plucking.

This trellis is known as vertical shoot positioning. It's probably one of the most traditional means of trellising grape vines. It seems to be the most suitable method for high quality pinot noir. We hedge it to keep it reasonably thin — four or five leaves thick so sunlight gets on every leaf, into every bunch. And that's important in a cooler district like this. Other systems might use double canopies, vertical up and vertical down. Certainly that method produces very good quality commercial

wines at much higher cropping rates, probably three times the cropping levels I obtain here. But if we're looking for longer keeping, more intense wines, this vertical shoot positioning at lower cropping levels seems to be the one.

In building the winery, I wanted a very cool and humid environment, and I preferred to do that in a natural way. Rather than air-condition the rooms, I chose limestone blocks as the building material because when they become damp with dew or rainfall and the sun shines, they act as a real coolant for the building. Also, I prefer to build an underground cellar, which we're doing at present, and have a cold and humid environment at less then 14 °C, rather than have an above-ground room which is air-conditioned. I guess my attitude is based on the principle that if ever there is a nuclear holocaust or serious energy crisis, I still want to be able to make wine here.

David Lance with Maryann Egan in Diamond Valley vineyard

Diamond Valley, a family-owned winery less than an hour's drive from Melbourne in the Yarra Valley, has three pinots produced by winemaker David Lance assisted by his son James, illustrating the reasons why premium pinot noir costs so much:

Starting from the top, we have our close-planted pinot. That's a very special wine, only made in tiny quantities from a very small, experimental vineyard that is very close planted like they are in Burgundy. The rows are 1.2 metres or four feet apart, which makes them very, very narrow, and the vines are a metre apart in the rows. There are 2,300 vines in that two-thirds of an acre — a huge number of vines — and most of the work on them is done by hand, so it's very labour intensive. A little bit of speciality equipment we had to make just to operate that little vineyard cost more than the equipment we use for the rest of the vineyard. But it was an experiment in trying to optimise the things I thought were important in growing the absolute best pinot noir. This is the fifth vintage made off that planting and it is proving to be exceptionally good wine.

This wine is our so-called estate pinot, that we've been making from the grapes we grow here since 1980. This is the one that's won so many trophies and made us so famous for pinot. I firmly believe that the quality has to be in the fruit, otherwise you've got no hope of making good pinot. And I guess that we were really lucky. Our site has quite a significant north wind component. The wind just roars up the hill and it has the effect of rolling the canopy of the vines on the trellis, and that exposes the fruit to the sun. I think that has been a significant, though accidental, characteristic of this vineyard which, with the very lean soil

OPPOSITE:
Yarra Valley

that we have here, keeps the vigour of the vines very low and allows them to produce fruit rather than leaves and wood.

One of the characteristics in this wine is 'stemminess'. We did some stem return to this wine — about a third, I think it was, in which the stems were returned to the fermentation. We do get a bit more tannin, a bit more structure and complexity in the wine, but it certainly comes through as a stamp on this particular wine, that 'stemmy' character.

Lance stresses the importance of site in comparing this wine with the least expensive of the three, made from grapes grown by other vineyards in the area:

Those wines are made with very similar techniques. The stem return is different, but I don't think that adds a significant amount to the wine. I think it's site specific, basically.

This Blue Label Pinot Noir, made from fruit we buy from other growers in the Yarra Valley, is a slightly lighter wine and there is a perceived quality difference, even though this particular wine won a

Wine & Wherefore

WHAT IS A SOMMELIER?

Sommelier, derived from an ancient French word, originally meant packhorse. It became the word used for the butler of a nobleman's chateau and, when restaurants came into being, the word was applied to the person in charge of the wine.

⏏ Nowadays, every licensed restaurant has a wine list and in many good establishments it is the role of the sommelier to choose the wines for the list and maintain the cellar. It is the sommelier's duty to inform the staff of his or her choices. This involves them tasting food with the wines so that diners' questions about the menu and the wine list can be answered with confidence by staff with firsthand experience.

⏏ Under the sommelier's guidance, staff are taught to serve wine at suitable temperatures and to open and pour wine into suitable glassware. But it is the sommelier who can answer the widest range of questions about the wine list and help you match your food choice with the most appropriate wine.

⏏ Restaurants in Australia have suffered in the past because of lack of true sommeliers. Times are changing. Training courses have been established and the position of the sommelier is now being treated as a career. Going to restaurants where skilled and knowledgeable sommeliers are employed will add extra pleasure to the dining experience.

trophy for best pinot of the show last year. It is a lovely wine. It's a bit of a shame: this wine suffers because of the other two. If we only had this one, we'd be pretty pleased with it — it's just a matter of degree.

Pinot noir was nothing like as popular a variety when Lance began planting it.

When we established our vineyard in 1976, the Yarra Valley was quite a different place to what it is now. There were very few wineries and vineyards in the Yarra Valley and the driving force for us was to try to emulate those classic European wines. The climate in this area was seen as being very similar to Bordeaux and Burgundy in France and other European classic areas. Our intent was to capitalise on that climatic similarity to grow those same classic varieties. And so we planted some Bordeaux varieties and we planted pinot noir. It's interesting that there was very little other pinot noir grown in Australia in the mid-70s. It was, in retrospect, quite a pioneering thing to do, I suppose. But that was the driving force — those classic European wines and the possibility of being able to grow wines of similar quality in this cool climate around Melbourne.

Gary Farr, winemaker, Bannockburn, with a burner during pruning

Pinot is challenging from two points of view. One is the viticulture. Because of the lack of vigour in the vines, it is a hard variety to grow and it is very important to get it well ripened and well flavoured. The quality of pinot is very much determined by the quality that's in the fruit at harvest time. But it's also challenging in the winery because it's extremely important to maintain the quality in the fruit through the winemaking process. In many ways, the winemaking is a custodial sort of process where you're actually trying to look after the quality that you're starting off with and not have it frittered away during the making process. It's challenging also because it's really important that a pinot be a very good pinot because a second-rate pinot hasn't got a lot going for it. A second-rate cabernet can still be quite a reasonable wine, but not a pinot. And this is related very much to its being a lighter bodied wine, I think: if you take away the exotic characters of pinot, you're left with just a very lightweight, pretty uninteresting pink wine. And I think that's probably the real reason why it's that challenging. It has to be good, otherwise it really hasn't got much going for it at all.

Pinot is certainly regarded as a speciality wine. Those early days were pretty interesting and pretty exciting. There was only a very small number of people who understood and drank pinot noir and they tended to be enthusiasts for it. Everybody else saw it as being light,

FOLLOWING PAGE:
Maryann Egan with Sairung and Phillip Jones, winemaker

pretty uninteresting, almost a rosé style which didn't have much merit at all. And particularly in the Australian context of the classic Australian big, gutsy red wine syndrome, pinot was considered to be a pretty wimpy wine. But I think that's changed enormously over the past ten, 15 years, where we've had good pinots appearing, plus the educational thing that people have suddenly realised that there's more to life than big, gutsy cabernets or shirazes — that pinot can be a pretty exotic drink, a very enjoyable drink, but it just needs a little bit more brain power.

Gary Farr, winemaker at Bannockburn, in the Geelong region southwest of Melbourne, was one of the many former students of Roseworthy Agricultural College who had to unlearn the old method of making pinot noir like any other red grape:

The only way to learn how to make really good pinot, I thought, was to go to France and see how they did it there. And so, in 1983, I made my first trip to Burgundy, which is an area where they exclusively make a wine from pinot noir grapes. I spent nearly three months working there and handling pinot noir, and it was quite an eye-opener to me as to the methods they used. Their ideas were very basic, very traditional winemaking methods and we'd missed the whole point with lots of cooling and added years and lots of … technology, one would call it.

Where I worked at Domaine Dujac, they didn't even own a crusher to crush the grapes. They relied on people's feet, in a tank — so that was the most basic of methods of actually crushing the fruit and turning it into wine. This was the sort of simplicity that impressed me and then the wines I saw — naturally from that vintage, but also from previous vintages in their cellar — impressed me so much with the flavour and finesse of wines that we were never likely to achieve with the winemaking methods we were using in Australia. It was difficult to change immediately, so we changed bit by bit. We were fully fledged into Francophile ideas by '86 and producing wine that made the Australian pinot drinker stand up and look at what we were doing — because the wines were so different, they had so much more character and finesse to them.

I went back to France for a number of years in a row and I was actually determined to outdo the French at their own game. I believed that I could make wine as well as they could and sell it for the prices they were selling it. I went to the extent of planting a close-planted vineyard, a metre by metre planting. I duplicated all their methods. I bought the same oak and basically followed along all of those lines. But now I believe, after many years of trying to emulate them, that that's not what it's all about. I'm much better off saying: 'This is Bannockburn.

Food Match

PINOT NOIR

There are many different styles of pinot noir being made in Australia, so it's impossible to set any hard rules when matching with food. But generally speaking, the gamey flavours of pinot noir enhance the gamey flavours of food, particularly duck. The sweetness is drawn out from both the wine and the rich duck flesh. One of the classic partnerships is pinot noir and Peking duck with its crispy skin. Or try the gamey flavours of quail or lamb.

Pinot noir is also renowned for its rustic characters — for its truffley flavours of the forest floor. With these pinots a mushroom dish can be quite sensational. Even a simple mushroom risotto can bring out these companionable flavours. An enormous range of mushrooms is available at the market and, in autumn, some specialist stores have wild mushrooms.

This is Bannockburn's terroir, or soil, or climate. We produce grapes that taste like this and from those grapes we produce wine that tastes like this.'

And this is very much what is happening right around the world now with winemakers from California through Oregon, and right through France. I mean, France has always said they will not even put on the bottle what grape variety they have. They call it by the village or the area because it's so important to them. There are many winemakers now in America that are naming vineyards and saying: 'This is a wine from a particular vineyard, it has particular characters.'

Pinot noir is still very much in the development stages and I think this generation is going to do extremely well with it, but I think the next generation maybe is the one that's going to find the microclimates and the really specific areas where pinot does well. Because pinot is that sort of grape. It takes very specific microclimates and positions within a vineyard and it does extremely well. Our best wine actually comes off the close-planted vineyard, but it comes from the middle of the close-planted vineyard and we've found this after making it since 1989. It's always the tank of grapes that comes from the middle of the vineyard — the most protected part of the vineyard, where it's created its own particular microclimate.

Farr stresses the importance of two aspects in his approach to making pinot noir: using natural yeast that forms on the skin of the grape rather than adding a single form of packet or dried yeast, and the use of stems, in which he has pulled back from his earlier method of using whole bunches exclusively.

We think we're making better wine by destemming about 75 or 80 per cent of it and having only a very small portion of whole bunches in there. To facilitate that we have a crusher outside the winery and we destem a lot of the fruit into that crusher, then into bins underneath. We want to achieve as many whole berries as possible. We don't really want to crush the fruit at that stage, all we want to do is take the berries off the stems. We then pick up the bin and tip it into an open top fermenter. And this allows us to have a very progressive fermentation. Because we haven't actually crushed the berries and released all the sugar to the yeast, the whole process is drawn out much longer: we have fermentations that can last up to three weeks. Because of the gradual crushing of the fruit using either foot stomping or a pneumatic peiaging machine, we can gradually break the berries and release the sugar, thus extending the fermentation.

The yeast that has naturally come in on the skins of the berries starts to work on the juice and the sugar, and cause the fermentation. You can end up with whole bunches down the bottom of the tank, even after three weeks, that haven't fermented. You can chew into those and they still have sugar in them. So we have to get down there by the method of peiaging, which is stomping the grapes. Traditionally, it was done by foot in France and that's how I started doing it there in 1983 and did it here for many years. We'd climb in the tanks and stomp around there to crush the berries off. Because naturally the unbroken bunches tend to float to the top and form a cap, and you'd punch that cap down with your feet. Now we've become a little more sophisticated in that we use a pneumatic ram that does the process for us and is a little less labour intensive. To have ten or 12 tanks of pinot noir fermenting in the winery and peiaging it three times a day is a lot of work. An enormous amount of work.

But how exactly is the stomping in the tanks carried out?

You put boards across to hang on to basically, and then you just get in there and swim in it. That's part and parcel of small winery winemaking and extracting the flavour and colour from the fruit. It's done like a time-honoured method: this is how it's been done before and this is how we get the good results. The French know this is the way to feel the warm patches and the cold patches in the fermentation and mix them up with their feet to even the temperature. Where the fermentation of the yeast finds a better environment, it grows quicker in one spot than another and so, in the initial three or four days, there are a lot of warm spots and cool spots that can be mixed together.

So what does Farr think makes a great pinot noir?

I think a wine that reflects its upbringing, its terroir and its climate, maybe some of its winemaker — his style, his character. This is all part of great pinot. It's a wine that has far more feeling to it, far more character than shiraz or cabernet. It really reflects a lot more than is put into it. The fruit, I suppose, is really the initial thing, which turns more into aromas and perfumes as the wine takes on some bottle age. So, I really like a wine that has three to five years of bottle age on it. It's showing some earthy characters and some feral characters to enhance that perfume. It's got to have a rich middle palate and length to it. When you find a wine with those sorts of characters, I think it matches food extremely well. My aim is to have pinot noir that matches food.

Characters of the Industry

Pam Dunsford, winemaker, with Maryann Egan in Chapel Hill vineyard
OPPOSITE: *McLaren Vale*

Pam Dunsford

Pam Dunsford is an Australian pioneer in the study of winemaking. She was the first woman to be accepted into, and graduate from, the oenology course at Roseworthy Agricultural College. That was 25 years ago, at the start of a career of achievements as winemaker, wine consultant, judge and importer of French oak barrels – with her chief occupation since 1989 being winemaker for Chapel Hill Wines in South Australia's McLaren Vale. Her student days are worth recalling, however, as a reminder of the breakthrough women have made in the wine industry since then.

Dunsford was studying agricultural science when she became interested in wine — through drinking it. Instead of taking animals as a subject in her last year, she asked to do plants. 'They said, "Well, as long as you don't interfere with the rest of the guys in the class, you can come."' And she did. One female student and 180 males, of whom 20 were winemaking students. There was no accommodation for women, so they put her in the infectious diseases ward.

Inevitably, people ask her about being a woman in what was then a man's world — and still is, to a great extent, although the barriers have been lowered. Pam says she has had no obvious sexist problems in her career: 'When I know what I want to do, I get on with it, and it doesn't worry me what other people think.' Even so, she has to cope with attitudes from outside the business that would seem outdated in any arena.

Although she hates generalisations, Dunsford admits that she thinks women have better palates than men. 'My explanation is that they're actually better at cooking, they've had more experience with putting flavours together and balance.' In wine tastings attended by husbands and wives, she has observed the men wanted to have answers so they could go away and talk about the wines with their mates, whereas the women 'were actually more interested in finding out what the flavours were all about. Women tend to be more open to different styles … Men feel comfortable with what's de rigueur.'

After working for Wynns for twelve years, Dunsford decided to go to France for a year of winemaking experience. She

asked Len Evans if he would be a referee for a Churchill Fellowship and he promptly gave her introductions that led to her doing a vintage for one of the world's greatest champagne makers, Krug. She calls it 'one of those quirky fates' and, although she did not go into sparkling wine when she came back to Australia — 'I did want to, but the sparkling wine industry in Australia was really dominated by the multinationals, so I left it alone' — she discovered attitudes that apply to any style of winemaking and completely changed her approach:

I went away with a very strict idea of what méthode champenoise winemaking was all about because I'd been making it for twelve years. What I really wanted to do was study the technology in Champagne. In fact, I ended up in a traditional house and it really turned upside down all of my ideas about winemaking. It made me look at empirical knowledge rather than technical theory, and just alerted me to a lot of things that, had I gone on the path I'd anticipated, I would have never thought about. So it was fantastic!

The French say, if you ask them a question that's technically based, 'It's because it's like that.' And for them that's an answer, because they say the grapes were given by the good Lord and you only start to work with them after they've been fermented. I spent a year in California as a scientist, studying for my masters, and the American approach to winemaking is to understand everything down to the last carbon atom. Yet, if you look at the history of wine, the organic chemistry doesn't necessarily stack up against how the wine flavour matches. If you look at the French, they'll say: 'We

don't know what the reason is, we don't care what the reason is, but we know if we do this it works — we know if we go out to that vineyard it's different from going out to this vineyard.' And so they're happy. And I think that's a really important component of winemaking.

They understand trusted information, whereas we have a different culture which says, go out and question it — and don't trust anybody except your own experience. Therefore, I think, you miss out on a lot of other, previous knowledge. When you've got generation after generation accepting the family business, then you get a respect that we probably don't have in our very young country.

Shiraz and verdelho varieties are Dunsford's particular focus in the range of wines she makes at Chapel Hill in the South Australian region of McLaren Vale, which is scenically, climatically and conveniently well placed between the southern end of the Mount Lofty Ranges and the sea, about an hour's drive south of Adelaide. Verdelho comes from Portugal, so it is suited to the 'maritime Mediterranean' climate that applies equally to McLaren Vale, which has already made a name for its shiraz. As Dunsford says:

If you look at the big vineyards of the world, the most famous, they're all maritime. It's because you need to have good sun during the ripening period, but you want coolness as well. So, you want ultraviolet radiation, but you don't want the vines to get overheated. If you've got coastal influence then you get some sort of moderation from the water, and you also get, at night, cooling breezes coming from the land on to the sea and vice versa. So all the vines get respite, which is terribly important in a Mediterranean climate. It's also important for the winemaker because after work, you just go to the beach.

Although Chapel Hill is partly housed in the heritage buildings that give the winery its name, there is nothing old-fashioned about the technology employed, which is both plentiful and the very latest.

I don't think that we should be doing arduous jobs when a machine can do better, so our philosophy is to try to do things in a way that is technically most advanced, but not sacrificing anything simply because it can be done by nuts and bolts. I mean, we wouldn't ever sacrifice anything that we thought was critical to flavour, but we wouldn't make a person do a job that we can do better with a machine. So even though we're now making quite a substantial amount of wine, we only have three fulltime people in the winery.

What we want them to do is monitor, make sure everything's right. We have everything that we can pump from A to B, all processes that can be motorised are motorised. Therefore, I think we get a high calibre of cellar hand or staff person because they don't get distracted trying to do physical things, they're only distracted doing the things that require brain power.

Dunsford might still be tagged with the 'first female' of her student days, but change and learning are obviously still part of her winemaking. For instance, she is turning away from the traditional Australian maturing wood of American oak and moving more towards French oak:

I actually like French oak in shiraz because I think it allows the fruit to do the talking. One of the problems with American oak, although it's terribly popular and an easy way to win accolades in the Australian wine show system, is that it tends to dominate. The flavour is a bit too strong and a bit too mono-dimensional.

And when, where and how does Dunsford think she's learned most about making wine?

Probably from the worst vintages. One of the weird things about the wine industry is that when you have a great wine, it's usually because the grapes have made themselves — and everyone thinks you're a wonderful winemaker. And when you have your worst wines, it's usually because you've had absolutely terrible fruit, you've worked your butt off, done a fabulous job — and everyone thinks you're passé. But no, I think we've learned more in bad vintages than we have in good vintages.

Characters of the Industry

Brother John May, winemaker, in the Sevenhill cellar
OPPOSITE: *St Aloysius Church, Sevenhill*

Brother John May

Sevenhill Cellars, in the Clare Valley of South Australia, is the only commercial Jesuit winery left in the world. Not only does it make sacramental wine for churches in Australia, India, Indonesia and Papua New Guinea, but also a whole range of table and fortified wines for sale to the public. Many of its religious activities over the past century and a half have been financially underpinned by its winemaking.

It isn't, of course, just a winery. Sevenhill, named after Rome, the city of seven hills, was settled by Jesuit Austrians seeking freedom from religious and political persecution. They arrived in 1848, planted vines in 1852 and established a boarding school five years after that. Construction of St Aloysius Church began in 1864 and was eventually ready for consecration in 1875. One of the brothers was killed when blasting stone in the quarry for the building, the roof arches are local red gum timber, the flagstones from nearby Mintaro and the slate roof from Wales. Although some additions have been made this century, the church still lacks a belfry and steeple.

The winemaker at Sevenhill Cellars, only the seventh since 1851, is Brother John May, who says that when he was called to understudy for the position in 1963, he didn't even drink 'wine or any beverages of that nature'. And since his predecessor didn't die as people had feared, he was recalled to Melbourne and didn't take up the position until he was suddenly summoned back in February 1972, one month before vintage. 'The Lord was on my side because I didn't know much. Although I was here for seven years, I actually hadn't made a decision. I didn't sleep much that vintage, but we survived — and my dry red shiraz cabernet of that year won a gold medal in Perth. So I say the Lord was with me, it wasn't my work.'

But Brother John has obviously done all right since then. In 1997, Sevenhill Cellars won 54 medals — seven gold, 19 silver and 28 bronze — and four trophies. About 30,000 people come to the cellar door each year, a stark contrast to when he was first at Sevenhill in 1963: 'We would knock off work if a car came up the drive.' The 16 grape varieties grown over 59 hectares are

pedro ximinez, riesling, traminer, chenin blanc, chardonnay, verdelho, semillon, grenache, frontignac (red, white, black and brown), cabernet sauvignon, cabernet franc, shiraz merlot, ruby cabernet, malbec and touriga. Altar wine is 25 per cent of the annual 500-tonne grape crush. As Brother John says:

It is the minority, and the sale of the table wines — the dry reds, dry whites and the fortified wines — help to subsidise the altar wine, which has the privilege of not incurring a sales tax so it is not sold over the counter. It cannot be purchased by the ordinary citizen. We supply wine to the Lutheran Church, the Church of England and other church bodies who use wine in their services or the sacrifice of the mass.

Our sacramental wine is a sweet red wine which is made from pedro ximinez and grenache, and we make a sweet white altar wine that hasn't got the pigment in it and therefore it doesn't stain the altar linen. We also make a dry altar wine that is mainly for priests who are diabetic, so there's no sugar in it. The difference from other wine is that it's the purest product we can make — we don't have any artificial colouring or sweetening and the sulphur dioxide is absolutely minimum. It's matured for two to three years in wood, so it has a bit of age on it and the style is a sweet or dry sherry style.

When I'm attending mass at another parish, it's quite interesting for me that the wine being offered up has been made here. And I think it is very symbolic — the whole vineyard and the whole scriptural context of wine. When you see the vineyard as you've seen it today it's dormant, being pruned. Then spring comes and the new leaf, the grape — and when you talk about the work of human hands, a place like this is very conducive to the religious life which I lead because it's so close to nature. We have sheep, there are crops, there are all those sort of things around us. I feel that one can live and be close to God in these circumstances. Part of my life is that, and working with people.

Yet the commercial side of Sevenhill Cellars is uppermost. How did that come about and how is it balanced with religious aestheticism? 'We made a decision about 1972 to either stay as we were or move with the industry. We could not produce altar wine and run a place of this magnitude — and wine was moving, people were drinking it.' Revenue was the key to deciding to modernise the winery and market the wine.

We're here to try to raise funds for the Society of Jesus and that finance goes back into educating our young men, it helps with our Indian mission, it helps with our other apostolic work. We work with street kids in Melbourne, and with various people in Sydney's Kings Cross area. In Melbourne, we have a home for alcoholics — this might sound funny, running a winery and having a home for alcoholics, but these men are beyond treatment — and we help them to die in dignity. It's wonderful work, they can die in peace and it doesn't matter what religion they are, we're there to help them have a peaceful end to their life.

I classify wine as a gift to men from God. I have no problem whatsoever in aligning myself with the wine industry because we use it at mass, and it's like everything else in moderation. It can be a help to health — a good meal, company and, as you know, the old scripture says wine gladdens the heart of man. And that's true. But too much of it doesn't do much good for anyone.

Pruning at Sevenhill

Characters of the Industry

Peter and Lyn Serventy at their Valley Home Vineyard

Peter and Lyn Serventy

Peter and Lyn Serventy were in Darwin when cyclone Tracy hit and it changed the direction of their lives. 'That was one of those experiences which make you realise the value of life — and huge values that, perhaps, you don't realise in your everyday, humdrum existence. Having gone through that and deciding we wanted to live in the country and live a different lifestyle, we were more open to searching for things.'

They came to Margaret River the following year, 1976, attracted by the area and the idea of living on the land. They ran sheep before they planted a vineyard to grow grapes organically. Lyn explains:

I think anyone coming into agriculture in Australia these days really needs to farm sustainably — and I mean really sustainably, not half-hearted efforts. So far, agriculture in Australia has not exactly been a resounding success, in as far as what we've done to the country and the future. And so, that's really the basis of it. We've got to find a way of farming sustainably. In viticulture your soil is your principal asset and it's doubly important that you learn to care for that and look after it.

We did have to spend a lot of time on improving the soil because Australian soils are really old, they're really leached. This was a karri valley, it grew trees that were 50 metres high. But once they were cut down the soil lost all its humus and its life. It's a matter of getting that life back into the soil, so Pete set about making hundreds of tonnes of compost to get into the vineyard.

It's essential that you use as much carbon as you can get in the soil. It's very necessary. It feeds everything in the soil, all the micro-organisms, the bigger soil life, your earthworms. You need the humus in there or your soils are going to go back to being desert soils with no life in them at all. And what we find, interestingly, is that we put on less and less fertiliser, even a natural fertiliser, each year because the soil is working. So in the long run it does pay. You may have to put a lot of effort into it at first, but it brings its own rewards.

Local seaweed is one of the compost ingredients, as well as being made into a fungicide spray by Peter. 'I have an ethical problem about removing seaweed from the beaches, but I do make a small quantity of fungicide. It doesn't take very much seaweed and it's a valuable contribution to the vineyard — it has an importance out of all proportion to the input, really.'

Lyn picks up the thread:

A small amount of seaweed has a somewhat miraculous effect. You put a bit of seaweed in the compost and it'll really make a difference. I think they're only just starting to look into the properties of kelp, which humans have valued over the years for medicine, food and other things. But what is it in kelp that actually gets enzymes working in the soil?

And it's not only the compost in the earth, but companion plants with the vines.

You want some things that are going to put nitrogen into the soil, so you want your clovers and perhaps lupins and things like that. You want grasses because they go deep down into the soil and they will start activating the soil further down, otherwise your soil will remain shallow. And then you want flowering plants because they will attract insects and, basically, in an organic vineyard you want as wide and varied an insect life as you can. We've got some mustard planted here. And that's a plant which gives out a natural fumigant as it comes into flower. So in the early spring when this is slashed, it acts as a fumigant — we hope against some nasty weevils in the vineyard that we don't want at that particular time.

As certified organic growers, Peter and Lyn Serventy have to follow strict regulations in their Valley Home Vineyard, 300 kilometres south of Perth:

We can't use any synthetic chemical herbicides, any pesticides, any fungicides in the vineyard. If you're using naturally occuring chemicals such as sulphur as a fungicide, you treat it as a restricted input. So you never use it as a general preventative, you look at other methods as well.

Their organic outlook evolved from experience. The name Serventy has been made famous in Australian conservation by the naturalist Vincent Serventy, who is Peter's uncle. His father is the ornithologist Dominic Serventy. So they had a background in the natural world, even though Peter had been involved with tin prospecting and mining, and Lyn with theatre production and education:

At first we ran sheep here. It was a process of elimination of chemicals as we saw what they did — and I suppose we knew what they did. It really is a process of knowing a bit deeper down when you have your own bit of turf and you see how beautiful it is, you see that it's been beautiful for a long time and you want it to go on in that way. You see yourself as a temporary guardian of it, not owning it.

We're lucky. We have two permanent creeks running through our place and the water's really clean. It isn't saline. To us, they need as much protection as anything else and we get worried about the fact that, with the spread of viticulture in the area, there's a tendency for people to dam the creeks and rivers, and you see the impact of that. We've got a few rare native fish in this creek and we worry about whether they're going to survive.

The organic making of chardonnay, shiraz and pinot noir means that some chemicals used in modern winemaking are banned. There is a strict limit on the amount of sulphur dioxide you can use. Egg whites are used to soften the tannins of the reds, milk to fine the whites and an edible clay to eliminate unstable proteins.

We find we always have a good, clean finish to our wines. I've talked to other organic winemakers and they say the same thing. I think it's possibly because when you grow organically you get a good sugar–acid balance. So we never have to add acid to our wines, and often it's added acid which will give a nasty finish to the wine. You get a true varietal character which I suppose is because you're growing grapes as they've been grown over thousands of years. You generally have a good nose to the wine, too. People talk about vitality, but that's hard to quantify.

And are there qualities which might help people who are allergic to wine?

I think we have so much sulphur in our food and our air that suddenly the body becomes sensitive to it. So somebody who for years has been able to enjoy their glass of wine will suddenly start reacting to it and that can be the key. There can be sulphur reacting to other things in the wine. A sort of chemical cocktail.

Recently I read that the amount of potassium that goes into soils in chemical fertilisers increases the amount of histamines which a grape will take up. So we'd had people coming to us saying: 'I can drink your red wines and not get a headache, whereas normally I'll get a headache with red wines.' With red wine, who would think that was histamines, and we do a very full carbonic maceration on the skins and so they should have plenty of histamines. And then I suddenly twigged that perhaps what they're picking up is grapes which have been produced with a lot of chemical potassium put on the soil.

Along with an enviable lifestyle in beautiful surroundings and the sense of doing something in a way that doesn't harm the environment, the Serventys have a surprising house in Georgian style made of recycled materials. It was built by Peter:

I'm very interested in history and quite interested in the 18th century and its architecture. Coming down here gave me the opportunity to carry out this fantasy of building. I didn't know it was going to be a double-storey house until I saw the staircase in a building being demolished, a nurses' home. And that set me on the two floors, which I jumped into without really thinking of the consequences of how to get bricks and things up that high and that sort of stuff. But it came together. I was very dogged and took about ten years to do that and start the vineyard at the same time. I'm glad I did it, although at times I wondered why I started.

New Regions

Geelong

Geelong is not so much a new region as an old region that's new again. Seventy-two kilometres southwest of Melbourne on the Bellarine Peninsula, it was one of the first areas in Victoria to be planted with vines in 1842, developing into what was probably the largest grape growing area in Australia in its time — sadly and suddenly brought to an end in the late 1870s by the outbreak of phylloxera. The shiraz and pinot noir from Geelong, so highly prized by wine drinkers of the time, were gone.

But not forever. In 1966, the great-grandson of one of the Swiss community which settled in the Geelong region from the 1840s to the 1860s decided to bring the winemaking alive again. Daryl Sefton and his wife Nini began planting vines with the aim of making and selling wine back to their ancestral homes of England, Ireland, Scotland and Switzerland — which they did. And their Idyll Vineyard became the first of about 30 vineyards and 16 wineries that are now scattered throughout the Geelong region, which has since been precisely described and internationally recognised.

'It's a small property,' says Nini Sefton. 'Only 56 acres, and it had been used as a horse stud, a sheep stud, an orchard. Until we came, nobody had actually done any intensive farming. We particularly wanted something that was in the heart of the old wine region and this is just that. We wanted hills and dales, aesthetics as well as practicality. This whole valley is called the Moorabool Sands, it's a fabulous area and just perfect for what we wanted. In fact, it has an old wine cellar just on the base of the hill down here.'

And that cellar was Daryl Sefton's introduction to the place, as it turned out. He was still working as a vet then, on a very cold and rainy day in the early 1950s:

I came out to treat a little pony stallion that was in here, and none of the beauty of the surrounding area was visible. It was late at night and I was probably pretty grumpy. The little stallion was decidedly grumpy ...

The cellar has been here since the mid-1800s or thereabouts, and it's typical of the so-called cellars that are in the area of Geelong where there are hills. It's cut into the bottom of a hill and the soil has been heaped against one wall so that it provides a ramp up for the drays to bring the drums or casks or buckets of grapes that were crushed on the top storey, of which very little remains. In those days, it was all gravity feed and the fermentation would've gone on in this lower part. This was all brick paved and quite spectacular.

Sefton's great-grandfather Jakob Just, and his wife Rosine, came out with a group of Swiss and, after first working in the goldfields, bought La Pension Suisse in Geelong, a popular meeting place for their many compatriots in the area. Madame Just, who was called Rosina in Australia, also planted grape vines. It might seem surprising to find Australia was a magnet for Swiss settlers in the 19th century. The fact that Governor La Trobe's wife Sophie was Swiss may have had something to do with it. Many of them brought knowledge of growing grapes and making wine, which they put into practice, bringing their discussions of work into Sefton's great-grandparents' La Pension Suisse:

Daryl and Nini Sefton, Idyll Vineyard

This was kept alive, as far as I was concerned, by my father, who was also a vet. I used to go out with him on country calls after school or in holidays and on weekends, and he would recount to me these wonderful stories of the old days and the people. 'There's so-and-so's place ... that used to have vines on it ... that's another one over there ... that's so-and-so's place ...' All these names I grew up with, they were quite familiar to me.

Problems other than phylloxera played havoc with the area, according to Sefton. First the gold rush robbed it of labourers, then there was an economic slump, religious bigotry and finally the terrible disease brought in on infected cuttings from Europe:

There was a government proclamation to the effect that the vines would be ripped out from infected vineyards and from vineyards within a three-mile radius. So there was much sadness in some cases and joy in others because vineyards that were relatively unproductive ... well, there was a money-back vine pull deal and, for people whose heart wasn't in it, this was eminently valuable. Phylloxera mostly got the blame, but it was a transition time. There is also another fact that many of the bigger vignerons had daughters, and in those days daughters did not run vineyards. Times have changed.

After 32 years of achievements, disappointments, innovations in the winemaking process, awards for wines and exporting, the Seftons have decided to leave Idyll Vineyard. They say they have a lot more living to do — the decision revolved around Daryl's 70th birthday — and that it's time for new blood to take over.

Another wine lover from the area with a dream to fulfil, Geelong businessman Stuart Hooper, was already 70 when he decided to help revive his local wine district in the 1970s, and he sought out a younger winemaker to help realise that dream. This was Gary Farr, and the winery is Bannockburn, which is best known for its pinot and chardonnay, but also makes an elegant shiraz and a refreshing saignée.

Farr recalls the choice of the land:

There's a lot of soil with a limestone base which is very well recognised as being excellent for pinot noir and chardonnay. So that was one of the prime drawing factors. Also, the fact that there were some sandy gravels which suit shiraz and some sandy soil that suits cabernet. So we have four or five major soil types here. The only real drawback is that they can vary throughout one vineyard site, and that we can have the four soil types in a 20-acre block. This gives us a great deal of variation in the wines that we make.

I think one of the biggest problems is the climatic variables that we have here — principally wind — and that's why Bannockburn has built up a reputation of having some of the biggest and strongest pinot noirs. They have a lot of strength and backbone to them because of the very low-yielding vineyards. So it's the weather conditions combined with other factors, not so much the soil probably, that influences the level of vigour. We have a natural vigour — we don't have to go out and manipulate the vines by leaf plucking or hedging or taking crop off. Some would say it's too low a level to be economic, but then it really depends on whether you want to produce a fine wine — I mean, the best you possibly can — or be in that mediocre group of producing wine for the sake of producing it.

I think the future could be quite interesting. There are several reasons why Geelong hasn't been as popular as the Mornington Peninsula and the Yarra Valley. Production is one of them in that Geelong has always been seen as a relatively low-yielding area. Most people these days are planting vineyards that they believe have to be economic and have to produce three or four tonnes to the acre. And that's very difficult — not impossible, but difficult — to achieve down here. The other thing is the siting of the Yarra Valley and Mornington being close to Melbourne and people see it as being more acceptable and a nice place to have a vineyard. With Geelong, you've got to go through some pretty ordinary suburbs before you actually get here.

But I think it's coming. I mean, it's definitely coming. There's a big vineyard only a few kilometres away as the crow flies. Now that's a couple of hundred acres and another one next door to it that will probably be a hundred acres. I just hope that it comes more from small producers rather than multinationals moving in and planting huge blocks of vineyards. I really think it has a good future if people seek out particular sites, particular microclimates and sites to plant their vineyards. This willy-nilly planting on flat or easy planting ground really upsets me. People do things that are easy rather than do things for the sake of producing a better product. If people really look for the piece of ground they're going to plant, choose something specific for a specific grape variety and seek help from locals who have been here for a few years, I think there's great potential to grow some magnificent wines down here.

I had a fantastic opportunity here: an owner that was willing to back somebody that had the initiative and the drive to really produce some great wine. I was very fortunate to have someone like Stuart Hooper, who owned Bannockburn till he passed away in 1997, who had this attitude that, if you keep working hard, I'll keep supporting you. And that went with travelling and learning about wine overseas. And so we had a much broader outlook than many other producers I think — not only within Geelong, but throughout Australia — as to what wine should taste like and what we should strive for in a much cooler climate. We wanted something that people would say: 'This is different, this has its own particular character and flavour.' We went about making wine that we thought was quite complex and had the right balance and a lot of length to it and went really well with food. Stuart never said to me: 'This venture has to make money.' It was more: 'Let's do the best we can, let's show people what Bannockburn can produce.'

Bannockburn wines tend to be kept back for a few years before they are released:

The cool climate means that everything develops more slowly. The wines develop much slower and the attitude to winemaking is that we try to extract as much flavour and character as we can. All those flavours and characters need to settle down in the bottle so the chardonnay and the pinot are given a year in barrel — a little bit more — then a year in bottle to really come together before they are released.

Slowness of ripening in a climate kept cool by the proximity of the ocean and the winds led to the planting of shiraz on a south-facing hillside being a mistake, and there is a balancing act in choosing the direction of the vine rows:

> We have experimented with placing vineyards facing north–south, but running east–west. And we've found that we get better wind protection by doing that. The vine actually creates its own microclimate within the vineyard. But really the answer to that is to plant more windbreaks around the property and thin out the wind a bit to create it that way — and still have the vine running north–south so it gets most of the sun during the day as the sun goes over from east to west.

Gary Farr, winemaker, Bannockburn, tasting saignée with Maryann Egan

Another challenge in the cooler climes is to get weight of colour and richness in the wine. Farr explains the secret:

> Saignée is a trick that I picked up in France, it's quite common in Burgundy. It means to bleed or take blood. In ancient French times, they believed that by bleeding someone, they could make them well. So the winemakers took this on as a way of getting the flavour and richness of their pinot noir or shiraz type wines — to drain some juice off very early on in the process. It's got a lovely pink hue, a salmon hue. We put the juice directly into some older wood and then ferment it just like chardonnay. And we end up with this very soft rosé style. It's rich but soft and very perfumed. It's a very pleasant wine to drink on a summer's evening.
>
> And because we have reduced the amount of liquid in the other wine, there is a greater skin-to-juice ratio, and the flavour and colour comes from the skins. Some of the French don't like to do this process because they believe that you're draining off the best juice from the richest grapes. Some of them would rather prune their vines or take some fruit off their vines to reduce the amount of wine they make for a vineyard. But this is just a different technique and I think we're enhancing the red wine that we make by taking this off rather than reducing its quality.

OPPOSITE:
Corio Bay and Geelong skyline

Scotchmans Hill is on the highest point of the Bellarine Peninsula, a source of benefits and disadvantages according to winemaker Robin Brockett:

The benefits are, we don't normally have very cold winters. To have a frost is quite rare, so we don't even have to think about it. The problem is mainland wind and that does have a huge effect on the vineyards here, mainly through damage, especially in spring when we get severe northerlies. As a consequence of this, we do find crops are reduced — which is an advantage to winemaking. So we do have some problems but, at the end of the day, we plant a lot of windbreaks to try to cut it down — and I think it does lead partly to some of the character we have in our wines.

We tend to find we have very high colour in the wines and a lot of flavour, and this is also due to the heavy soils we have here. A combination of the climate ... the wind cutting down on cropping levels, slowing the ripening down because in midsummer, when we have very warm days, it tends to be quite a bit cooler here, and the interaction of the wine with the heavy soils ... overall making quite a big robust style of wine with lots of flavour.

Brockett buys grapes from other growers, but it is all local and bought for reasons in addition to keeping up volume:

Especially with pinot noir, we're finding that different vineyards are giving different characters to the wine and we're trying to make a very complex wine so by utilising fruit from vineyards grown in different areas, we're finding we're getting quite different wines. The second consideration is trying to get our volume up so, until our vineyards come on stream, we certainly need a supply of fruit. Presently, probably 50 per cent of our vineyards are producing. Our supply is well and truly outstripped by demand.

A lot of changes have taken place at Scotchmans Hill since Brockett arrived at the beginning of 1988, starting with the need to bring it up from 'pretty poor condition ... from a vineyard that had no crop, even after five or six years of being in the ground, to cropping at an economic level which is sustainable for us. We're aiming at a cropping level of around three tonnes to the acre and by doing this we're able to get fruit that is very high in colour, flavour and very clean. Having the raw product and the base there to work with, we're able to turn out what I think are excellent wines.' Judging by the success of Scotchmans Hill, wine lovers agree.

At the moment, we have a huge expansion program in place, both vineyard and winery. We're looking at expanding our plantings probably threefold over the next three years. We're doing this to get high quality fruit, but also to have a lot more control over what's happening with our wines by growing a lot of the fruit ourselves. We'll still buy in high quality fruit from growers, and that's very important as far as the blending aspect of the winemaking is concerned. It's very important to have control over what we're doing to maintain that high quality. I'm a firm believer in low crop per vine … that's where the flavour comes in. There's only so much flavour that can go round and, if you overcrop, you dilute, especially with pinot noir. That's our main variety, and that's where the majority of our developments will be. Certainly, this year there are around 20 acres of pinot noir going in at different climes, so we're really putting a huge investment into that variety and it's a variety of the future.

Robin Brockett, winemaker, Scotchmans Hill, making a trellis

Rotten grapes can make exquisite wine. That is, if it's the

or noble rot may look like a disaster on the vine, but it is

Botrytis

lovingly by winemakers who know how to turn

fungus-covered grapes

Botrytis

flavour is so distictive and delicious that they could

Botrytis

kind of rot and a skilful winemaker. Botrytis cinerea

Botrytis

rich golden wine of intense flavour and complexity. Dessert wines, some people call them, but they

Botrytis

well be a dessert on their own.

Botrytis

*R*otten grapes can make exquisite wine. That is, if it's the right kind of rot and a skilful winemaker. *Botrytis cinerea* or noble rot may look like a disaster on the vine, but it is nurtured lovingly by winemakers who know how to turn these fungus-covered grapes into a rich golden wine of intense flavour and complexity.

Darren De Bortoli is one such winemaker. His botrytis semillon, the Noble One, is Australia's most acclaimed sticky — the affectionately mundane nickname for these superb sweet wines. Dessert wines, some people call them, but their flavour is so distinctive and delicious that they could just as well be a dessert on their own.

The De Bortoli family vineyard where it all began is just outside Griffith in the Riverina district of New South Wales, not far from the borders of Victoria and South Australia. It's a hot, dry area dependent on irrigation for its bountiful crops of grapes and fruit. Vittorio De Bortoli settled there from Italy in 1924 and, with his wife Giuseppina, established what was to become one of Australia's largest family-owned wine companies.

Their grandson Darren, now managing director of De Bortoli Wines, became interested in sweet wines when he was studying oenology at Roseworthy Agricultural College: 'I absolutely fell in love with a French sticky, Chateau Coutet '75, which was one of the great years in Bordeaux, and I was fascinated by the complexities and length of flavour.' He and fellow students such as Tim Knappstein and Joe Corelli were getting the botrytis fungus to grow in special rooms with humidity and temperature control.

Back home in the Riverina, Darren De Bortoli told his grandfather how much he would like to make sweet wine. He'd assumed the climate would probably be too hot and dry, but grandfather Vittorio assured him the fungus would grow in the area and pulled out a bottle of McWilliam's botrytis semillon, the first made in Australia in the mid-1950s. In 1982, Darren decided to give it a go, simply leaving some semillon vines with their grapes well beyond normal harvest, inviting the fungus to attack the ripe grapes through the berry skin, evaporating their water content and concentrating their flavour and sweetness.

'We didn't know whether they would just shrivel up and we'd lose the crop. We watched these grapes week after week, month after month, then finally we got into a situation that the noble rot, the fungus started spreading quite nicely.'

The timing turned out to be perfect.

At the same time, one of the local wineries had run into financial difficulty and they'd left a lot of their growers stranded with semillon hanging on the vines at that stage. A lot of these growers heard that we were taking these rotten grapes and they thought we were crazy. So we were inundated with all these growers saying, 'My grapes are rotten' and that they'd heard we were paying good prices. It was quite funny, because we'd go to the vineyards and, lo and behold, some had fantastic noble rot infection … though others were not so good. So, in 1982, we were very fortunate, we had a reasonably large pool of grapes to select from.

Darren De Bortoli, winemaker

Given the grapes, he knew there were characteristics of making the sweet wine that were different from normal wine, but he wasn't sure precisely what they were, so a lot of trial and error went into that pioneering 1982 vintage. 'The first year, I remember it picking up something like seven gold medals and it started to cause a bit of a storm in the wine industry. The second year it picked up more, and I think its total of medals is in excess of 50 or 60 in its show career. It's probably one of the most awarded wines ever made in Australia.'

Times were tough for the wine industry in 1982, but the Noble One was a challenge that Darren De Bortoli couldn't pass by. Although money was tight and some people thought it was 'sheer lunacy to go on with a harebrained idea of developing this classic wine style', the choice turned out to be inspired — and inspiring. 'Besides becoming a classic in its on right, the style gave us the confidence to pursue some of our other dreams. One was to establish a winery and vineyard in the Yarra Valley, which we were able to do in 1987.'

The success of the De Bortoli Noble One botrytis semillon has triggered similar ventures by other companies without topping its dominance, but keeping its makers on their toes. It's a tricky style to make for a variety of reasons:

One of the hardest problems is to know when to pick. Once you've got that right, then everything else is just a question of making sure you don't make a mistake in making the wine. There are enormous technical problems with making these sweet wines.

The botrytis fungus is no different to most moulds: they like high humidity and warm temperatures. We're fortunate that once we get to late April, early May, we start to get those ideal temperatures, ranging from six to seven degrees Celsius minimum up to about 22°C. We've found that over the years we've been making this, there's probably one in three years tends to be a very wet year. And with a very wet year, you tend to find there's a sort of secondary mould infection occurring in the wines so that they have an extensive botrytis influence and will probably be a lot more complex.

One in three years as a rule tends to be a bit too dry, and those years we may not pick grapes until June, which is getting exceptionally late and they tend to be more classical in style ... where you know the botrytis influence is there, but it's not as obvious as some wines of other years. And one in three tends to be an absolutely fantastic year where we get perfect botrytis influence in very clean growing conditions. It's interesting, though, that the one in three years that's extremely wet, the wines tend to remind me stylistically more of European styles than what we'd take as our benchmark style.

De Bortoli's chief winemaker Steve Warne and senior winemaker Karen Leggett have mixed responses to their responsibilities in taking over the Noble One from Darren De Bortoli. Warne says it is 'just such a thrill to be working with it' and Leggett finds it 'nerve wracking', though 'really exciting too, really pleasurable'. As they talked, Steve was up to his fifth vintage and Karen was doing her third — and they were moving up to the vital decision of when to pick the grapes.

Making the wrong decision can lead to everything being too dry or not dehydrated enough. It can happen so fast that you can overshoot or undershoot pretty quickly. The wine is a quality wine that is made due to the unique conditions of this area ... so the result isn't entirely due to human efforts, it's a freak of nature that occurs in this area with our grapes.

There's a lot of luck involved, but we're trying to eliminate that aspect. We take regular samplings of the vineyards and there's a number of them so it's a big job — once a week then three times a week. We try to be methodical and precise about what we do each time, which involves walking through the vineyards and taking note of the condition of the fruit and sampling. Then, based on that, plus a lot of experience as to how the prevailing weather conditions will affect the dehydration of the rotted berries of the next few days, start to plan our picking sequence. We also work with the local Charles Sturt University doing ongoing research with them, trying to make the process a bit more predictable in terms of estimating picking dates.

Botrytis cinerea *or noble rot*

Just a single day can make a huge difference. 'We can have pretty heavy frosts, and following that the vineyards can dehydrate if we've got a sunny day ... and defoliate, and once the leaves have gone you haven't got a chance ... so you have these odd-looking vineyards with no leaves, packed with fruit with mould dripping off them.'

Although De Bortoli has experimented with machine picking for the

Noble One, it doesn't seem likely to be extended. Warne and Leggett explain:

Karen Leggett and Darren De Bortoli in the laboratory

> Hand picking is really the way we get them off here. Crushed in a crusher, put into a tank where they're left overnight in contact with the juice up to twelve hours. We make a decision when we see the grapes how long we leave that skin contact because that's where we get a lot of sugar out.
>
> Then after a day — or the amount of time that we've decided — the juice is drained off and settled in a tank. The skins go through a press, the juice is pressed out of those skins really hard. Both fractions are separated, usually they go back together later, then they're settled, centrifuged, and that gives you the sort of clean juice to start your fermentation with. So it takes about three days to get to the fermentation stage and then we use a special yeast that's tolerant to high levels of sugar and alcohol. We try to ferment it as quickly and safely as possible, and then it's a matter of cleaning up the wine, getting it bright and yeast-free. When it comes in, it looks like mud. It's amazing. Whoever first decided to make wine out of it must have had a vision …'

A vision indeed. After 12 to 18 months in wood, then another year's bottle age it will be ready for the market. But may be many years after that before the patient connoisseur will drink it. The clue to its possible longevity — depending on the many climatic and technical elements involved in making it — is offered by Darren De Bortoli:

> I like to be surprised by the wine every now and again, and it certainly does that to you. We've tried to make the style something that has some aging ability. You see some of these older wines and you just don't know how lasting it will be. I sometimes think, aren't I fortunate? They really do surprise you. It's like everything, I suppose: when you get so close to something, you know that attraction starts to wear off — and then you see it in a different context and you really start to appreciate it again.
>
> The '82 is now 16 years old. It's still holding up. The colours are changing, it's starting to go to amber. The flavour's still there. I would think that the wine, even though the colours are changing, would still be intact for another ten to 15 years.

But how many people could wait that long to find out?

Grappa

Tony Zorzit pouring grappa

Grappa is a drink for all reasons and all seasons. It began as a fiery beverage made by peasants in Italy, who saved their grape skins after pressing them for wine and stored them away until less busy winter days for distilling into grappa with a distinctively mouldy taste. These days, commercial production is a much more sophisticated business using a copper still, stainless steel tanks, maturing in oak and flavouring with the herb *ruta* — rue in English — to get a softer, more aromatic result.

What has not changed is the spirit with which grappa is consumed. At the Fogolar Furlan Club in Sydney, Silvano Duri, Beppi Polese and Tony Zorzit compare memories and a tasting of grappa in robust good humour. Polese is, of course, renowned in Sydney for his restaurant Beppi's, but the family also produces three styles of Manzoni grappa from 15 acres of grapes at Orchard Hills in the city's west: the pure distillate, oak matured and flavoured with *ruta*.

This is what you call sipping grappa. I'm used to the old style — one gulp and you drink it down. It only burns you once. But if there's one drink I love, it's grappa. I don't drink it very often because it's a very strong drink, but it's also a very nice drink. If you take it in moderation, you can enjoy it for years and years, but if you indulge, it's going to get you. (Zorzit)

In the morning, you start with one. Sip it and then gargle and it kills the germs. But most of the time, in the villages, they used to go after dinner to play cards and there was the grappa, especially in the winter. They used to drink the grappa, but when they left it was very cold outside and warm inside, and your ears would crack — you could hear them cracking. It's true — the contrast between the heat and the grappa intake. But you sleep well, too, after that. (Polese)

You know what they used to do, maybe 70 or 80 years ago, when a young kid was sick with flu or something, one or two nips of grappa and tomorrow it was fixed. No problem. (Duri)

I started drinking grappa when I was 14 because everybody had grappa in the family — they used to make it themselves, out of the wine, out of the grapes. Every family used to make grappa. It was a common drink that we grew up with. (Zorzit)

Our villagers had two or three hectares of land — they used to grow everything for the family. They used to grow white and red grapes, and mix everything together to produce a wine of nine or ten per cent alcohol. After ferment, they used to just squeeze or drip the grape, then they have a second or third pressing, and they would have a by-product to produce the grappa. They picked the grape around September, stored the skins away in some container and covered it with sand. They used to distil the grappa in the winter, around December. Because the dry pressing was mouldy, they would use a pot and put timber on the bottom so the skins wouldn't stick, put in some water and steam. That is why the grappa is slightly mouldy. (Polese)

The reason it's not very popular with the young generation is because they've got more fancy name drinks now. These days, the kids don't go back to the roots like we do and drink the grappa. 'It's too strong,' they say. 'Yuck.' As they grow older, they'll enjoy it more. (Zorzit)

The grappa we produce ourselves is from muscatel grape. They separate the stalk then squeeze, separate the juice and ferment. In the end, we put 50 per cent skin, 50 per cent juice and distil it. This is the pleasure of the grappa because you get the combination, and the flavour being muscatel grape. This is not mouldy. This is an elegant grappa. Like everything in life, what you eat and what you drink is nice if you can enjoy it. (Polese)

Silvano Duri, left, and Beppi Polese

Characters of the Industry

Brian Croser, winemaker, company executive and industry leader

Brian Croser

There are many reasons to know the name Brian Croser. Born and educated in South Australia, he has based his career there by establishing Petaluma, producing a range of premium table and sparkling wines that has been reinforced and expanded through Australian acquisitions in the 1990s. Concurrently with his dual role as Petaluma's winemaker and executive chairman — since it was listed as a public company in 1993 — Croser has moved into the United States, where he is founder and chief executive of the Dundee Wine Company near Portland, Oregon.

This international spread of wine production responsibilities hasn't stopped Croser from involvement in Australian industry matters, which have occupied him for much of his professional life. He was re-elected president of the Winemakers Federation of Australia in 1997, having held that position from 1991 to 1995. He has been president of the Australian Winemakers Forum and the Australian Society of Viticulture and Oenology. He was a member of the Industry Commission's inquiry into the wine industry and a director of the South Australian Development Council.

So, when Brian Croser talks about the Australian wine industry, it's from a position of considerable knowledge and experience. What has brought him from the winery to the meeting room?

A sense of responsibility first of all, because I think this industry does have an enormous potential, for itself and for Australia, and I hate to see potential truncated. It needs to be fully exploited for the benefit of those in it and for Australia. It's one of the few things that Australia can do much better than almost anywhere else in the world. And specifically South Australia, too. It's very important for South Australia.

The second issue is that if you create a dream and an image, as I have, of Petaluma being a top-class world company making some of the best table wines made anywhere in the world, it needs the right environment in which to do that. You can't do that if you don't have the right research and education inputs. If you don't have the right economic environment in which to act with governments. If the government has got the wrong taxation system imposed on the industry. If the Australian wine industry has the wrong image overseas. So Petaluma needs an environment in which to work, as does every other Australian wine company — and to help mould that environment is one of the motivations.

Taxation is a big issue for the industry, but it's not the biggest issue. It's an emotive and divisive issue. Government in Australia — and this is generalising all governments — has an appallingly inconsistent approach to taxation on the wine industry and doesn't understand what the wine industry is. But there are much bigger issues than tax. There is research and development and education. There's the international connection, the trade barriers. There's the image of Australian wine overseas. There's the domestic economy and how that supports domestic sales, which is the basis for export success. They're more important than tax. But tax certainly gets the wine industry motivated.

And how does he view the wine industry today?

I'd like to see less complacency than we have now. There are a lot of newcomers to the industry — and I think there should always be that — who fundamentally have walked into probably the most prosperous era the industry has ever had in its existence. And to some extent, those people think that's the way it always is, has been — and that's not the case. To some extent, these people are harvesting

the investment of previous generations in what this industry is — in research and education and in attitude and culture and image overseas and so on — and are not making a contribution to it. In fact, are beginning to think they invented it, which is not the case. I'd like to see more from those people, more recognition that more has to be done, that they're not just here to harvest the rewards. And more has to be done in all sorts of aspects of industry administration and in enhancing the image of the industry.

Conversely, at a practical level of winemaking, he praises the way that knowledge is shared amongst his colleagues and competitors:

There's a spirit of generosity which prevails and everybody in our industry, especially the Australian wine industry, understands that as much as you give away, you get back. It's really an evolving science if you like, and there are lots of contributors around the world. The great thing, though, the most satisfying thing, is to pass on some of the experience and some of the attitudes and some of the science to younger people. I've got a team of young people down here — it's a bit like a university in itself in a funny sort of way — who are enormously energetic and enthusiastic, and I enjoy seeing them develop.

I think we have not only embraced technology, we've also given it a shove here and there and made it move along. There is a sort of an anathema amongst the wine media of the world to the word technology. That's almost antithetical from their viewpoint to art, creativity, tradition. Science and tradition seem to be in conflict. That's absolute rubbish. The best of technology enables you to nurture wine more than even the traditional methods have allowed very good winemakers of the past to nurture their wines. Where technology is abused in overprocessing and overproduction, it gets a bad reputation. Whereas, used properly, it really advances the cause of the art of science, the art of winemaking — the science of wine advancing the cause of the art.

The first stage of a winemaker's career is to learn to be competent scientifically and to approach grape growing and winemaking in an orderly fashion. That first phase is incredibly important. The art of wine can only be built on the science of wine. The second phase is to recognise that, however technically competent you are and however much you're at the cutting edge of things, other people will copy you. So, if you want to stay ahead, you've got to own something unique. And the uniqueness of a vineyard — where it is, where it looks towards the sun, its soil and its climate — is the one thing that other people can't copy readily. People who want to make Petaluma Chardonnay would have to own this vineyard to do that.

Petaluma, which Croser established in 1976, has vineyards in three grape-growing regions of South Australia: the Clare Valley for riesling, Piccadilly Valley in the Adelaide Hills for pinot noir and chardonnay, and Coonawarra for cabernet sauvignon and merlot.

We've inherited this need to draw a line around our regions in Australia from our bilateral trade agreement with Europe.

And Europe is a highly constrained industry. It's all tied up in the chains of appellation, where you can only use certain varieties grown at certain crop levels, managed in certain ways and in certain districts. And we've tried to avoid that. Our bilateral trade agreement means that we've had to draw lines around our regions. Australia's as regionalised in wine as California, South Africa or Chile. Not as regionalised as Europe. And regions are very valuable things.

But do they cause friction? 'When you draw a boundary, someone is always left on one side and somebody else is left on the other. It tends to be that the ones left on the right side get richer and the ones left on the wrong side get poorer. So you get into some pretty emotional arguments about where those boundaries should go. And of course that's been the case in Coonawarra and a couple of other notable issues.' As Croser is personally aware, since Petaluma's vineyard interests in the Coonawarra area are outside the region's traditional boundary.

And how does he see his future?

I think that making wine is a lifelong process and the older you get, the more experienced you get. The more grape vines you've seen and the more harvests you've been through, the more wines you've made and, especially if you're dealing with a defined number of vineyards as I do — and I know those vineyards like my own children — the better you get, the better the wines are. I don't think there's ever been a revolutionary young Turk who has instantly made great wine. I guess a small percentage of the old-timers get through to the point where they've been dedicated for long enough and are able enough to have made a collection of great wines, like O'Shea for example. I hope I'm making the transition along that pathway. Time will tell.

Right at the core of everything that I've done with Petaluma has been my insistence that I have to remain very much in the cellar, in the vineyard, and I've managed to achieve that. My connection to the product is absolute and, if it wasn't, I wouldn't be interested in the sort of growth that either Petaluma or the Australian wine industry is going through. In other words, if I had to sacrifice my role in the cellar, then I wouldn't go up the scale to being president of the Winemakers Federation or the CEO of Petaluma. I'd rather stay right where I was, which is as winemaker. Fortunately, I've been able to accommodate the two.

The wine industry around the world is a wonderful industry. It's in the best climates, the best looking geography. It's got restaurants, it's got culture, it's got great people. Great cellars. You can always find good food and great wine. And people are generous and open in the world wine industry. I feel privileged to be part of it.

Characters of the Industry

Allan Watson, wine merchant, restauranteur and son of Jimmy

Jimmy Watson

There are plenty of awards and medals for Australian wines these days, but none of them equals the legendary aura of the Jimmy Watson Trophy for a young red wine. It wasn't always that way — but then the wine industry itself has changed a lot over the last three decades as well. And the Watson family has been there all along, with the third generation now taking turns behind Jimmy Watson's wine bar in the Melbourne suburb of Carlton.

When Jimmy Watson opened his bar in 1935, most of the wine consumed in Australia was fortified. But Watson's father had Italian blood, so he was familiar with the pleasures of table wine accompanying food. He opened his bar with an Australian Wine Licence, which permitted only local wine to be sold, and people would bring sandwiches and sit in the garden or around the few tables inside.

Allan Watson, son of the founder, recalls that his father found there were:

> … a lot of wineries making table wines that they couldn't sell and didn't market — people like Brown's. So he used to call himself a 'wine distributing centre' and he would get these wines, bottle them down here and invite people to come and taste them, then sell them to take home.

> It was an interesting period because the Services were based in Melbourne and those people basically knew about wine, so we had the heads of departments coming down. We had a room which is outside — now the kitchen — and that was prized as a convention area. We once had very senior-ranking people from the Air Force come down and they wanted that room for a particular function. They walked in and they found the Navy in there. Actually, it was the Air Marshal who walked in, and he opened the door and said 'Bloody Navy'. In those days we had to ask all the drivers to park around the corner because it looked very bad to have the admirals' and officers' cars out front.

The clientele at Jimmy Watson's was always a great mixture, reflecting the gregarious attitude of the man himself, with his dislike of pomposity and his genuine enthusiasm for people, his sense of humour and his love of a good story. His customers regarded themselves as friends, and he treated them with kindness and generosity. When he started the wine bar, still well within the days of six o'clock closing, he continued to work as a musician in the evenings, and he always had musicians, as well as actors and artists, amongst his regulars, along with truck drivers, lawyers and salesmen. With an address of 333 Lygon Street, Carlton, it was natural that he attracted students and academics from nearby Melbourne University. It was a place for lively exchanges in addition to its relaxing qualities.

Jimmy Watson was only fifty-eight when he died. As well as running his bar for twenty-six years, he loved to go sailing and was a member of the Royal St Kilda Yacht Club. He was a keen photographer and showed unexpected talents for renovation, and making and repairing things with the woodworking and metal-working machinery he had at home. He had friends and skills ranging over many walks of life.

The Jimmy Watson tradition of tasting young red wine was the cue for the trophy that has become his memorial:

When my father died in 1962, the people here at the funeral decided to honour his memory by having something to remember him by. So they organised a trophy which was not meant to be what it is now, it was just something honouring an honest wine merchant. But now it's just exploded into such a marvellous experience. It's left to Victoria's Royal Agricultural Society to administer and it is for the best eighteen-month-old red wine of the Royal Melbourne Wine Show.'

The first 16 Jimmy Watson Trophy winners were South Australian and this State has continued to dominate the competition, with Victoria and Western Australia dipping in a toe a few times.

Food came into Jimmy Watson's wine bar in 1962, but it was only secondary to the wine in those days. Now there is a much greater emphasis on food, especially in promoting partnerships between food and wine. In 1996, in addition to its traditional hearty fare, Jimmy Watson's opened a restaurant upstairs for dinner, matching vintage wine with a sophisticated menu devised by chef Steve Szabo. Simon Watson, one of the third generation, says the clientele is as diverse as it has always been, with its mix of lecturers and students, and people coming out from the city for lunch and dinner.

'We've introduced a lot more wine', he says in naming changes from his grandfather's time to today. 'We used to bring wine down from the vineyards and siphon it off out the back, and sell a lot of wine that way. We've certainly diversified our range of wines and we have a lot of estate bottled wines from various areas across Australia.'

And does he enjoy wine? 'Oh yeah, absolutely. I love wine. It's certainly been a great deal to do with my upbringing and, you know, a lot of winemakers are really lovely, genuine people — great people to know and passionate about their product. It's a pleasure to sell their wine.'

Collecting Wine

Wine lovers' heaven would probably be something like James Halliday's cellar. Line after line of dusty bottles with vintages going back decades, wine that has been stored with care to reach its mature potential before it is consumed. Anyone can do it — anyone strong enough to resist tasting before time — as Halliday points out in a short guide to collecting wine, a topic about which he has written a book.

I started with wine under a bed, many, many years ago when I was a university student. So storage doesn't have to be grand. You don't have to have a formal room dedicated as a cellar. If you get styrene boxes, which are extremely good insulators, or even cardboard cartons — if you can resist the temptation of continuously opening them and getting into them. Stack those cartons one on top of the other and, providing they're in a dry place, you'll find that both of those are good thermal barriers. And they'll also keep out the other enemy of wine, which is light.

Halliday's cellar is 'towards the Rolls Royce end', as befits a man whose career in wine has embraced vigneron, winemaker, wine judge, journalist, author and wine consultant.

It's got double brick: two brick walls with insulation between the bricks. The ceiling is concrete, it's got a house on top of that, it backs into the side of a hill and is partly underground. We are in southern Victoria and you would think that the temperature would vary very little. I keep a thermometer which tells me the truth. Here we are at 14.2°C, when you will find that it has been as high as 19°C in the summer. So even in a preferred circumstance like this, you do get variation. It doesn't matter nearly so much if the temperature gradually shifts warmer in summer and cooler in winter. The killer is if you have got high day time/low night time temperatures. Because that leads to rapid expansion and contraction of the wine in the bottle.

If you decide to air condition your wine collection, there is another problem:

Unless it is refrigeration type cooling, you do need a humidifier. Because a normal house air conditioner will do quite a good job on temperature, but it will reduce the humidity well below the 75 per cent that's desirable and your corks will dry out. It's quite dramatic. High humidity in a cellar may lead to the labels looking like they've got some dreaded fungus growing on them and falling off. That's aggravating, as well as being unsightly, but it's certainly not harmful to the wine. A damp cellar is, by and large, better than an excessively dry one.

Wildlife can also damage your wine — even empty the bottles:

I have here the consequence of a rat attack on a lead capsule — probably trying to get the glue underneath it. I had some old bottles which a rat took a particular liking to and ate his way through the capsule. Then started with the cork. I was away for six weeks and came back and found six bottles of 1918 sauterne empty because the rats had pushed all the corks in. It was unbelievable.

And cork moth. I don't have too many like this, but on the top you can see crumbling, like you would see with any borer insect — the sign

Wine & Wherefore

GLASSWARE

There seems to be a trend these days to serve wine in the largest glasses possible. People appear to think bigger is better. Whilst this is not necessarily true, certain wine styles and grape varieties are suited to particular shaped and sized glasses.

Try tasting wine out of a cafe latte glass and see how much you enjoy it. You just do not get the flavour of a full-bodied wine. The aroma simply vanishes with the open shape of these glasses. This is an extreme case, but even a standard bistro wine glass will not help wine to show all its characters. Wine is much better suited to a glass with a long, slightly tapering barrel or you may wish to use a large shiraz glass when the wine is big in flavour. The biggest glass will concentrate and highlight the intensity of the wine.

Never pour too much wine in the glass — one-third full at the most. You need that space so that you can swirl the wine around in the glass and release the bouquet.

A more delicate red wine variety such as pinot noir has sweeter fruit with lighter, more perfumed characters. It is better suited to a bowl-shaped glass to trap this perfume.

Modest wine, however, will get lost in these big bowls. So if you are about to open a cheaper wine, do not think that a large, deluxe glass will improve the flavour. It has to be there in the first place.

White wine is typically less intense than red and is best suited to a medium-sized glass that bowls out in the middle, but tapers at the top to trap the bouquet.

Whatever shape or size glass you use, cleanliness is paramount. Any glass can be tainted through lack of care in washing and storage.

of activity — and you can even see at the side of the cork that the cork moth has been active. I have pest strips in the winery to deal with that.

As for uninvited guests of the human variety, all serious wine collectors keep their wine secure and are confident that it would be very hard to dispose of stolen wine because the auction houses can be alerted to it.

White wines are more susceptible to heat or slightly adverse storage conditions. Red wines are that little bit more robust. Fortified wines — it doesn't matter. Sparkling wines are normally not kept for a long period anyway, and certainly there is no particular trap about that. Sometimes you have people asking: 'I put a bottle of sparkling wine into my refrigerator and I kept it there for a month: is it dead?' and the answer is no, it has virtually no effect on it.

Part of James Halliday's wine collection

What are the joys of collecting wine?

Well, there is this thing that drives us collectors of stamps or works of art or anything — so there is the pure collecting element of it. I'm very opposed to the show-and-tell type of cellar that is exposed to too much light and typically too much heat, which you find is constantly used as a place of entertainment. I mean, normally I come into a cellar for one purpose and one purpose alone — well, two. One is to put wine in, but, more relevantly, it is to take wine out. One of my mottos is that when I take a bottle or a number of bottles out of this cellar, it doesn't cost me a thing. It costs me when I put it in, but it costs me nothing when I take it out, and that's why I'm never hesitant about drinking the good bottles. And what an awful thought that someone less deserving than me, after I'm gone, should be drinking them. No, not really … but you get the drift.

There is also the pleasure of a bargain:

Chassagne-Montrachet for $12.95, 1982 vintage, bought in 1984. It was a time when the dollar was very strong against the French franc, about double the exchange rate of today, give or take a little bit, favourable to Australia. So I bought quite a lot of that and, even if it cost me $12.95, it's not very expensive. That's one of the joys of the cellar. We're all human at the end of the day and you know that if you bought something wonderfully well, perhaps it adds to the pleasure when you drink it. I'm not sure it affects me too much, but that bottle today … well, the current vintage of a Chassagne-Montrachet would be

not less than $70 or $80 and an '82, which was a good year
in white burgundy, would bring more at auction.

Halliday has about 15,000 bottles in his collection:

*James Halliday in his
cellar*

Every bottle of wine that I have bought, has been bought with
the intention of drinking. Clearly, I'm not going to drink them
all and maybe someone, somewhere along the line, might
make a decision to sell them. I might do so. I don't think I will,
but … You don't set out with the idea of creating an enormous
cellar, you get infected by the wine bug and you start realising the
enormous diversity of wonderful wines that there are, not only from
Australia, but also from all around the globe and there's so much to
choose from. And that's been particularly marked in recent years with a
much wider selection of higher quality European, Chilean and Italian
wines coming into the country, so the choice and the scope for
collecting continues to widen all the time.

There are two sorts of collectors. One buys wine because they really
love it and they intend to drink it. Then there is the investment collector.
Now I think one of the great pities of the price hike of wines like
Grange and Hill of Grace is the realisation that it's estimated that 60
per cent of Grange is bought by investors who do not have any
intention of drinking it. That, to me, takes wine away from the thing that
it ought to be, which is the source of enormous pleasure, infinitely
variable, always exciting, always fun, to something which it ought not
to be. But if you think about it, people can't go on collecting 60 per
cent of Grange as an investment forever, it's finally got to start coming
back on the market. When it does come back in, you'll probably see
prices soften. You won't see these crazy rises of the last few years.

It was said of Andre Simon that, wasn't it wonderful, he died when
he was 90-something with only one bottle left in his cellar. My answer
to that is that's exactly why he died — because he realised he had only
one bottle left. And, by having 15,000, I'm going to ensure myself
immortality.

About the Presenters

Maryann Egan

Maryann Egan

It was almost as if Maryann Egan were born to make wine. As a child, she toured the great wineries of France with her parents and sister — two unwilling young travellers on an adult quest. Her father, a lawyer, was so entranced by the making of wine that he had planted a vineyard the year before she was born and took up winemaking fulltime in 1984.

On leaving school, Maryann qualified in physical education then set off on a solo trip to France. 'When I was overseas, it occurred to me that physical education was not really my bag, and I couldn't get passionate about it.' Instead, she decided to study French and enrol in a winemaking course at university there. She got as far as being accepted, but changed her mind on the grounds that the course was too narrow and the whole venture would be too expensive. She came back to Australia and studied wine science at Charles Sturt University instead.

She laughs when she recalls how she and her sister — now a chef running Becco, one of Melbourne's leading restaurants, with her restaurateur husband — grumbled about being 'dragged around vineyards' and taken into 'boring, cold, underground cellars'. They would be working on their father's vineyard every Saturday, when friends were doing other things that seemed to be much more appealing.

These days, Maryann shares the management of that vineyard, Wantirna Estate, with her father. She is responsible for the winemaking and overseeing the vineyard and vintage procedures. Less than an hour from Melbourne, in the Yarra Valley green belt which is increasingly being hemmed in by suburbs, Wantirna Estate produces chardonnay, pinot noir and cabernet merlot.

It was quite a journey, however, from university course to family winery. At Charles Sturt University, wine science was a correspondence course with hands-on experience because you had to be working in the wine industry to qualify. After that, she was in between jobs and contacted the winemaker at Domaine Chandon, whom she had met, to ask if he knew anyone who needed winery help. His reply was: 'I do. Can you come tomorrow?' What started as a couple of days a week turned into seven and, when the winemaker took a break, she was left in charge. But Maryann was also going away: suddenly she found herself with a formal job offer, which she accepted, working for Domaine Chandon Australia between 1990 and 1996.

'When I joined, they were making just on 22,000 cases of premium sparkling wine. When I left, it was 88,000 cases, including table wines. I learned an immense amount about wine — sparkling wine. But things you can take over into making table wine as well.' For example? 'When you are blending a sparkling wine you can fiddle around with one or two per cent, and it can make a tremendous difference to the wine. And just checking things: everything was always perfectly checked.'

In formal terms, she was responsible for the production of the Domaine Chandon sparkling wine and the Greenpoint Vineyard table wine range. This included coordination of the harvesting, production and quality control of each stage of the winemaking; blending; controlling laboratory activities such as microbiology, wine chemistry and research; and promotion of the wines through interstate trips, visiting clients and hosting wine seminars and dinners.

Maryann resigned after the birth of her first child, but is now working again for Domaine Chandon as a consultant. In this role, she develops food and wine matching concepts for its wines and trains staff in this subject. She is also a guest speaker for the company and involved with its approaches to export markets.

Earlier in her career, she set up and advanced a wine education series under the auspices of the Stephen Hickinbotham Wine Trust, raising money for research and innovation within the wine industry. She also spent four months in the Medoc, the most famous red wine district of Bordeaux, making wine for Chateau Chantelys.

Although it's been only a decade since she embraced winemaking as a fulltime job, Maryann has seen many changes in the industry and predicts a great many more. She is delighted that 'all those technocrats of the 1970s, the white-coated laboratory winemakers' have actually discovered a way to make more interesting wine. 'Revelation! If you go out and taste the fruit, and look and see what is happening on the vine …'

As to the future of Australian wine: 'I just hope the current boom doesn't see lots and lots of mediocre wine being made. I think we have seen, in the past, any variety planted anywhere. We are now getting much more regionalised, seeing certain areas can make very different wines. Portuguese and Italian varieties are making a bit more of a show in Australia.' So, a greater breadth of grape varieties, more distinctive regions and a careful eye on quality seem to be the way to go.

And for herself as a winemaker? 'It is a frustrating thing. It really is agriculture which is made into something more glamorous called wine. But you can't control what comes out of the sky. You can't control what happens. The wool industry doesn't value-add, but the wine industry does.'

Yet, even as she attempts to demystify her chosen career, she gives it the fascinating quality that makes it special. 'You wish you could set aside a small parcel of fruit to try something different. It is very exciting to try something different. But in a small winery, you can just try a little bit of a diversion on a theme.'

Meanwhile, in her wide-ranging working life, she is a contributor to *The Wine Magazine* and has had her first experience as a TV presenter with *Wine Lovers' Guide to Australia*. At the time the programs were made, she and her husband — a project manager for Optus — had two children under three. After the first week, she said, she came home exhausted and told everyone it was such hard work. 'It became easier and less terrifying. It was great meeting all sorts of people — just being exposed to so much. And I will never look at TV the same way in my life …'

Grant Van Every

Grant Van Every

Grant Van Every sounds as though he has the world's most wonderful job for anyone who loves wine. He earns a living by thinking about it, discussing it, tasting it and recommending it. And his career came about as much by chance as anything else. It could almost be the definition of serendipity.

Brought up in a family where alcohol wasn't a part of daily life, Grant drank beer as a student of psychology and arts at the Australian National University. A resident at one of the colleges, he and some fellow students rebelled at the monotony of the food and went out in search of the few restaurants that Canberra boasted in the late 1970s. They were BYO and, by this time, he had discovered the joys of wine through working in the college bar.

'All beer tasted the same,' he recalls. Buying stocks of beer at the local cellar warehouse, he saw the variety of wine labels and would buy a mixed dozen. His interest in wine had begun. It took a big jump when he abandoned his university course after two years, got a job in the public service and began taking holidays with a wine retailer friend in France. They toured wineries and three-star Michelin restaurants, having a great time and learning 'heaps', as he puts it.

'There is nothing like tasting wine at the winery. Nothing that equals knowing the wine you are tasting comes from grapes grown on the vines outside the door. You smell the cellar and the winery. They have their own humidity and dampness. You feel it through your skin. Every cellar has its own personality. The wines, to a large extent, are like their makers.'

Grant's passion for wine was growing as his enthusiasm for his job was diminishing even further from the low point where it started. It wasn't until a few holidays later, however, in New Zealand in 1985, that there was 'a defining moment', as he describes it. The situation wasn't exactly set up for it, as the three-member self-styled Precision Eating

Team had selected New Zealand primarily because there were Rugby
Union and League Tests in Auckland within a couple of days of each
other. They would go to these and try the food and wine around the
country while they were there.

They found they could drink well and very cheaply, though
interesting restaurants were not exactly plentiful. Then they came upon
one on Lake Taupo. Only two diners other than themselves were there
that evening and they finished up making friends with the chef, who
talked with them long into the night, drove them back to their motel
and insisted they come back for breakfast — an eight-course banquet of
specialities accompanied by champagne.

The chef recommended the food of a colleague in Auckland, who
again turned out to be great company. He also drove them home after a
long night in the restaurant. You sense it was this mixture of
camaraderie, a shared passion for food and wine, and the pleasure of it
all that inspired Grant. 'It was a defining moment. I knew I wanted to
be in this business.'

His first thought was to be a chef, and he composed a letter to send
to leading chefs asking if they would take on a mature-age apprentice.
But fate stepped in. He didn't even get to send it before he was invited
to compile wine lists for Len Evans' restaurant in Sydney and work as
sommelier in the Tasting Room. He had no formal training and had
never worked in a restaurant before, but his knowledge and love of
wine carried him through and he was already good at talking to people
about wines.

Len Evans became his mentor, leading by example more than
instruction. 'It was enough to see how he works with crowds, how he
enjoys wine,' says Grant. The pay was 'lousy', a point agreed on by
Evans himself who said to him only recently: 'I didn't pay you much,
Grant, but we drank well.' Not only was this job an opportunity to taste
the best wines from around the world, but it was also a chance to mix
with the big players in the wine industry, building up a valuable
network of contacts. If building projects hadn't closed the restaurant in
1989, Grant reckons he would probably still be there.

The same year, he assisted the small Victorian winery of
Bannockburn in its winemaking process, which he has done almost
every vintage since. In 1990, he assisted during vintage at the Domaine
Dujac in Burgundy. Two years later, he moved to Melbourne and
helped to establish and manage Blakes in the new Southgate complex.
One of its chief attractions and distinctions from other restaurants was
the recommendation of wines to match items on the menu and served
by the glass. Grant believes he introduced this style of wine
presentation and it is a pivotal part of Stella, the restaurant he launched

in 1994 as a partnership with Andrew Blake, of Blakes, and Geoff Lindsay, former head chef at Blakes and Stephanie's. Stella has been a tremendous success with the public and the critics, winning awards locally and commendations at home and internationally.

Grant runs a consultancy, for which his clients include other restaurants, wine companies and marketing groups. As a writer, he produced wine recommendations and an outline of his wine and food matching process for the book *Blakes Food*, which has gone into reprint, compiled the Australian Dairy Corporation's *Cheese and Wine Guide* and is published regularly in *The Wine Magazine*. He was elected inaugural president of the Victorian Chapter of the Australian Sommeliers Association, for which he has coordinated and conducted seminars.

Now he has made his debut as a TV presenter. And it's different from all the rest: 'It's so much harder. The camera is inanimate. It doesn't get the jokes.'

Pria Viswalingam

Pria Viswalingam

Pria Viswalingam is a familiar figure on SBS TV, with a decade of regular appearances in a variety of roles. He was first seen in 1989 hosting a weekly current affairs program, *Asia Report*. In 1990, he presented the current affairs program *Tonight* and, in 1991, the weeknight program *Dateline*. Since 1992, he has concentrated on his quirky travel program *A Fork in the Road*, which is seen worldwide.

Born in 1962 in Malaysia of Sri Lankan background, Pria was educated in his homeland, Britain and Singapore before coming to Australia in 1978 and completing his studies at tertiary level. An interest in theatre took him to the West Australian Academy of Performing Arts, where he graduated with an associate diploma in performing arts in 1987. His broadcasting career began in radio, where he worked as a newsreader and reporter, specialising in politics and international affairs.

But he is best known in his current, travelling role in a series he developed himself. *A Fork in the Road* is based on the concept that his best travel experiences were staying with friends and fitting into their lives for a week, sharing their conversations and getting to know their friends and favourite places, especially restaurants and pubs. Taking that idea, he translated it to television and extended it to a wider range of people.

In the first series, screened in 1993, his journeys took him to Egypt, Italy, Scotland, Hong Kong, France and New York. Since then, he has been to Greece, Buenos Aires, Zimbabwe, Sumatra, the Rhine Valley, San Francisco, Chicago, Sicily, Kerala, Malta, Paris, New Zealand, New Orleans, Budapest, Brazil, Japan, Malaysia, Marseilles, Spain, Washington, Jamaica and Ireland.

After nine years of living in Sydney with his wife and their young twins, he had been no further north in Australia than Newcastle and only as far south as Melbourne. *Wine Lovers' Guide to Australia* changed all that, as it introduced him not only to Australian cities, but also to the fascinating and often beautiful parts of the country where grapes grow best. To add to his new knowledge of Australia, *A Fork in the Road* also concentrates on his adopted country in its 1999 series.

While he relishes good food and wine, Pria stresses that he comes to *Wine Lovers' Guide to Australia* 'very, very much from a layman's point of view. I am really impressed by the quality and range of wine that we have in Australia: that you get in Australia anything you want. And that the people who make it are so passionate about it.'

While Pria had inadvertently shaped his taste buds for the task by sampling some of France's greatest wines on trips overseas, as well as setting aside a few of Australia's top reds for future consumption, his role in the program was to talk to some of the characters in Australian winemaking. He observed hardworking lifestyles and a few glamorous country establishments, as well as sampling the occasional drop of wine. Without too much prompting, he recalls a 'liquid velvet' tokay in Victoria, and his conversion to shiraz and sparkling white on the same day in South Australia. As he warms to his subject, good memories flood back.

Above all, it was the people that impressed him. 'And the goodwill in the industry. People talk to each other and help each other. And what a great advertisement for wine. Quite a few of them were in their 70s and 80s — imagine how much wine they must have drunk. And they're still laughing.'

About the Editor

Jill Sykes AM is best known as a commentator on the performing arts. She was named in the Australian honours list in 1995 for her contribution to the arts in Australia as a writer and broadcaster. She has been dance critic of *The Sydney Morning Herald* since 1972, and is author of the book *Sydney Opera House: From The Outside In*. A freelance writer since 1979, she has written on dance, music and theatre for newspapers, magazines, encyclopedias and specialist books published in Australia and overseas.

While the arts have always been her particular interest, her journalistic career has covered all aspects of reporting, from political profiles to chasing fire engines. She started her career at *The Advertiser* in Adelaide — where she was cookery editor at the age of eighteen, long before her culinary skills were honed — before moving to London and spending six years working in Fleet Street, where her dance reviewing began. On her return to Australia, she joined *The Sydney Morning Herald* as a news reporter, going on to become a feature writer, columnist and arts editor before leaving to work freelance.

Having grown up in Adelaide in a family of wine lovers, she had a youthful education in the pleasures of Australian wine. Her grandfather had an enormous, well-filled cellar and was an early enthusiast for Max Schubert's Grange Hermitage, as it was called in its controversial early years. She remembers going as a child with her parents to McLaren Vale with a cargo of freshly washed flagons to be filled with red wine from giant barrels, and is fascinated by the sophisticated developments in winemaking since then. She thoroughly enjoys monitoring the growing diversity and quality of Australian wine, and has said that, if she hadn't been a writer, she would like to have been a winemaker.

Index